Invisible Scars

Studies In Canadian Military History

Series editor: Andrew Burtch, Canadian War Museum

The Canadian War Museum, Canada's national museum of military history, has a threefold mandate: to remember, to preserve, and to educate. Studies in Canadian Military History, published by UBC Press in association with the Museum, extends this mandate by presenting the best of contemporary scholarship to provide new insights into all aspects of Canadian military history, from earliest times to recent events. The work of a new generation of scholars is especially encouraged, and the books employ a variety of approaches – cultural, social, intellectual, economic, political, and comparative – to investigate gaps in the existing historiography. The books in the series feed immediately into future exhibitions, programs, and outreach efforts by the Canadian War Museum. A list of the titles in the series appears at the end of the book.

CANADIAN WAR MUSEUM
MUSÉE CANADIEN DE LA GUERRE

Invisible Scars
Mental Trauma and the Korean War

Meghan Fitzpatrick

UBCPress · Vancouver · Toronto

26 25 24 23 22 21 20 19 18 17   5 4 3 2 1

Printed in Canada on FSC-certified ancient-forest-free paper (100% post-consumer recycled) that is processed chlorine- and acid-free.

Library and Archives Canada Cataloguing in Publication

Fitzpatrick, Meghan, author
    Invisible scars : mental trauma and the Korean War / Meghan Fitzpatrick.

(Studies in Canadian military history, ISSN 1499-6251)
Includes bibliographical references and index.
Issued in print and electronic formats.
ISBN 978-0-7748-3478-0 (hardcover). – ISBN 978-0-7748-3479-7 (pbk.)
ISBN 978-0-7748-3480-3 (ePDF) . – ISBN 978-0-7748-3481-0 (EPUB)
ISBN 978-0-7748-3482-7 (Kindle)

1. Korean War, 1950–53 – Medical care. 2. Korean War, 1950–53 – Psychological aspects. 3. Military psychiatry – Commonwealth countries – History – 20th century. 4. Psychic trauma – Commonwealth countries – History – 20th century. 5. Soldiers – Mental health – Commonwealth countries – History – 20th century. 6. Soldiers – Mental health services – Commonwealth countries – History – 20th century. I. Title. II. Series: Studies in Canadian military history

DS921.25.F58 2017   2017 951.904'27   C2017-902085-4
                                                               C2017-902086-2

Canadä

UBC Press gratefully acknowledges the financial support for our publishing program of the Government of Canada (through the Canada Book Fund), the Canada Council for the Arts, and the British Columbia Arts Council.

This book has been published with the help of a grant from the Canadian Federation for the Humanities and Social Sciences, through the Awards to Scholarly Publications Program, using funds provided by the Social Sciences and Humanities Research Council of Canada.

Publication of this book has been financially supported by the Canadian War Museum.

Printed and bound in Canada by Friesens
Set in Minion and Helvetica by Apex CoVantage, LLC
Copy editor: Frank Chow
Indexer: Margaret de Boer
Cover designer: George Kirkpatrick

UBC Press
The University of British Columbia
2029 West Mall
Vancouver, BC V6T 1Z2
www.ubcpress.ca

Contents

List of Illustrations / vi

List of Abbreviations / vii

Acknowledgments / xi

Introduction / 1

1   Brave New World: Organization of Wartime Psychiatric Medicine, 1914–50 / 9

2   Together We Stand: Inter-Allied Cooperation and Quality of Care / 23

3   For the Common Good: Mental Health and Maintaining Morale / 39

4   Weathering the Storm: Psychiatrists and Soldiers in the Field, 1950–53 / 61

5   Forever Changed: The Korean War, Veterans, and the Pensions System / 85

Conclusion: Korea and Its Legacy / 102

Appendices / 107

Notes / 114

Bibliography / 153

Index / 167

Illustrations

Map of the Korean Peninsula (1950–53) / xiii

1 Captain A.J.M. Davis of the Royal Canadian Army Medical Corps, 1945 / 18

2 British Commonwealth General Hospital in Kure, Japan, 1947 / 26

3 Australian Lieutenant General Sir Horace Robertson, December 1950 / 33

4 Major General Jim Cassels, 1952 / 41

5 Australian soldiers leaf through mail from home, 1953 / 50

6 Navy, Army and Air Force Institute (NAAFI) mobile canteen, 1951 / 52

7 British soldiers at Kookabura Club, June 1951 / 54

8 Canadian soldiers play hockey in Korea, March 1952 / 57

9 Australian soldiers set up for film screening, March 1951 / 57

10 American serviceman comforts fellow soldier, August 1950 / 62

11 Private Heath Matthews of the Royal Canadian Regiment, June 1952 / 70

12 3rd Battalion Royal Australian Regimental Aid Post, April 1952 / 76

13 His Majesty's Hospital Ship *Maine* in dry dock, 1951 / 80

14 A group of Commonwealth soldiers demonstrate a convalescence exercise regime, May 1952 / 81

15 Aerial view of Ste-Anne-de-Bellevue hospital, Quebec / 83

Abbreviations

1 RAR	1st Battalion Royal Australian Regiment
1 RCR	1st Battalion Royal Canadian Regiment
16 NZ Fd Regt	16 New Zealand Field Artillery Regiment
25 FDS	25 Canadian Field Dressing Station
3 RAR	3rd Battalion Royal Australian Regiment
AACS	Australian Army Canteen Service
ACPMH	Australian Centre for Posttraumatic Mental Health
ACS	Army Council Secretariat (UK)
ADA Psych	Assistant Director of Army Psychiatry (UK)
ADMS	Assistant Director of Medical Services (1 Commonwealth Division)
AG	Adjutant General
APA	American Psychiatric Association
BCCZMU	British Commonwealth Communications Zone Medical Unit
BCFK	British Commonwealth Force Korea
BCGH	British Commonwealth General Hospital
BCOF	British Commonwealth Occupation Force
BEF	British Expeditionary Force
BGH	British General Hospital
BKVA	British Korean Veterans Association
BMA	British Medical Association
BMJ	*British Medical Journal*
CASF	Canadian Army Special Force
CF	Canadian Forces
CIGS	Chief of the Imperial General Staff (UK)
CMA	Canadian Medical Association
CMAJ	*Canadian Medical Association Journal*
CO	Commanding Officer
COS	Chiefs of Staff

DA Psych	Director of Army Psychiatry (UK)
DDMS	Deputy Director of Medical Services (1 Commonwealth Division)
DGAMS	Director General of Army Medical Services (UK)
DGMS	Director General of Medical Services (Canada)
DHH	Directorate of History and Heritage (Canada)
DND	Department of National Defence (Canada)
DSM	*Diagnostic and Statistical Manual of Mental Disorders*
DVA	Department of Veterans' Affairs (Australia)
ECAC	Executive Committee of the Army Council (UK)
FARELF	Far Eastern Land Force (UK)
FDS	Field Dressing Station
GAC	Gerontological Advisory Council (Canada)
GOC	General Officer Commanding
GSO	General Staff Officer
GSW	gunshot wound
HMAS	Her Majesty's Australian Ship
HMCS	Her Majesty's Canadian Ship
HMHS	Her Majesty's Hospital Ship
HMS	Her Majesty's Ship
IAMS	Indian Army Medical Service
ISAF	International Security Assistance Force
ISMC	Inter-Service Medical Committee (Canada)
JRAMC	*Journal of the Royal Army Medical Corps* (UK)
KOSB	King's Own Scottish Borderers
KSLI	King's Scottish Light Infantry
LAC	Library and Archives Canada
MAOI	monoamine oxidase inhibitors
MO	Medical Officer
MoD	Ministry of Defence (UK)
MPNI	Ministry of Pensions and National Insurance (UK)
NAAFI	Navy, Army and Air Force Institute (UK)
NATO	North Atlantic Treaty Organization
NCO	non-commissioned officer
NHS	National Health Service

NKPA	North Korean People's Army
NS	National Service (UK)
NVC	New Veterans Charter (Canada)
NVRP	National Veterans Resource Project (USA)
NZ	New Zealand
OFP	Ordnance Field Park
OR	Other Ranks
OSI	operational stress injury
OTSSC	Operational Trauma and Stress Support Centre (Canada)
OVO	Office of the Veterans Ombudsman (Canada)
PAC	Psychiatric Advisory Committee (UK)
PIE	proximity, immediacy, expectancy
PO	personnel officer
POW	prisoner of war
PPCLI	Princess Patricia's Canadian Light Infantry
PTSD	Post-Traumatic Stress Disorder
PULHEMS	Physique, Upper limbs, Locomotion, Hearing, Eyesight, Mental functioning, Stability
R22er	Royal 22e Régiment (Canada)
RAAF	Royal Australian Air Force
RAAMC	Royal Australian Army Medical Corps
RAChD	Royal Army Chaplain's Department (UK)
RADC	Royal Army Dental Corps (UK)
RAEC	Royal Australian Educational Corps (UK)
RAMC	Royal Army Medical Corps (UK)
RAOC	Royal Army Ordnance Corps (UK)
RAP	Regimental Aid Post
RAR	Royal Australian Regiment
RASC	Royal Army Service Corps (UK)
RCAF	Royal Canadian Air Force
RCAMC	Royal Canadian Army Medical Corps
RCASC	Royal Canadian Army Service Corps
REME	Corps of Royal Electrical and Mechanical Engineers (UK)
RMO	Regimental Medical Officer

RNZASC	Royal New Zealand Army Service Corps
RNZEME	Royal New Zealand Electrical and Mechanical Engineers
RSL	Returned and Services League (Australia)
RTU	return to unit
SIW	self-inflicted wound
TCA	tricyclic antidepressants
TNA	The National Archives (UK)
UNC	United Nations Command
VAC	Veterans Affairs Canada
VIP	Veterans Independence Program (Canada)
VRMHP	Veterans and Reserves Mental Health Programme (UK)
VVAW	Vietnam Veterans Against the War (USA)
VVCS	Vietnam Veterans Counselling Service (Australia)
WHO	World Health Organization
WO	War Office (UK)
WOSB	War Office Selection Board (UK)
WPC	war pensions committee

Acknowledgments

WHEN I FIRST BEGAN writing this book, I could not have anticipated the many struggles and trials that lay ahead. Equally, I could not have predicted the many extraordinary people whom I would meet and who have been instrumental in my success. I must first take this opportunity to thank my editors, Emily Andrew, Randy Schmidt, Megan Brand, and the entire team at UBC Press, for their invaluable guidance through the publishing process. Thanks must also go to Dr. Andrew Burtch of the Canadian War Museum for taking a chance on *Invisible Scars*. My supervisors and examiners at King's College London were pivotal in shepherding this project through its early phases, and for this they too have my gratitude.

Over the past few years, I have had the pleasure of interviewing and corresponding with both Korean War veterans and their families. They have been exceedingly generous with their time and candid in sharing their memories with me. Thanks go to Dr. David Oates, who helped me establish a network of contacts and arrange interviews. Former Royal Army Medical Corps (RAMC) personnel Bill Trevett and Kenneth Davison invited me into their homes and helped me better understand daily life in a warzone. Dr. Fraser and Dr. Bartlet both served as psychiatrists in Korea. I am indebted to them for answering my many lengthy questions and allowing me to read their personal letters and correspondence from that time. In addition, I must thank Professor Anthony Rosie, whose father served as Director of British Army Psychiatry in the early 1950s. Through our correspondence, I learned a great deal about his life and came to better appreciate the significance of his achievements.

It is always challenging to take on a project of multinational dimensions. Having said that, I have been able to manage the difficulties of international research with a little guidance. The reference and archival staff at Library and Archives Canada were vital in helping me to find the right materials within a very tight timeframe. I am also obliged to Professor Thomas Nesmith of the University of Manitoba and Dr. Tim Cook of the Canadian War Museum, who kindly arranged for research assistance when I needed it. Master's student Michel Legault of Carleton University located and photocopied indispensable archival records. Thanks also go to Douglas Chalke, whose father, Major Franklin Cyril Rhodes Chalke, served as divisional psychiatrist from March to October 1952.

Mr. Chalke graciously responded to my letter of inquiry, and I am grateful to have learned more about an exceptional doctor and father. Throughout this project, I have also had the joy of corresponding with Leslie Peate of the Korea Veterans Association of Canada and Vic Dey of the Korea Veterans Association of Australia. Without the help of both groups, I would not have been able to answer many critical questions.

Finally, I need to thank my circle of friends and supporters for their unflagging encouragement. In particular, Dr. Robert Young and Dr. Kathryn Young have continually inspired me and provided a model of what I hope to achieve moving forward. I have spent many happy hours in their company discussing history and all manner of subjects. Last but not least, I must thank my mother and father, Cheryl and Michael Fitzpatrick. They deserve more praise than I can possibly convey. I thank them for helping me to pursue my studies so far from home and for listening to countless drafts of the book without complaint. Most importantly, I thank them for believing in me before anyone else did and inspiring me to become the best version of myself.

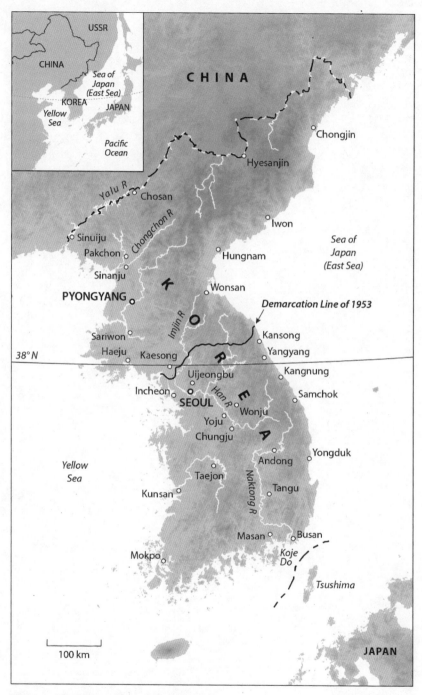

MAP 1   The Korean Peninsula (1950–53).

Source: Australian War Memorial, "Out in the Cold: Australia's Involvement in the Korean War," https://www.awm.gov.au/exhibitions/korea/ (last modified, 2015)

Invisible Scars

Introduction

Nations customarily measure the, "costs of war," in dollars, lost production, or the number of soldiers killed or wounded. Rarely do military establishments attempt to measure the costs of war in terms of individual suffering. Psychiatric breakdown remains one of the most costly items of war when expressed in human terms.

– RICHARD GABRIEL, *NO MORE HEROES*

As COALITION OPERATIONS in Afghanistan have come to a close, there is growing concern for the health and well-being of soldiers and veterans. Since 2001, Western countries such as Canada have incurred significant physical and psychological losses on the battlefield. Recent reports in the press suggest that an alarming number of veterans are experiencing service-related mental health problems. Numerous authors have expressed the fear that a record number will present with conditions such as Post-Traumatic Stress Disorder (PTSD).[1] The debate over how best to address the needs of returning servicemen and women has become highly contested. Over the past decade, it has also generated unprecedented interest in combat, trauma, and the historical development of military psychiatry. Considering the implications for public policy and the planning of future military operations, interest in this subject will undoubtedly continue to grow.

The body of literature available concerning the history of military medicine and psychiatry has expanded in response to these developments. Extensive research has been conducted in connection with the experiences of soldiers during both world wars and the Vietnam War. As a result, the image of the shell-shocked soldier has come to define how we understand and conceptualize the destructive effects of industrialized warfare. The battle-exhausted troops of the Second World War and the struggling Vietnam veteran have also come to represent the human impact of war and the long-term repercussions of trauma in a uniquely intimate way. Other pivotal historical events have largely escaped notice. Widely referred to by commentators and veterans alike as the "forgotten war," the Korean War (1950–53) has received almost no attention. Although there are numerous books on the topic of war and mental health in the twentieth century, Korea receives scant mention. It is frequently characterized as an

American conflict with no regard for the activities of other key participants, such as the 1st British Commonwealth Division. This lack of scholarly attention may appear to suggest that there is little worth studying, but nothing could be further from the truth. By ignoring Korea, writers and commentators have ignored a crucial piece of the puzzle. This work not only extends historical coverage of the Korean War experience but does so in a largely novel way – by addressing the subject of soldiers and trauma.

The Korean War was a brutal conflict that resulted in roughly four million casualties in the space of only three years. In the early hours of June 25, 1950, communist North Korea launched an invasion of South Korea in a bid to forcibly unify the two countries. Although the attack was widely unforeseen, the United Nations responded quickly to an assault on one of its member states. Events in Korea represented the first time that the Cold War turned hot. The invasion was also the first significant test of the UN as an arbiter and organ of international security. American troops based in occupied Japan were hastily assembled and dispatched to defend South Korea from further aggression. Initially overwhelmed by the enemy, the Americans were compelled to retreat to a perimeter around the coastal city of Busan.[2] Shortly thereafter, ground, air, and naval forces from fifteen other countries arrived in support of their efforts. Under the command of General Douglas MacArthur of the US Army, UN forces quickly regained the initiative and pushed the North Koreans back across the border by October 1950. Their success was short-lived. Fearing an invasion of neighbouring Manchuria, the authorities in Beijing decided to enter the war as an ally of North Korea the following month. Truce negotiations were initiated less than a year later, in the summer of 1951, but peace talks would drag on for over two years. During this period, soldiers and civilians alike were caught up in a grinding and destructive war of attrition.[3]

Around 145,000 troops from the United Kingdom, Canada, Australia, and New Zealand were deployed to the Far East from 1950 to 1953. They formed a unified division in July 1951. Working closely together, the 1st Commonwealth Division was also an unprecedented experiment in integration and inter-allied cooperation. Together, the members of the division confronted innumerable challenges.[4] Rugged and mountainous, Korea was an unforgiving country. In winter, temperatures regularly plunged below −20°C and the summers were marred by humidity, flooding, rodents, and insects. In the early 1950s, there was little basic infrastructure to compensate for these realities.[5] Soldiers were also initially ill-provisioned in terms of both clothing and kit. Simply surviving was a formidable struggle. As journalist Max Hastings has pointed out, troops "suffered privations of almost Crimean proportions."[6] Furthermore, the reasons for the war were often unclear, and public support for UN forces waned as peace negotiations stumbled.[7] Accounting for one in twenty wounded or sick Commonwealth soldiers, psychiatric casualties were an all too familiar reality.[8] They suffered from a range of conditions, including psychoneurosis, character disorder, and battle exhaustion. Doctors grappled with self-inflicted wounds, cold injuries of suspicious origin, and a variety of unexplained somatic disorders.[9]

Despite the many hardships they encountered, the Commonwealth Division has received minimal attention from the academic community, and the medical aspects of the conflict remain largely untouched. In the decades following the war, only a handful of articles and books have addressed Commonwealth health and psychiatric practice, or the related topic of trauma.[10] In 1954, Captain J.J. Flood penned a short piece for the *Journal of the Royal Army Medical Corps* outlining the basic medical provisions made for British troops and the nature of early casualties.[11] A year later, Flood's Canadian counterparts, Colonel J.E. Andrew and Brigadier Ken A. Hunter, related their version of events.[12] Historian Bill Rawling touches on psychiatric practice in Korea as part of a larger discussion on postwar Canadian military medicine in his books *Death Their Enemy* and *The Myriad Challenges of Peace*, published in 2001 and 2004, respectively.[13] Professor Edgar Jones and his colleagues at the King's Centre for Military Health Research have also highlighted the role of psychiatrists in the Far East by exploring Commonwealth policy, treatment methods, and common mental health problems.[14]

Throughout the Korean War, Canada and Britain were chiefly responsible for providing the division with medical support. Prior to the summer of 1951, psychiatric casualties were generally evacuated to Japan for treatment. Between December 1950 and November 1951, Captain Flood reported that among the British contingent roughly thirty-five men in every thousand were admitted for a mental health problem.[15] Edgar Jones has argued that "the initial peak in psychiatric casualties owed something to the nature of the troops that deployed."[16] Many were hastily screened volunteers who received little training before embarking for the Far East. Others were veterans and reservists disgruntled at the idea of returning to a life in uniform. Early patients were principally admitted for anxiety and fatigue states. In July 1951, a divisional psychiatrist was appointed to offer clinical guidance to forward medical units. Following this development, the number of patients requiring treatment and evacuation began to fall steadily. As the war became static, behaviour- or character-related problems were increasingly common. Nonetheless, the divisional psychiatrist regularly reported that over 50 percent of soldiers treated were successfully returned to duty.[17]

For the most part, the 1st Commonwealth Division had a relatively low rate of psychiatric illness. As time passed, medical officers became increasingly skilful in properly identifying and caring for those in need. Nevertheless, Edgar Jones has argued that many psychiatric cases went unrecorded. In the book *Shell Shock to PTSD,* Jones and co-author Simon Wessely have pointed out that "unexplained medical symptoms were a feature of the Korean War."[18] For instance, a significant number of Commonwealth soldiers suffered from hypothermia and related cold injuries during the winter months of 1950–51. Jones and Wessely have hypothesized that these men may have consciously or unconsciously exposed themselves to injury in response to "situations of intolerable stress."[19] They further illustrate their case by highlighting the most common reasons for admission to hospital. During the war, servicemen were predominantly admitted to base hospital for skin reactions, gastrointestinal conditions, and respiratory problems. Jones and Wessely maintain that "it is likely that some of these cases represented a somatic expression of psychological distress."[20]

Although Jones presents compelling arguments, he leaves many questions unanswered. His arguments are also based on a limited number of published and unpublished sources. The division included troops from several Commonwealth countries, but Jones uses archival materials from the British National Archives alone. These records are only one part of the story. The Canadians played a crucial role in divisional medicine and psychiatry. Between July 1951 and July 1953, three out of four divisional psychiatrists were officers from the Royal Canadian Army Medical Corps (RCAMC). The division's psychiatric ward was also attached to 25 Canadian Field Dressing Station (25 FDS). Neither Jones nor his colleagues make use of Canadian war diaries, unit records, policy documents, or medical files.[21]

Invisible Scars breaks new ground as the first extended account of Commonwealth Division psychiatry in Korea and provides a portrait of mental health in that theatre. It is also the first publication to make use of source materials from Canada, the United Kingdom, Australia, and New Zealand. The book addresses several principal questions. First, how were soldiers treated for psychiatric disorders in the field, and what efforts were made to bolster mental health? Second, how successful were Commonwealth doctors in treating the psychologically traumatized in both the short and long term? Finally, what impact, if any, did the Korean War have on the evolution and subsequent development of military psychiatry? Although sailors and airmen made significant contributions to the UN war effort, this book focuses on the activities of ground forces, as they dominated the campaign. I argue that while the division was reasonably successful in returning psychologically traumatized servicemen to duty in the short term, the Commonwealth countries failed to compensate or support returning veterans sufficiently. Public ignorance of the war also deprived veterans of the opportunity to grieve and process trauma openly. The experience of returning home and the acknowledgment of society is as pivotal to recovery as any clinical treatment. While the book centres on one particular conflict and its legacy, the Korean War is only a starting point. Chronologically, it sits at an important crossroads dividing up a hundred years of war. Events in Korea reflect both the past and help us consider what followed. Indeed, *Invisible Scars* is intended as a wider-ranging reflection on the treatment of traumatized soldiers and veterans throughout the twentieth century, and the long-term repercussions of living with trauma.

The book is at the intersection of a number of historiographies: the Korean War and its place in the wider Cold War; the medical-military history of Canada, the United Kingdom, and Commonwealth forces, and post–Second World War social history, particularly with regard to demobilization, austerity, and the development of welfare states. It also addresses the longer history of combat stress from the First World War through to contemporary wars, and the understanding of PTSD as a medical term or condition. While the book addresses a wide range of subjects, the wounded soldier is at its heart. Individual suffering is central to the war experience.

My work is informed by the research efforts of numerous historians, social scientists, and medical professionals. Scholars from across the disciplinary spectrum have made substantial contributions to the study of the military and mental health.[22] In common with many of these authors, I argue that combat stress reactions like PTSD are universal and emerge as a result of exposure to trauma, rather than physiological or psychological predisposition. What is more, they cannot be separated from their "specific socio-cultural context."[23] As historian Roger Cooter asserts, "theatres of war and medicine must be studied as part and parcel of the societies and cultures in which they were set."[24] This setting determines how mental health problems are interpreted, categorized, and treated. It also shapes the manner in which military authorities, patients, and medical professionals interact with one another. Diagnostic language and categories have changed radically since the Korean War. For the sake of clarity, I have strictly employed the terminology used by military medical officers and civilian psychiatrists at the time. As a historian, I am also interested in the evolving relationship between psychiatry as a medical discipline and the military as a social institution. Officers and doctors often have competing agendas. An officer's primary aim is to win battles. Meanwhile, physicians are focused on the preservation of life and optimal health. How do these two parties come together within the confines of the military establishment and respond to the realities of war?

The pool of published work on the Commonwealth Division is relatively small. It is primarily confined to a selection of official histories and a number of key academic works, such as Professor Jeffrey Grey's seminal 1988 study of the division.[25] Grey and his fellow authors generally portray a closely integrated, well-disciplined, and combat-effective division, but one still deeply impacted by differences in nationality and strategic priority.[26] Historians like Bill Rawling who explore the activities of the medical services or support branches are in a distinct minority.[27] Consequently, *Invisible Scars* principally relies on unpublished archival sources. Medical records, casualty reports, unit war diaries, and other relevant documentation help us to form a picture of events in the Far East. The majority of the research work was conducted at Library and Archives Canada in Ottawa and the British National Archives at Kew. My arguments and conclusions are largely based on information gathered from central governments and the military. This reliance on official sources is both positive and problematic. On the one hand, official documents are essential to any historical study and provide an intimate first-hand account of events. Away from public scrutiny, officers and policymakers candidly discuss casualties, the development of medical policy, and the challenges that the division faced. On the other hand, there is always the possibility that the documents may be misleading. For example, unusual events are more likely than the habitual to have been recorded.

Relying on archival sources presents a unique challenge, but these obstacles are far from insurmountable. In line with good historical practice, all of the sources have been carefully evaluated with regard to authorship, intended audience, and the purpose of the document. Moreover, the vast majority of the evidence has been corroborated. Commonwealth medicine was an inter-allied venture and psychiatry was the joint responsibility of Canada and the United Kingdom. A more balanced picture of the division begins to emerge when one compares Canadian and British records. Newspapers and other contemporary publications such as the *British Medical Journal* and *Lancet* have also been useful for comparing and contrasting civil and military medical practice. In addition, interviews have been conducted with a number of British veterans who served as ambulance orderlies, nurses, and medical officers. Correspondence has also been maintained with representatives of the Korea Veterans Associations of Canada and Australia. The published and unpublished memoirs of nurses, doctors, support troops, and combat soldiers held at the British Library, the Imperial War Museum, the Liddell Hart Centre for Military Archives, and the Wellcome Library have also proved invaluable. Human memory is far from perfect. As historian John Tosh has noted, memories are "filtered through subsequent experience. They may be contaminated by what has been absorbed from other sources (especially the media); they may be overlaid by nostalgia ('times were good then') or distorted by a sense of grievance."[28] Nonetheless, witnesses have been key in clarifying confusing and contradictory records and providing insights into the realities of life in Korea.

The book is roughly divided into two sections. The first four chapters review and examine events before and during the war. Chapter 1 looks at how the treatment of psychologically distressed soldiers evolved during both world wars and explores how understandings of trauma changed over time. In addition, it reviews how the armed forces struggled to preserve medical knowledge and institutional memory in times of peace and in the face of challenges like demobilization and budgetary cuts, with the goal of assessing how well the Commonwealth countries were prepared to meet the mental health needs of the troops deployed to Korea. Chapter 2 considers how Commonwealth forces were organized in theatre, why the division was formed, and the impact of inter-allied relations on the quality of healthcare.

During the war, the Commonwealth Division had an enviable reputation for high levels of morale and combat efficiency. By all accounts, the troops were well disciplined and motivated.[29] Although historians agree that the Commonwealth countries were initially unprepared for deployment in 1950, the members of the division worked well together on the ground. Since the First World War, both medical and military commentators have recognized that morale is central to the management of mental breakdown in war and is therefore crucial to the maintenance of manpower.[30] Chapter 3 considers how leadership, the development of key policies to foster group cohesion, and the provision of welfare services contributed to improved levels of mental health. Within the context of two world wars and previously unprecedented casualty figures, post-war military leadership needed to be extra vigilant in stressing a more careful approach to wastage. This encouraged the creation of policies and practices designed to limit casualties and nurture strong bonds.

Chapter 4 outlines and assesses the effectiveness of front-line psychiatric care by considering matters such as organization, staffing, common mental health problems, and the composition of the patient population. The Korean War was a pivotal turning point in the development of battlefield medicine. By employing new surgical techniques and evacuating patients through the use of helicopters, medics were able to appreciably lower mortality rates. Fewer advances were made in psychiatry. This chapter compares Commonwealth practice in Korea with techniques employed during the Second World War and with contemporary American methods. Throughout the twentieth century, the military has suffered from a certain degree of organizational amnesia with regard to psychiatry, with a perennial need to relearn the lessons of the past. This was also the case in Korea, where Canadian and British doctors were initially heavily reliant on their colleagues from the US Army Medical Corps.[31] This reliance had an impact on both the disposal of early casualties and how clinical practice evolved as the division took greater responsibility for patients. Doctors claim to have returned over 50 percent of psychiatric patients to duty, but Edgar Jones has argued that there were many unrecorded casualties; for example, men were admitted for cold injuries, self-inflicted wounds, and unexplained somatic disorders. However, divisional authorities were well aware of the psychological considerations in relation to these cases, and this guided both medical and disciplinary policy.

The final chapter reflects on events since the end of the Korean War. Chapter 5 reviews the evolution of the postwar pension system and the challenges that mentally ill veterans faced in obtaining compensation. This is a traditionally controversial area and one in which official systems have been found wanting in the past. Largely designed to address the needs of the physically disabled serviceman, the pension system frequently failed to accommodate the psychologically wounded. This chapter looks at how the experiences of Korean veterans compare with those of their predecessors and assesses the impact of subsequent legislative and medical advances on what is currently available to veterans across the Commonwealth.

This is a story about the human dimension of war. Even today, there is still a stigma surrounding mental illness and those who suffer from it. Within the military, the psychologically traumatized challenge concepts of courage, cowardice, masculinity, and normality. As an organization, the armed forces nurture a culture of resilience, strength, and toughness. In this space, psychological problems can easily be interpreted as weakness or lack of willpower. By studying these casualties of war, we can learn about everything from conditions on the ground and individual experiences of trauma to the culture of major social institutions. The voices of the most vulnerable members of society are difficult to hear, but they often tell us the most about ourselves.

There has been little written about the Commonwealth Division, but it is more than deserving of attention. The troops deployed to Korea endured brutal conditions. They performed their duties far from home, in the face of extreme weather, difficult terrain, and a determined enemy. Moreover, they were called on to work together as an integrated and close-knit team. When they returned home, they found a public with limited interest or sympathy for the sacrifices they made. Over the past decade, Commonwealth troops and their colleagues from around the world have once again been deployed on operations together. Multinational coalitions have become the hallmark of today's operating environment. Like their predecessors of the 1950s, servicemen and women face harsh conditions and uncertain support. This will more than likely continue to be the case moving forward. The world shows no sign of becoming a less volatile or violent place. Consequently, there is more reason than ever to learn from the experiences of the 1st Commonwealth Division. The guns have fallen silent, but a hard-won legacy remains.

1

Brave New World

Organization of Wartime Psychiatric Medicine, 1914–50

ON OCTOBER 16, 1916, Private Harry Farr of the 1st Battalion West Yorkshire Regiment stood alone in the cold early morning light. Refusing a blindfold, the twenty-five-year-old quietly faced a firing squad of fellow soldiers. Court-martialled for cowardice, his trial lasted a mere twenty minutes. Despite his best efforts, there was no reprieve and he was found guilty.[1] As the Battle of the Somme continued to rage, Farr's death occurred without drums, pomp, or military glory. Its impact was keenly felt, however. Following his execution, Farr's "family received no military pension and his widow and daughter were forced out of their house, suffering financial hardship, stigma and shame."[2]

Born in London in 1891, Harry Farr dutifully volunteered for service when hostilities first broke out in 1914. Although he was eager to serve his country, the war soon began to take its toll. Prior to his trial in the autumn of 1916, Farr was hospitalized for shell shock on three separate occasions but managed to return to the front each time.[3] On the morning of September 17, he finally had enough. As his battalion marched towards the front line, Farr asked for permission to fall out and report to the medical officer. With no sign of physical injury, he was told to return to his unit. When discovered at the rear later that evening, he confessed to Regimental Sergeant Major Hanking that "he could not stand it."[4] Hanking had little sympathy for the young man and ordered him to rejoin the battalion. At 11:00 p.m., a final attempt was made to escort him to the front line, but a melee soon broke out and he ran away. The next morning, Farr was arrested and charged with "showing cowardice in the face of the enemy."[5] In spite of his history, no medical evidence was presented at trial several weeks later. Badly wounded at the time, the medical officer who had previously treated him for shell shock was unavailable to testify before the court martial. Farr's commanding officer acknowledged that he was generally of good character and that combat had destroyed his nerves, but understanding was in short supply.[6] As the British Expeditionary Force (BEF) struggled for survival, Harry Farr became another tragic casualty.

The advent of industrialized war exacted an unprecedented human toll that resulted in devastating physical and mental injuries. While very few men met the same fate as Harry Farr, many returned home with lasting psychological scars. Both the military and the medical community scrambled to understand how best to treat those in need and help them recuperate. This chapter reviews how the treatment of psychologically traumatized soldiers evolved during the first half of the twentieth century, prior to the outbreak of the Korean War, and explores how understandings of trauma changed over time. It also looks at how the armed forces struggled to preserve medical knowledge and institutional memory in times of peace, and examines how military medicine is impacted by challenges such as demobilization and budgetary cuts, with the end goal of assessing how well the Commonwealth countries were prepared to meet the mental health needs of troops deployed to Korea in 1950.

Coping with Trauma (1914–45)

When Harry Farr was executed in 1916, clinicians and officers alike were still struggling to understand the bewildering impact of total war on the human body and mind. As early as 1914, previously healthy young men began to present with a variety of mysterious symptoms that could include anything from anxiety and heart palpitations to tremors and functional blindness.[7] In December, the BEF reported that from 7 to 10 percent of its officers and 3 to 4 percent of other ranks were suffering from nervous illnesses.[8] Initially, medical officers speculated that these symptoms were the result of concussion following exploding ordnance, and the popular term "shell shock" was adopted in publications.[9] At first, most servicemen were evacuated back to hospitals in the United Kingdom for treatment. This proved to be an ill-conceived decision, as patients only seemed to worsen when they were moved further away from the front lines.[10]

By early 1916, the medical community began exploring the possibility that the majority of "shell shock" cases were the result of emotional or psychological distress as opposed to physical injury. In fact, only 4 to 10 percent of cases were directly tied to a concussion or bomb blast.[11] Clinicians theorized that the long-term stresses and strains of front-line life were actually to blame. As debate continued, the term "shell shock" was deemed to be misleading and was generally abandoned by doctors in favour of older diagnostic labels such as neurasthenia and hysteria.[12] In any case, "shell shock" continued to dominate popular discourse and remains a part of our modern lexicon of trauma.

Confusion regarding the etiology of nervous disorders presented doctors with a conundrum as to how best to treat patients. Were they offenders to be punished or victims in need of sympathy? At the beginning of the twentieth century, there was still a strong stigma against the mentally ill, who were primarily relegated to large asylums for care. Psychological problems were seen as character failings passed down through hereditary taint. In a rigidly hierarchical society, mental illness was also principally associated with the lower classes and the weaker sex.[13] Consequently, there was little prestige associated with psychiatry as a discipline, and the profession was in its infancy in 1914. However, the war led to an unprecedented mobilization of the medical profession in support of a common cause, and stimulated advancement in fields such as surgery. Parallel developments occurred in psychiatry, involving experiments on everything from talk therapy to the use of physical treatment methods such as electroshock. The nature and the quality of treatment varied widely, depending on the clinicians involved.[14] Officers were generally dispatched to private institutions and could expect more attentive nursing. In contrast, other ranks were primarily sent to general hospitals, where specialized assistance was unavailable and doctors were ill prepared to care for men suffering from psychological distress.[15]

The common goal of all treatment methods was the preservation of manpower. Doctors therefore focused on relieving destructive symptoms that interfered with combat performance, rather than on alleviating the underlying condition. This was a pragmatic approach shaped by the necessities of modern war, and ultimately led to the development of forward psychiatry. Pioneered by French and British medical officers on the Western Front, this system of treatment was further refined by Thomas Salmon of the American Expeditionary Force.[16] The principles of forward psychiatry are best encapsulated by the acronym PIE, which stands for proximity, immediacy, and expectancy. In other words, casualties should be treated as quickly and as close to the front lines as possible. Patients should also expect to recover and return to duty.

Around 200,000 British servicemen were "discharged from active service due to various mental disorders" from 1914 to 1918. With the end of the war, authorities in Britain and around the world had the unenviable task of determining how best to compensate those men who were mentally scarred by their experiences. It was not readily apparent how to measure the impact of psychological injury on earning capacity or quality of life. Over the next two decades, this had a clear impact on the public purse. For example, 35,000 British veterans were still drawing pensions for a psychiatric disability attributable to war service as late as 1937.[17]

The end of the First World War also signalled the departure of doctors and psychiatrists in uniform. Demobilized rapidly, most chose to return to civilian practice rather than remain in the military. Whereas the war presented opportunities for clinical experimentation and professional advancement, peacetime service did not offer the same prestige. This resulted in a significant and lasting loss of expertise and institutional knowledge, the repercussions of which would become noticeable only as the armed forces mobilized for war once again in 1939.

Fearing the inevitable toll of war and the associated cost of pensions, Britain and its allies invested heavily in the development of psychological selection and screening programs at the beginning of the Second World War. With the help of modern science, they believed that it was possible to identify men who were vulnerable to breakdown and screen them out of the armed forces before they posed a risk to themselves or others.[18] It took several years before similar investments were made into the development of military psychiatric programs in the field. The principles of forward psychiatry were only rediscovered and employed at divisional level during the Western Desert campaign of 1941.[19] As the war expanded, the role of psychiatrists grew and evolved in response. Besides delivering clinical care, they were involved in everything from officer selection to efforts to boost and maintain morale. They also conducted experiments in the use of new treatment techniques (e.g., group therapy and occupational therapy) and drugs (e.g., sedatives and amphetamines).[20]

Back to the Future (1945–50)

On Victory in Europe Day in May 1945, there were millions of men and women in uniform on both sides of the Atlantic. Separated from family and friends for years, they demonstrated immense dedication to duty and were now eager to return to life in Civvy Street. In both Canada and the United Kingdom, there was immense pressure to demobilize service personnel as quickly as possible. Tentative plans for demobilization were first drawn up in 1941 with the goal of designing a transparent and equitable release system. Policymakers were well aware of the unrest and rioting that had accompanied demobilization at the end of the First World War and were determined to avoid the same mistakes.[21] After careful consideration, the final arrangements stipulated that soldiers would be released in staggered groups based on a calculation of age and length of service. The oldest and longest-serving troops would be released first. Service personnel were eligible for early release only if they were members of professions deemed valuable to postwar reconstruction efforts and economic development, such as mining, building, and teaching.[22] As historian Rex Pope has pointed out, "the virtues of this arrangement were its obvious justice (long service promised early release) and its simplicity. It was easily understood and not readily open to manipulation."[23]

Both Canadian and British politicians promised a speedy demobilization and were expected to deliver in 1945.[24] There were additional incentives, especially in Britain, where economic concerns played a critical role in determining the speed of demobilization efforts. Canadian finances were relatively stable in 1945, but seven years of total war had taken a toll on the British economy. Throughout the war, the United Kingdom suffered heavy financial losses and amassed huge foreign debts. The Americans loaned their British counterparts nearly US$4.3 billion in the final year of the war alone.[25] Nevertheless, the War Office,

Admiralty, and Air Ministry were still spending over £100 million a week in order to maintain the armed forces.[26] Prompt demobilization would reduce spending significantly and return productive labour to the civilian job market. This in turn would restore the country's industrial base, increasing tax revenues and exports. A fast demobilization was both politically expedient and economically necessary.

In spite of their professional qualifications, medical officers and psychiatrists did not qualify for early release and were subject to the same system of demobilization as everybody else.[27] Healthcare professionals were in high demand, however. The war had put the civilian healthcare system in both Canada and Britain under incredible strain. As early as 1942, reports of hospital staff shortages began to surface. The problem was largely attributed to the unprecedented number of medical students and young doctors enlisting in the armed forces.[28] Writing to the editors of the *Canadian Medical Association Journal*, an anonymous correspondent anxiously confided: "We all know how hospital staffs have been drained of their strength and are still being drained. To carry on the routine of work throws on the reduced staff a strain which is nearly intolerable."[29]

British hospitals were also suffering. On November 3, 1943, the secretary of the British Hospital Association, J.P. Wetenhall, wrote to prominent Member of Parliament Sir William Jowitt. A government adviser on postwar reconstruction and a former solicitor general, the Labour MP was influential with those in high office. Wetenhall pleaded with Jowitt to press for a speedy demobilization at war's end and expressed serious reservations as to whether hospitals could continue functioning in their current state.[30] By 1945, there were 6 doctors for every 1,000 men in the British Army. In contrast, the ratio of general practitioners to civilian patients was 1:2,400 in rural areas and 1:3,000 in urban centres. Meanwhile, a third of all Canadian doctors were in uniform by war's end, and nearly 58.3 percent of those remaining in civilian practice were over the age of forty-five.[31] Along with other pressing considerations, rapid demobilization was in the interests of public health.

Throughout the demobilization process, government officials attempted to strike a balance between the interests of the public and those of the armed forces, but military requirements were no longer a priority. Furthermore, the new Labour government in Britain promised extensive welfare reform and the establishment of a comprehensive health system as part of its platform in the general elections of 1945. Prime Minister Clement Attlee and his ministers originally promised to release 31 percent of medical officers between June and December 1945. This figure was increased by a further 15 percent following a cabinet meeting in September.[32] At this meeting, the Secretary of State for War and the First Lord of the Admiralty argued that the military would be adversely affected by such a decision. Both men believed that proceeding too quickly would have a lasting, detrimental impact on the armed forces. Although their concerns were acknowledged, the rest of the cabinet sided with Attlee and the service ministers were overruled. Secretary of State for Dominion Affairs Christopher Addison even argued that "there was good reason to believe that the services of doctors were wastefully used in the Forces."[33]

The Second World War triggered an unprecedented mobilization of medical and psychiatric manpower. From 1939 to 1945, talented and ambitious clinicians from leading institutions such as McGill University, the University of Toronto, and the Maudsley Hospital and the Tavistock Clinic in Britain all volunteered for service. Fulfilling a variety of roles, they screened new recruits, helped select officers, and consulted on disciplinary cases.[34] The war presented unique opportunities for clinical innovation and advancement. Peacetime service was a different matter altogether. As with their predecessors, the end of hostilities presented an opportunity to depart in favour of more comfortable civilian appointments. As Edgar Jones and Simon Wessely of King's College London have pointed out, "psychiatrists who had volunteered in a spirit of patriotism, were keen to re-establish themselves."[35] As the demobilization process moved forward, the elder statesmen of Canadian military psychiatry departed for prestigious posts across the country, including appointments at the Allan Memorial Institute, the Canadian Mental Health Association, and the World Health Organization. Rising through the ranks to become Canada's first Surgeon General in 1959, consultant psychiatrist Ken A. Hunter was the only major wartime figure who was still in the army by the early 1950s.[36]

There was an equally high turnover of senior staff in Britain. From 1945 to 1948, there were three different Directors of Army Psychiatry (DA Psych) and four Assistant Directors (ADA Psych). After serving as DA Psych since 1942, Brigadier H.A. Sandiford was succeeded by Colonel Alfred Torrie in 1946.[37] Although Torrie "had practised at a base hospital during the Western Desert campaign, at Northfield [military psychiatric hospital] and ended the war as command psychiatrist of London district, he was not an innovative clinician or researcher and was chosen for his administrative skills."[38] He was replaced in December 1948 by Brigadier Robert James Rosie, who, although a seasoned medical officer, had never served on the front lines as a psychiatrist and lacked the same degree of experience as his predecessors.[39]

Neither the Royal Canadian Army Medical Corps nor the Royal Army Medical Corps was ever able to recover from the loss of personnel following demobilization. This did not appear to present a problem initially. Throughout the late 1940s, several committees were convened in both countries to estimate the number of medical personnel required to meet future demand. Following the end of conscription, the Canadian Army Active Force began to shrink dramatically and experts anticipated that only a few hundred doctors would be needed.[40] Meanwhile, the 1946 Nathan Committee predicted that the British Army would require 1,310 doctors for a force of 320,000 British-born soldiers and 55,000 colonial troops.[41] Recruitment levels of doctors plummeted in the late 1940s and early 1950s, however. Once again, military service during peacetime presented few opportunities for young and ambitious doctors. There were many disadvantages to joining the armed forces, and the services had a poor reputation as an employer.[42] In October 1950, Mr. Morrison of the Canadian Department of Labour was dispatched to Montreal to speak with medical students and ascertain their opinion of the military. He reported to his superiors that the students were overwhelmingly negative about a career in uniform, believing that medical officers had very few opportunities for further education and were forced to make undue sacrifices because of successive postings. He also found that "there [was] a general idea that the calibre of doctors in the Service [was] below the general average."[43]

The following year, a series of articles in the *Journal of the Royal Army Medical Corps* suggested that British medical students and doctors had similar feelings about the armed forces. The author, Colonel R.H. Robinson outlined the many reasons why he believed that medical professionals were deterred from joining the RAMC. He recognized that service life entailed certain "social and domestic" sacrifices and that a career in the army could involve an "unavoidable loss of professional experience and skill due to the limitations of peacetime military medical practice."[44] Most importantly, medical officers were not well paid.

On September 6, 1946, the Canadian Inter-Service Medical Committee (ISMC) convened to consider problems with pay and compensation. In its final report, the committee concluded that "salaries offered by municipalities [and other government departments] ranged from $4,000 to $6,000 annually."[45] It failed to specify how much medical officers were paid in comparison but underlined that it was much less than what was available in the civilian job market. In 1951, another committee was assembled to study and review the RCAMC's manpower and recruitment practices. It too noted that service pay compared unfavourably with civilian compensation. In their final summation, the committee members argued that "the most valid proof that Service rates of remuneration for the medical profession are below the civilian average is the fact that there is a serious shortage of doctors in the armed forces."[46]

Across the Atlantic, repeated requests for better pay were summarily rejected on the grounds that the current economic climate precluded the possibility of increases.[47] The War Office acquiesced to a modest pay increase in April 1950 only under pressure from the British Medical Association (BMA). Throughout the late 1940s, representatives of the BMA lobbied Members of Parliament, cabinet ministers, and officials from the War Office on behalf of their service colleagues, without success. They prepared to publish a biting critique of army policy in the *British Medical Journal*. Recognizing that this would be "politically embarrassing," the Standing Committee of Service Ministers agreed to an immediate pay raise to mollify the BMA.[48] This positive decision was eclipsed by developments in the National Health Service (NHS), however.

On March 25, 1952, Minister of Health Harry Crookshank announced a substantial pay increase for NHS doctors. Several years earlier, in response to vocal criticism from the medical community, Lord Justice Harold Danckwerts had been appointed to investigate whether doctors were fairly remunerated. His report concluded that physicians were not well paid in light of the rising cost of living and the average number of patients they treated. He recommended that they should be awarded roughly £10 million more per annum. For the average general practitioner, this represented a salary increase of £300 to £500 per year. However, although a victory for the medical community as a whole, the decision did not apply to doctors serving in the RAMC, and delivered a lasting blow to their professional ambitions.[49]

As the gravity of the situation became apparent, Canadian and British recruiters resorted to increasingly inventive tactics in order to attract medical students and young doctors, promising financial incentives and fully funded postgraduate programs. Beginning in 1946, the Canadian armed forces even dispatched representatives overseas to countries like Britain, hoping to entice young men dissatisfied with working conditions in the NHS to seek adventure abroad.[50] The RAMC countered by creating the short-service commission, allowing doctors to join the army for four years of active duty and four in reserve. At any point in time, they could switch to a regular commission of five years in active service and seven in reserve. The short-service program was designed to be flexible and appeal to individuals who might not have considered a career in the forces.[51] Despite creative tactics, the RCAMC failed to boost its recruitment figures. Attracted to better terms of service, most British medical students who joined the Canadian Forces enlisted in the air force rather than the army. The RAMC also failed to convince its target audience of the merits of service. By 1951, only 154 out of 461 short-service commissions had been successfully filled.[52]

Resolved to field a large standing army in order to meet growing international obligations, the British government maintained conscription in the 1940s and 1950s. Indeed, conscripts were the backbone of the Royal Army Medical Corps during this period. From 1948 to 1960, over 50 percent of medical officers were conscripts. Under the terms of the National Service Act, medical students could choose to enlist before or after completing their education. Conscription was a useful answer to the RAMC's recruiting woes in the short term but was not a good long-term solution. Young and inexperienced, National Servicemen were not qualified to meet the RAMC's insatiable need for highly qualified specialists. As the members of the Army Council lamented, they were "unable to provide more than a sprinkling of specialists. Moreover their limit of two years in the Army precludes their being trained" as such in future.[53]

At a meeting in May 1950, Director General of Army Medical Services (DGAMS) Sir Neil Cantlie stressed the scale of the RAMC's recruiting problems to his colleagues. Of the army's 357 specialists, only 43 percent were fully qualified consultants. Furthermore, Cantlie estimated that the RAMC would need 98 more doctors to meet minimum requirements.[54] Specialties in dire need of new personnel included psychiatry, anesthesiology, radiology, surgery, and otology.[55] There was also evidence that staff shortages were already having a negative impact on job performance and quality of care. For instance, over 350 soldiers were waiting for surgery or orthopedic treatment as of May 1, 1950.[56] Nearly a year earlier, the Standing Committee of Service Ministers predicted this development when it concluded that "the soldier will [soon] receive medical care which is of a lower grade than he would receive in civil life."[57] On the eve of the Korean War, Secretary of State for War John Strachey warned fellow ministers that "unless effective steps were taken ... in the near future, a public scandal would develop."[58]

Manpower shortages and budgetary cuts had an effect on all aspects of military medical care. Psychiatry was one of the hardest-hit specialties. Despite gains during the Second World War, it remained a relatively young discipline with vocal detractors and therefore presented an obvious target for further cuts. On September 23, 1946, the Canadian Director General of Medical Services (DGMS), Brigadier Clifford S. Thompson, responded by letter to an inquiry from officials at the American Psychiatric Association (APA) about psychiatry in the Canadian Army. Writing to Dr. G.H. Hutton of the APA, he confirmed plans to dismantle the RCAMC's neuropsychiatric division following demobilization.[59] Although psychiatrists played a key role in "conserving manpower, in building morale, in developing treatment units and [disposing] of difficult cases" during the war, their services were no longer needed.[60] Thompson explained the army did not require full-time psychiatric staff or dedicated mental healthcare facilities going forward. He argued that these arrangements were superfluous, considering that the "strain of battle no longer exists and it is probable that army life in peacetime is no more hazardous than many civilian occupations."[61] In other words, Canadian troops were no longer actively engaged in combat operations overseas and so there was no need to maintain a psychiatric program. The army also planned to replace psychiatrists with well-trained personnel selection officers in areas like recruit screening (see Figure 1).[62]

FIGURE 1   Captain A.J.M. Davis of the Royal Canadian Army Medical Corps lectures a service audience on mental health in March 1945. Throughout the Second World War, psychiatrists provided expert advice on issues such as personnel selection and discipline.

Source: Library and Archives Canada, R1196-14-7-E

Thompson's initial confidence proved woefully misplaced. Within a year, medical officers across the country reported growing "behavioural and morale problems" and complained that they could not access "expert [psychiatric] advice" to effectively address the issue.[63] There was overwhelming consensus that personnel selection officers routinely failed to recognize mentally substandard and unstable recruits. In a 1948 article titled "Memorandum on Psychiatry in the Canadian Army," Assistant Director of Organization Lieutenant-Colonel G.D. Dailley explained that personnel selection officers "had been called on to assume responsibilities, for which they are not equipped by training and experience in connection with the assessment of emotional fitness."[64] Thompson yielded to increasingly vocal dissent by appointing Major Franklin Cyril Rhodes

Chalke as an adviser on matters of "personnel selection and allocation, operational treatment and handling, and mental hygiene."[65] In short, he was appointed to reconstruct the psychiatric program that Thompson had so quickly dismantled. An experienced medical officer and Second World War veteran, Chalke was a natural choice for the position. Nonetheless, he had qualified as a psychiatrist only in 1946 and was still completing his postgraduate studies at the prestigious Menninger Clinic in Topeka, Kansas, when he first secured the job.[66]

Despite financial problems, the British Army's Directorate of Psychiatry survived demobilization intact. British troops were regularly deployed on operations overseas and there was no reason the directorate should close its doors. Nevertheless, money was always in short supply and from 1945 to 1950 the RAMC focused on reorganizing for greater efficiency. Although it went to great pains to protect the quality and availability of clinical care, postwar efforts to economize had unintended consequences.

During the war, psychiatric consultants in uniform served as senior administrators in each theatre of combat. As experienced clinicians, they also determined the direction of policy and were instrumental in shaping psychiatric practice in the field.[67] The majority of these men planned to leave the armed forces following demobilization. Recognizing this, Director of Army Psychiatry Brigadier Hugh A. Sandiford wrote to DGAMS Major General Sir Alexander Hood about his concerns for the future in July 1945. He recommended appointing civilian consultants to serve as replacements. Shortly after, a seven-person Psychiatric Advisory Committee (PAC) was formed.[68] The group originally included well-known academic advisers like Professor D.K. Henderson of the University of Edinburgh and Dr. Aubrey Lewis, clinical director of the Maudsley Hospital. As impartial observers, committee members were to advise the army about developments in psychiatric medicine and suggest directions for future policy.[69]

At first glance, the Psychiatric Advisory Committee appeared to be an efficient and inexpensive substitute for wartime consultants. However, there were problems with the plan from the outset. Acting in a voluntary capacity, committee members were not paid for their efforts and were compensated for travel expenses only. Weighed down with other professional obligations, they met only sporadically.[70] As a result, the group had few opportunities to interact with serving medical officers or troops. Furthermore, the committee did not hold any executive authority, and so lacked the power to implement programs or make critical decisions. The PAC was ultimately an ineffective consultative body limited by circumstance and design.[71]

Efforts to economize also restricted plans to expand psychiatric training in line with postwar demand. Proposals for a school of army psychiatry were first presented in 1945, and Assistant Director of Army Psychiatry Lieutenant Colonel N. Copeland lent the idea his support by arguing that the RAMC was in critical need of such an institution.[72] Over the next two years, extensive plans were drawn up for the school. Attached to a three-hundred-bed hospital near Aldershot, it would offer postgraduate courses for officers specializing in psychiatry, training for mental health nurses, and additional instruction for general duty officers.[73] Senior officers insisted that the new school was a necessary expense, arguing that "no civil institution can teach the prophylactic side of Psychiatry, which is the essence" of military practice.[74]

On June 6, 1947, the Executive Committee of the Army Council (ECAC) met to consider whether to approve funding for construction. The psychiatric school was only one of many proposals that the RAMC presented; others included schools of health, physiotherapy, dispensing, field training, and hygiene.[75] During heated discussions, committee members debated the expense of the project and roundly criticized the RAMC for being "too ambitious."[76] On the subject of psychiatry, they agreed that it was "a young science and its basic principles were still being explored by the medical profession,"[77] and concluded that "it would be cheaper to pay the cost of such instruction by way of fees (to civilian institutions)."[78] The ECAC would not consider supporting the school or allocating additional funds for psychiatric training as long as defence spending continued to fall. Introductory courses were available through the Royal Army Medical College at Millbank, and officers who wished to pursue further education could do so through civilian channels.[79] This decision severely restricted the RAMC's capacity to offset low recruitment figures by training existing personnel.

Efforts to expand the scope of psychiatric activities were further undermined by the profession's detractors within the armed forces. During the war, War Office Selection Boards (WOSBs) were responsible for selecting candidates to undergo officer training. The boards consisted of a president, a military testing officer, and a medical officer. Beginning in 1941, they also included a psychiatrist. Psychiatrists who were unavailable to sit on the board could act as outside advisers, providing the panel with guidance on a candidate's mental capacity and stability. From 1945 to 1946, several investigative teams were assembled to consider accepting psychiatrists as permanent members of the board.[80] Sir Alexander Hood was very supportive of the idea, writing to Adjutant General Sir Richard O'Connor on December 4, 1946, that selection boards without a psychiatrist overlooked an average of one in three suitable candidates, and pointing out that

assessment of psychological fitness and capacity to bear strain is essentially psychiatric since through his [the psychiatrist's] professional training and experience he is concerned with strains, which cause breakdown and their psychological mechanisms. His training and approach is Scientific [sic] and from this follows that he is specifically equipped to advise a selection board on the capacity of candidates to bear strain.[81]

Hood's endorsement fell on deaf ears. Shortly thereafter, the Army Council Secretariat (ACS) voted decisively against the idea, for several key reasons. First, the army could ill afford to spare existing staff for additional duties in the midst of a manpower crisis. Second, there was limited financial support for such a venture.[82] Finally, the ACS members suggested that there was a "widespread distrust in the Army of the function of psychologists and psychiatrists," and that they took this into account during their deliberations.[83] Adjutant General O'Connor wholeheartedly agreed with his colleagues. Responding to a letter from Hood, he argued that "it is unquestionable that there is a mistrust of these officers in the Army," and that "I do not think, therefore, that they should be restored for the present, at any rate until this mistrust has been removed."[84] O'Connor even recommended referring to psychiatrists as special selection officers to encourage greater trust in their abilities.[85] It is unclear whether this mistrust was as widespread as the Adjutant General and the ACS believed. The War Office's Advisory Committee of Psychologists vocally protested that it was not the case, and characterized the decision as unfair and uninformed.[86] The ACS did not waver, however. Throughout the first half of the twentieth century, psychiatrists and the military were uneasy bedfellows. Referred to derogatively as "trick cyclists," the former were not well received by the army officers or medics with whom they worked. Despite significant progress in dispelling misconceptions about the profession by the early 1950s, psychiatry remained misunderstood by many and maligned by some.

At the end of the Second World War, Assistant Director of Army Psychiatry Copeland estimated that the army would need to retain at least 80 of the 197 psychiatrists on staff to meet minimum peacetime requirements. Five years later, only 12 consultant psychiatrists remained, a deficiency of close to 66 percent.[87] Despite these reduced numbers, however, demand for psychiatry in the armed forces was growing. Early in 1947, the British Army adopted a new recruit-screening system first developed by the Canadians: PULHEEMS, which stands for physique, upper limbs, locomotion, hearing, eyesight, mental functioning, and stability.[88] During the initial enlistment process, personnel selection officers were expected to assess recruits in each category and award points accordingly. Intelligence and psychological fitness formed an important part of the overall evaluation and the examiner could request further testing when deemed necessary.[89] This meant that an average of around 17 percent, or 1,800 recruits, were sent to see a psychiatrist each month. Due to National Service, there was always a steady stream of servicemen awaiting an appointment.[90]

The late 1940s also witnessed a substantial rise in the number of troops receiving treatment for a mental health problem. The *Report on the Health of the Army 1949–1950* concluded that "psychiatric disorders [had become] a major source of manpower wastage" since the end of the war in 1945.[91] It argued that "this [was] certainly the feature of post-war discharges which contrasts most strikingly with pre-war invalidings, when the total discharges were averaging about half the present level, and the rate for psychiatric discharges was about 1.3 per 1,000 as against six or eight times that number now."[92] By 1949, psychiatric discharges rose to a staggering 10.74 men per 1,000. The report attributed this to "an increasing awareness of the psychiatric element in many diseases."[93] It explained that "many men formerly discharged through administrative channels as unsatisfactory soldiers are now discharged on medical grounds as psychiatric cases," and argued that "the tempo of the modern scientific army is such that it is less able to tolerate individuals of lowered intelligence or with the lesser degrees of mental deficiency."[94] The report predicted that in the future these figures would either remain the same or continue to rise steadily.

Reflections

In 2006, the British government formally pardoned Private Harry Farr and three hundred other men executed during the Great War. Looking back, we now regard Farr's sentence and execution as barbaric and cruel, but we cannot judge his contemporaries by our own values and standards. Industrialized warfare produced casualties on an unprecedented scale and left lasting psychological scars. Both before and after Farr's death, doctors and officials around the world struggled to adequately understand trauma and treat those in need. In its desperation to return to peace, the military also failed to preserve critical medical knowledge, and institutional memory faded over time. Despite improvements by the late 1940s, key patterns of behaviour recurred in the wake of demobilization. Free from the strain of war, peace can lead to a certain degree of negligence. In the summer of 1950, Canadian and British medics were unprepared for what they would soon face in the Far East. It was only by working together that they could hope to succeed.

Together We Stand
Inter-Allied Cooperation and Quality of Care

ON JULY 21, 1953, an article titled "Commonwealth Forces Record in Korea: A Successful Experiment" appeared in the *Times of London*. A correspondent for the newspaper praised those in uniform for their efforts, asserting that "history will record that this 1st British Commonwealth Division was an experiment well worth making."[1] As members of a multinational division, soldiers from Canada, the United Kingdom, Australia, and New Zealand worked closely together for two long years. By the end of the war, they had acquired an "outstanding reputation" for their fighting prowess among both their allies and their enemies.[2] Like their counterparts in the teeth arms, Commonwealth medics were widely respected for their professional skills. In Korea, mortality rates were relatively low (34 per 1,000 wounded) compared with those recorded during the Second World War (66 per 1,000). Psychiatric casualties accounted for only 5 percent of wounded or sick Commonwealth soldiers.[3] Success was by no means assured when war first broke out in the summer of 1950, however. At the time, Britain and the old dominion countries were growing apart and they shared few overall strategic objectives. Moreover, they were not prepared for a deployment of the size and scale of Korea. Compromise would be very difficult to achieve. Nevertheless, organizational and administrative choices are paramount in safeguarding the safety, health, and well-being of those on the ground, and these factors can determine the quality of operational medical care. Korea was no exception.

Caught Unawares (June 25, 1950 – July 28, 1951)
When the North Korean People's Army (NKPA) invaded South Korea in the early hours of June 25, 1950, the international community was caught unawares. There were signs of what was to come, but few observers predicted the fighting. The invasion presented a major challenge to global security, and it was the first time that the Cold War turned hot.[4] A few days later, the United Nations called on its member states to "furnish such assistance to the Republic of Korea [South Korea] as may be necessary to restore international peace and security in the area."[5] A battalion of American troops based in Japan was immediately dispatched to Korea as part of Task Force Smith. Shortly thereafter, General Douglas MacArthur of the United States Army was appointed Commander-in-Chief of UN forces.[6]

The Commonwealth countries were quick to respond to the UN's call for help, and were eager to support its efforts. Korea was the first test of the United Nations as a tool of collective security. Britain, Canada, Australia, and New Zealand also wished to foster closer political and defensive ties to the United States. The North Atlantic Treaty Organization (NATO) was a relatively recent creation and the ANZUS Treaty between the United States, Australia, and New Zealand was still under negotiation.[7] In light of these considerations, all four countries offered to deploy naval forces as soon as possible. Australian ships were the first to arrive in the region, on July 1.[8]

Several weeks later, American forces retreated in the face of overwhelming enemy opposition to a perimeter around the city of Busan on the south coast of Korea. By the first week of August, the US Army had suffered an astonishing fifteen thousand casualties. Task Force Smith was neither well equipped nor well prepared for the intensity of combat operations. The first Americans sent to Korea were principally based in Japan as occupation troops and had grown accustomed to comfortable living conditions.[9] The North Koreans, on the other hand, were much better prepared for the privations of an active campaign. Many had prior military experience and were battle-hardened veterans of the recent Chinese civil war (1946–50).[10] As casualties climbed, the Americans put pressure on their allies to contribute ground troops, and announcements to that effect were made in London, Canberra, and Wellington on July 26. The British government agreed to send a brigade to the area as soon as possible.[11] The Australians and New Zealanders promised to recruit men for the purposes of a "special volunteer force ... for Korea and for service in any other area to which the conflict might spread."[12] Although the Canadian cabinet originally dismissed the idea of deploying ground troops to the Far East for budgetary reasons, it reversed itself because of public opinion and fear of the political fallout from declining to support a major ally. Prime Minister Louis St. Laurent announced the recruitment of a Canadian Army Special Force (CASF) on August 7.[13]

The 27 British Brigade was the first Commonwealth contingent to land in Busan, on August 28. Commanded by Brigadier Basil Coad, the formation included troops from the 1st Battalion of the Argyll and Sutherland Highlanders and the 1st Battalion of the Middlesex Regiment.[14] In the summer of 1950, the brigade was "on active service defending the frontier of [Hong Kong] with China."[15] According to veteran and distinguished British historian General Sir Anthony Farrar Hockley, "almost three quarters of the brigade were national service officers and soldiers, many of whom had been posted from basic training just prior to embarkation. It was thus a relatively raw force."[16] Coad and his colleagues were therefore surprised when they were ordered to prepare 27 Brigade to depart for Korea. The British government first intended to send the

29th Independent Infantry Brigade Group (29 Brigade), which was based in Colchester and properly provisioned for deployment. However, the Americans needed help urgently and 27 Brigade was in a better position to travel to Korea quickly.[17] The hurried departure had its drawbacks. The formation was "sadly understrength" when it arrived in theatre and had to wait for its transport to catch up.[18] Moreover, the government would not allow National Servicemen under the age of nineteen to serve in Korea. Consequently, volunteers from the King's Scottish Light Infantry (KSLI), the King's Own Scottish Borderers (KOSB), the Royal Leicestershire Regiment, and the Staffordshire Regiment were hastily assembled as replacements.[19] 29 Brigade did not reach the Far East until months later, in November. In contrast to 27 Brigade, it was well supported by "armour, artillery, field engineers, signals and the administrative services – supply and transport, ordnance, a medical and dental element for the recovery and treatment of casualties, and electrical and mechanical engineers for the recovery and repair of the brigade's hardware."[20]

Deprived of additional manpower following demobilization, Canada, Australia, and New Zealand were in no position to deploy ground troops to Korea in August 1950. Although the latter two countries enforced forms of national service, legislation and public opposition precluded sending of conscripts overseas. There was no alternative but to recruit the necessary soldiers.[21] The numbers of volunteers who responded initially overwhelmed authorities in all three countries. Within a few short weeks, over ten thousand Canadians, "enlisted under the Special Force terms of service," and thousands of men "thronged the desks of recruiting offices" to join 16 New Zealand Field Artillery Regiment (16 NZ Fd Regt) and the Royal Australian Regiment (RAR).[22] This meant that the Australian Army could reject three out of every four men who volunteered to fight, and nearly six thousand New Zealanders ended up joining Kayforce, as it was called – six times the number originally required.[23] Most of the volunteers were Second World War veterans. For example, around 45 percent of CASF members had seen action from 1939 to 1945, and 42 percent of the New Zealanders who enlisted in Kayforce had prior military experience.[24]

When they arrived in Korea, new units were placed under the command of Brigadier Coad of 27 Brigade. The 3rd Battalion Royal Australian Regiment (3 RAR) was the first to land, on September 27. It was eventually joined by the 2nd Battalion Princess Patricia's Canadian Light Infantry (2PPCLI) in December and 16 NZ Fd Regt in January.[25] Despite intense preparation, however, none of these units had completed training when they first sailed for Korea, and they continued to drill in transit.[26]

Operational control of Commonwealth troops ultimately rested with the Americans,[27] but Lieutenant General Sir Horace Robertson was responsible for

FIGURE 2   Housed in facilities previously occupied by the Japanese Navy, the British Commonwealth General Hospital in Kure, Japan, was the centre of Commonwealth medicine in the Far East during the Korean War.

Source: Australian War Memorial Photo Collection No. P05195.137

administrative direction. He had commanded the British Commonwealth Occupation Force (BCOF) in Japan since 1946. This group included personnel from the United Kingdom, New Zealand, India, and Robertson's home country of Australia. By June 1950, the Australians were the only remaining contingent in theatre. The Joint Chiefs of Staff in Melbourne planned to withdraw BCOF at this time but changed plans when war broke out. Over the following months, Robertson and his team provided crucial logistical support to Commonwealth troops bound for Korea. BCOF was conveniently headquartered in the Japanese coastal town of Kure (see Figure 2). Located on "the southern tip of the main ... island of Honshu," Kure is only ten miles from Hiroshima and a day's journey by ship from Busan.[28]

Medical support was fragmentary and units were slow to arrive during the early months of the war. Regimental Medical Officers (RMOs) accompanied each group, but 26 British Field Ambulance was the first large medical team deployed. Arriving in support of 29 Brigade in November 1950, the field ambulance was commanded by Captain W.J. James and there were 13 officers and 125 men on strength.[29] Shortly thereafter, the 60th Indian Field Ambulance joined 27 Brigade. India's sole contribution to the Commonwealth war effort, it was commanded by Lieutenant Colonel A.G. Rangaraja of the Indian Army

Medical Service.[30] Around the same time, the 130th Australian General Hospital was renamed and converted into No. 29 British General Hospital. Based in Kure, it was ideally located to receive casualties. The Australian Army had originally commandeered the buildings and grounds from the Japanese Navy in 1945. Prior to the Korean War, the hospital was a small two-hundred-bed facility and performed an average of only four operations a month.[31] It expanded to accommodate an additional two hundred patients in December 1950.[32] The hospital was the "first integrated unit of its kind in the United Nations Command, staffed by British, Canadian and Australian personnel."[33] Although the commanding officer, principal matron, and registrar were British, the Canadians and Australians "each had their own matron and administrative officer."[34] The wards were uniquely "staffed on an integrated system, with the specialist being of a different nationality from the ward sisters."[35]

Awaiting the arrival of additional personnel, the Commonwealth countries initially relied on the US Army for logistical and medical support. American doctors regularly tended to Commonwealth patients in the field and took responsibility for evacuation and care.[36] This was a problematic arrangement. The United Nations Command included troops from Colombia, Belgium, France, Greece, Ethiopia, the Netherlands, Luxembourg, the Philippines, Turkey, and Thailand. These countries similarly relied on the US Army for resources, transport, and medical assistance. As the tempo of operations increased, the Americans struggled to keep up with demand. Furthermore, they did not have the personnel or the bed space to accommodate the growing number of sick and wounded,[37] and patients were evacuated to Japan or even the United States for treatment of relatively minor injuries and illnesses. The US Army Medical Corps often failed to notify Commonwealth officials of such evacuations, and it could take days or even weeks to locate a casualty within the vast American evacuation system.[38]

Lieutenant-General Charles Foulkes, Chief of the Canadian General Staff, was the first to suggest the idea of a Commonwealth division, on July 18, 1950. The government of New Zealand "was the first to raise the proposal for serious consideration with the other members of the Commonwealth," on July 26.[39] Despite Foulkes's endorsement, Prime Minister St. Laurent and Secretary of State for External Affairs Lester B. Pearson were both strongly opposed. Late in August, the Canadians communicated their views to the British government in the form of an aide-mémoire, copies of which were circulated to the other dominions. While they were more than willing "to serve alongside their comrades from the United Kingdom and the other Commonwealth nations as they had been accustomed to do in the past," they were against forming a division.[40] As historian Jeffrey Grey has noted, they "wished to stress the UN character of the operations to the maximum extent possible."[41] They were open to a formation that included other non-Commonwealth countries. Failing this, they would agree to participate in a Commonwealth division as long as it was not labelled as such, and suggested the title of 1st United Nations Division as an alternative.[42] Since the 1930s, the Canadians had slowly distanced themselves from Britain and cultivated closer ties to the United States. Canadian politicians were keen to highlight the country's sovereignty and independence from the United Kingdom.[43] In 1944 and 1946, Prime Minister Mackenzie King rejected proposals for centralized defence cooperation between the Commonwealth countries by arguing that any close ties to Britain "might prejudice defence discussions vis-à-vis the United States."[44] When the concept of a division was first proposed, both St. Laurent and Pearson were afraid that this suggested that Canada remained firmly within Britain's sphere of influence. Consequently, they continued to obstruct discussions throughout the autumn of 1950. As UN forces broke out of the Busan perimeter and won a series of significant victories against the NKPA, everyone believed that the fighting would be over soon anyway. These hopes were dashed in November, however.

On October 1, UN forces crossed the border between North and South Korea, commonly known as the 38th parallel. Throughout the month, they advanced northward, towards the Yalu River and the Sino-Korean border. Fearing that the Americans were planning to invade Manchuria after subduing North Korea, officials in Beijing decided to act.[45] Moving only at night, Chinese troops began crossing the Yalu River and marching southward. On November 1, "they struck with overwhelming force against US troops," forcing them into a hasty retreat.[46] Although Chinese Premier Zhou Enlai had warned the UN Command (UNC) that China would intervene if UN forces advanced towards the border, the attack took the Americans and their allies by surprise. By mid-November, approximately 250,000 Chinese troops were in theatre, with more arriving daily. Despite launching a sustained offensive, UN forces suffered heavy casualties and were compelled to abandon their positions.[47] China's entry dealt the UN Command a devastating blow and was a turning point in the war.

As Chinese troops streamed into Korea, the United States pressed Canada and its partners to dedicate more ground troops and establish a division. On November 15, General Robertson reported to the Chiefs of Staff in Melbourne, Wellington, and London that "General Walker commanding Eighth Army expressed to me the opinion that it would help him greatly ... if we would form a British Commonwealth Division which would take care of all British Commonwealth military units."[48] He pushed his superiors to come to a final decision, explaining that "the Americans are so used to us managing our own affairs that they cannot understand our present piecemeal organisation and from the top down I get the feeling that they hope we will take over all our own affairs."[49] Taking this into consideration, the Canadians finally agreed to the formation of division in December 1950.[50] Fresh obstacles to the union soon emerged, however. On February 21, 1951, the Canadians announced that they would send the 25th Infantry Brigade Group to the Far East. Reluctant to dedicate additional troops and resources to Korea, the British now saw an opportunity to withdraw 27 Brigade, but it was impossible to do so without serious political and diplomatic repercussions.[51] Less than a month later, General MacArthur highlighted the importance of British troops in discussions with Robertson: "I would be recreant to realities ... if I did not say that the command in Korea is woefully outnumbered and fighting under the severest handicaps and hazards. Its needs and necessity for reinforcement and steps to the contrary would not fail to increase its difficulties and jeopardy."[52] The British took MacArthur's words to heart and agreed to keep the formation in the field until the 28th British Commonwealth Brigade Group arrived in April. Negotiations finally moved forward without any further objection.

Shoulder to Shoulder: The Birth of the 1st British Commonwealth Division

The Commonwealth division flag "was formally hoisted [for the first time] at a ceremony" held on July 28, 1951, close to the front lines at forward headquarters in Tokchon.[53] The new division included 28 British Infantry Brigade, 29 Independent Infantry Group, and 25 Canadian Infantry Brigade Group. Commonwealth forces were under the operational control of Lieutenant General John W. O'Daniel of US I Corps, who was widely known as "Iron Mike."[54] British Major General Jim Cassels became the division's first General Officer Commanding (GOC). Since they fielded the largest number of troops, the Canadians and the British provided the majority of staff officers, but the Australians and New Zealanders were also well represented at headquarters.[55] Back in Kure, Robertson remained in administrative control, providing the division with supplies and facilitating the movement of Commonwealth troops in theatre.

The Canadians and the British also divided the chief medical appointments, although Colonel C.W. Nye of the Royal Australian Army Medical Corps (RAAMC) became the division's first Deputy Director of Medical Services (DDMS). Responsible for overall direction of policy, the DDMS was the highest medical authority in theatre. Nye's selection owed much to Australia's generous contribution of supplies and the divisional hospital,[56] but he was also a natural choice for the job. A knowledgeable and well-respected officer, he had previously served as the "senior administrative medical officer with BCOF" and as Assistant Director of Medical Services (ADMS) to Commonwealth forces from January to July 1951.[57] In a newspaper article, colleagues described him as a "wise ... and willing co-operator."[58] Nye's second in command was Colonel Geoffrey Anderton. Commissioned into the Royal Army Medical Corps in 1927, he had served throughout Europe, North Africa, and India. As ADMS in Korea, he was responsible for ensuring that orders were properly issued and executed by those on the ground. He also played an instrumental role in determining where medical units should be located, and organized everything from the transport of casualties and supplies to additional training for officers.[59]

There were four major Commonwealth medical units in theatre in the summer of 1951: 25 Canadian Field Dressing Station (25 FDS), 25 Canadian Field Ambulance, 26 British Field Ambulance, and 60 Indian Field Ambulance. Landing in Korea on July 8, 25 FDS was undoubtedly the most important, and it became the centre of Commonwealth medicine. Commanded by Major W.R. Dalziel, the unit admitted patients for the first time on July 21.[60] Initially housed in a school building in Seoul, it was originally established to "deal with the minor sick and wounded."[61] It eventually became "a general hospital in all but name," and could accommodate 122 medical, 44 psychiatric, and 11 venereal disease patients.[62] It was also home to the division's medical specialists and regularly hosted conferences on a variety of topics. In addition, there were three field ambulances in theatre at any one time. Consisting of a headquarters and three self-contained forward units, they toured the front lines and transported casualties from regimental aid posts to larger units like 25 FDS. These forward units or sections typically included a doctor, a sergeant, and several lance corporals and privates. Casualties were occasionally transported to Norwegian or American units for specialized surgical treatment.[63]

The Commonwealth Division's Japanese headquarters continued to expand over time. By autumn 1950, roughly four thousand troops lived and worked in the Kure area.[64] No. 29 British General Hospital grew and evolved in response to the division's needs and was renamed the British Commonwealth General Hospital (BCGH) in December, to better reflect its multinational composition. Commanded by British officer Colonel J.E. Snow, the hospital was "spartan" in appearance but housed over a thousand beds and was equipped with all the requisite diagnostic, medical, and surgical equipment.[65]

Inter-Allied Command

Although all four nations were initially reluctant to join the division, there were many benefits to inter-allied cooperation. Working as partners, they wielded greater political influence and could act in unison. They could also solve previously insurmountable "logistic and operational problems" through the pooling and sharing of resources.[66] This was particularly beneficial for the British contingent. For example, the Australians and the Canadians began providing air support to evacuate Commonwealth patients from forward locations like Seoul beginning in July 1951. The dominion countries were also useful allies when supplies were scarce. Based in Singapore, the British Army's Far Eastern Land Force (FARELF) was responsible for providing the RAMC with medical stores and equipment. Throughout the spring of 1951, FARELF fell well behind rates of consumption, but the Canadians and Australians procured the necessary items by drawing on their own independent supply chains.[67]

There were many advantages to working as a team, but there were also challenges and obstacles. Manpower remained a constant and pernicious source of friction. In the early 1950s, British defence commitments were widespread and the British Army struggled to meet global demand. Consequently, the manning of British infantry battalions in Korea "fell consistently short of establishment by up to twelve per cent."[68] At Whitehall, Chief of the Imperial General Staff (CIGS) Field Marshal Sir William Slim was forced to admit that "we have not nearly enough infantry battalions and have had to accept gaps in Germany and the loss of a strategic reserve in this country," in order to meet our obligations in the Far East.[69] General Michael West, who succeeded Cassels as GOC, expressed similar concerns in a letter to the Adjutant General dated October 29, 1952, pointing out that "when a British battalion relieves an Australian or a Canadian one it has too few men to fill the holes."[70] This was a source of tension between partners and exposed British troops to unnecessary risk.

The medical branch of the division also struggled to field an adequate number of personnel. When war erupted in the summer of 1950, neither the Royal Canadian Army Medical Corps nor the Royal Army Medical Corps was prepared for deployment. Although a staggering number of Canadians had enlisted to serve in Korea as infantrymen, very few doctors volunteered their services and the army was forced to shuffle existing staff members.[71] Meanwhile, over 50 percent of British medical officers were young National Servicemen who had only recently graduated from university. The British Commonwealth General Hospital in Kure was the "only source of replenishment" for medical units based in Korea.[72] Addressing the Royal Society of Medicine in June 1953, Major General A.G. Harsant acknowledged that the situation was further complicated by "the varying lengths of service of medical officers from the different Commonwealth ... countries."[73] Depending on nationality, MOs served an average tour of three to six months. As a result, levels of experiences varied and there was an exceptionally high turnover of staff.[74]

Manpower shortages significantly restricted the mobility of Commonwealth medical units. Based nearly thirty-five miles behind the front line in Seoul, 25 Canadian Field Dressing Station was one such unit. Early in the war, ADMS

Anderton recognized that 25 FDS was located too far back.[75] One news correspondent was generous when he described the Korean road network as a "churning nightmare of mud."[76] It could take hours to safely transport critically wounded patients from one point to another, but 25 FDS could not be moved closer to the front because it was responsible for controlling the air evacuation of casualties from nearby Kimpo airstrip. Brainstorming solutions, Anderton considered assembling an entirely new unit to replace 25 FDS but not enough doctors and nurses were available. For well over a year, the problem of the field dressing station remained unresolved. Exasperated, Anderton's successor, Colonel G.L. Morgan Smith, split 25 FDS into two in June 1952. An eighty-bed forward section moved to the Tokchon-Uijeongbu area around fifteen miles from the front lines on June 18. Headquarters stayed behind in Seoul. Several months later, September 16, a new British Commonwealth Communications Zone Medical Unit (BCCZMU) finally opened. Commanded by Canadian officer Major R.A. Smillie, it was multinational in composition and staffed by doctors and nurses reassigned from other units in Korea and Japan. Housed in the former headquarters of 25 FDS in Seoul, it could accommodate roughly a hundred patients. BCCZMU was chronically short of supplies, but the unit quickly proved its worth.[77] Over the summer months, an average of 458 men were evacuated every month from Korea to Japan. By October, this figure had fallen to 279 per month. Free from prior responsibilities, 25 FDS also relocated to a better position and was able to substantially improve the quality of patient care.[78]

National differences presented even greater challenges for the Commonwealth countries than the dilemmas associated with manpower. After all, the 1st British Commonwealth Division was a marriage of convenience. Following the Second World War, Britain and the dominions were beginning to drift apart from one another strategically. They were thrown together again by shared political concerns and financial necessity. Increasingly independent and confident, the dominions were eager to be recognized as the United Kingdom's equal partner. During the Korean War, they expected to be treated in a manner that accurately reflected the changing nature of this relationship. To their detriment, the British were not always sensitive to this consideration.

Throughout the war, Australian Lieutenant General Sir Horace Robertson (see Figure 3) held non-operational control of the division and was responsible for representing the Commonwealth in its dealings with the UN Command. Appointed largely because of his prior experience working alongside the Americans during the occupation of Japan, Robertson was a natural fit for the job, but the British quickly became dissatisfied with the arrangement and dispatched their own liaison officer to Tokyo. Representing the Chiefs of Staff, Air

FIGURE 3   Australian Lieutenant General Sir Horace Robertson (centre) visits Busan in December 1950. Administrative control of the Commonwealth Division rested with Robertson, who was based at headquarters in Kure, Japan. Throughout his tenure, he was a controversial figure who proved unpopular with British officials.

Source: Brian McMullan and Cecilia Mary McMullan/Australian War Memorial Photo Collection No. P01254127

Vice Marshal Cecil Bouchier was encouraged to foster a separate and "special relationship" with the Americans.[79] Over the course of his career, Robertson "had never been popular with Whitehall," having proved "too independent and ready to assert the rights of the Dominions."[80] On top of that, he had an abrasive and belligerent personality that landed him in hot water on more than one occasion.[81] Nonetheless, Bouchier's appointment was ill conceived. In appointing him, both the "Foreign office ... [and] the War Office attempted to undermine and isolate [Robertson] and, in the process demonstrated that the inability to recognise the sovereign rights of the dominions which had characterised British attitudes during the Second World War had not changed."[82] The Australians were understandably dismayed and insisted that the decision "was not in harmony with the established principles of co-operation in British Commonwealth Defence."[83] Ignoring these protests, the British continued to maintain an independent representative in Japan long after Bouchier had departed. Selected as Deputy Chief of Staff to the Commander-in-Chief of UN forces in July 1952, Major General

Steven Shoosmith did not officially speak on behalf of the Chiefs of Staff, but he maintained close contact with London. Uncomfortable with Robertson, the British took matters into their own hands, but the dominions were no longer willing to see Britain as a senior partner or accept unilateral decisions from Whitehall. Bouchier and Shoosmith inconveniently highlighted cracks in the alliance at a time when the division was in sore need of greater unity.[84]

Like the British, the Canadians regularly presented obstacles to smooth co-operation. When 25 Canadian Infantry Brigade arrived in Korea in April 1951, Brigadier John Rockingham was given very specific instructions, most important of which was that the "principle of the separate entity of the Canadian Force shall at all times be maintained."[85] Brigade staff acquired a reputation for keeping to themselves and "officers of other nationalities ... soon came to leave liaison with the brigade to the Canadians among them."[86] When Robertson recommended integrating divisional headquarters in Japan, the Canadians simply "declined to participate."[87]

In a 1954 study of Commonwealth medicine, former ADMS Colonel J.S. McCannel was asked to outline the major challenges that the division faced in Korea. He pointed to "nationalistic feeling" as one of the primary impediments to cooperation,[88] arguing that national differences undermined efficiency in the field. For instance, each contingent insisted on maintaining separate medical records, and British, Canadian, and Indian medical units recorded admissions, transfers, and discharges differently. For reasons that are unclear, the Canadians did not share these records with the division's Deputy Director of Medical Services in Japan. Instead, they forwarded the documents only to the ADMS and to the pertinent authorities in Ottawa, frustrating communications and making it exceptionally difficult for the DDMS and his staff to collect statistics on divisional health and formulate appropriate policies in response.[89]

"Nationalistic feeling" further restricted the mobility of Commonwealth medical units. In a 1955 article for the Canadian Medical Association, Brigadier Ken A. Hunter and Colonel J.E. Andrew reviewed events in Korea and pointed out that "throughout the two Great Wars, in which Canada has played a large part, it has been a policy of the ... Army to provide Canadian medical attention for Canadian casualties at all levels where such attention is necessitated."[90] They explained:

This ... has been based on the fact that the Canadian soldier expects treatment by Canadian doctors whenever it is possible to provide such treatment. This ... does not cast a reflection upon the professional ability of doctors and nurses other than those of Canadian origin but rather is based on a sentimental and natural desire of the wounded man for contact with people from his own homeland.[91]

The RCAMC vigorously defended and enforced this policy in Korea by positioning medical units close to Canadian infantry battalions. In the spring of 1951, the Canadians even considered erecting their own hospital but abandoned the plan because of budgetary constraints.[92] Popular with the public and politicians at home, the policy significantly limited the mobility of key medical units like 25 FDS and 25 Canadian Field Ambulance. Besides being poorly positioned due to manpower shortages, units were subjected to a policy formulated for sentimental rather than pragmatic reasons.

Compromise and Cooperation

By all accounts, the Commonwealth Division was an efficient force. In the book *Army, Empire and the Cold War,* well-known historian David French concludes that "the British and Commonwealth ground forces who fought in Korea gained a good reputation in the eyes of American commanders," who considered the division to be reliable and disciplined.[93] Existing documentary evidence suggests that US Army medics had a similar appreciation of their Commonwealth counterparts, with whom they worked closely during the war.[94] Despite the obstacles they encountered and their arguments with one another, the British, Canadians, Australians, and New Zealanders somehow managed to work together under great strain. There are several key reasons for this.

The division owed some of its success to the nature of the Korean War. During the first year of hostilities, the fighting was highly mobile and required manoeuvrability, but Korea soon became a war of attrition. Beginning in July 1951, large-scale offensives were rare and the "campaign became one of limited set piece attacks, supported by heavy artillery bombardments, and restricted fighting in which patrolling, field works, [and] barbed wire played a prominent part."[95] Casualties remained manageable and it was possible to house units like 25 FDS in more durable accommodations.[96] Although Commonwealth medical units were always understrength and lacked flexibility, this never seriously compromised the division's health. If the war had remained mobile, the division might not have been able to cope so admirably.

As members of the Commonwealth, Britain, Canada, Australia, and New Zealand also shared a unique bond. Similarly organized into distinct regiments, they had worked closely together in the past.[97] In the early 1950s, they continued to use the same equipment and operate "with the benefit of common doctrinal and organizational assumptions."[98] Furthermore, the dominions sent officers to study in Britain and vice versa. Canada's Royal Military College at Kingston and Australia's Royal Military College at Duntroon were also deeply influenced by British tradition. Both were modelled on the United States Military Academy at West Point but maintained robust links to the United Kingdom.[99] For example, the college at Kingston was "wholly British in administration and professoriate, was commanded by a British Army officer until the 1920s, and subscribed to the teaching of British strategic and tactical doctrine."[100]

There were equally long-standing ties between the Royal Canadian Army Medical Corps and the Royal Army Medical Corps. Throughout the first half of the twentieth century, Canadian doctors commonly studied in Britain because universities there were considered prestigious. Canadian Army medical policy was heavily influenced by these transatlantic connections. In the late 1940s and early 1950s, Canadian medics were frequently in contact with colleagues from the United Kingdom and were eager to encourage further cooperation.[101] Captain W.G. Clever explored this relationship in a 1954 article for the *Canadian Army Journal*. The Canadians were beginning to develop closer ties to their American colleagues, but Clever stressed the continued intimacy of Anglo-Canadian relations, pointing out that "the RCAMC field organisation was amended in 1947 to conform with ... British post-war policy. The changes included the adoption of one type of field ambulance ... the allotment of one field dressing station, reduced in size and function, to each infantry division; and the reinstitution of RCAMC other ranks in battalion establishments."[102] Historian G.W.L. Nicholson has underlined the links between Canada and Britain during the Cold War era. For example, the Canadians continued to use British training pamphlets and study materials to educate officers. The RCAMC also increased the number of non-medical officers and other technical personnel at the same time as the RAMC.[103] When the British made a major change in policy or organization, the Canadians would invariably follow suit.

Officer selection was the final key to Commonwealth cooperation. The interplay of personalities played a crucial role in smoothing ruffled feathers and ensuring that national differences did not become insuperable barriers to compromise. The senior officers who were chosen to serve in Korea were selected both for their experience and their ability to work effectively within a coalition environment. The division's first GOC, Major General Cassels was a man well suited to commanding a multinational force. As Australian historian Jeffrey Grey has commented, "a man better qualified to head the composite Commonwealth Division and deal with potentially troublesome dominion forces would have been hard to find."[104] Cassels, a Seaforth Highlander, joined the British Armed Forces in 1926. Throughout his career, "he had served on the North West Frontier ... had a knowledge of the Indian Army," and even spoke a little Urdu.[105] During the Second World War, he rose rapidly through the ranks to become the youngest divisional commander in the British Army, and, as commanding officer of the 51st Highland Division, he collaborated closely with the Canadians.[106] Prior to his appointment as GOC, he served as head of the

United Kingdom Services Liaison Staff in Canberra and forged strong connections with his Australian colleagues. Cassels's successor, General Michael West, was also well prepared for his role in Korea. Commissioned into the British Army in 1925, he served in India during the 1930s and "commanded an infantry battalion and two brigades in the Second World War."[107] When CIGS Field Marshal Slim was asked why he appointed West, he replied that it was because West "had a good record as an infantry soldier" but, more importantly, he "knew how to get on with all sorts of people."[108]

Brigade and battalion commanders were similarly chosen for their experience in working effectively as members of a multinational team. At forty-six years of age, Brigadier Thomas Brodie of 29 Brigade "had seen a good deal of active service, including command of a Chindit formation in Burma during the Second World War."[109] Born in Australia, Brigadier John Rockingham of 25 Brigade immigrated to Canada as a young man. He attended the staff course at Camberley and commanded both British and Canadian troops in action.[110] Lieutenant Colonel Francis Hassett of 3 RAR was a graduate of both Duntroon and the British Army Staff College at Haifa, and served in North Africa and the Pacific during the Second World War. A distinguished and decorated veteran, Lieutenant Colonel J.W. Moodie of 16 New Zealand Field Artillery Regiment had equally extensive experience working alongside officers from the other dominions.[111]

Senior medical personnel like DDMS Brigadier Nye also had experience operating within the confines of a coalition. During the occupation of Japan, Nye had served alongside other Commonwealth officers as ADMS. His second in command, Colonel Anderton, worked with officers from the dominions throughout his long career in Europe, North Africa, and India. Anderton's successor, Canadian officer Colonel Morgan Smith commanded a Canadian Army Hospital during the Second World War, and was attending the Australian Staff College in Queenscliff when he learned that he was going to Korea.[112] His replacement, Colonel J.S. McCannel, commanded the 24th Canadian Field Ambulance in Italy from 1944 to 1945. Before embarking for the Far East, he attended a staff course in Britain.[113] Beginning in May 1952, Colonel N.T. Meneces of the RAMC acted as Commandant of the British Commonwealth General Hospital. Maltese by birth, he commanded both British and Indian medical units throughout his time in Burma during the Second World War. Described as a "very cultured chap," Meneces was widely respected by close colleagues and hospital staff alike.[114]

Reflections

Today's operating environment is dominated by alliance politics and multinational cooperation. Countries rarely deploy in isolation. The members of the Commonwealth Division succeeded in achieving a positive, if flawed, working relationship in Korea. It is impossible to distill this success into an easily digest-ible and repeatable formula. Nonetheless, the Commonwealth experience underlines the value of fostering close links with one's military partners. The ties that these countries forged in the long term were pivotal to the achievement of short-term operational goals. Furthermore, these connections had an impact on the way that medical officers operated in the field, and the efficiency with which they worked. Administrative choices determined everything from where medical units were located to how, when, and where casualties were evacuated, and shaped the healthcare options open to physically and psychologically injured troops. These relationships would also prove pivotal in moulding the division's approach to issues of welfare, morale, and mental health.[115]

3
For the Common Good
Mental Health and Maintaining Morale

IN THE EARLY 1970s, American General Bruce Clarke was asked to reflect on his experiences during the Korean War. When asked which foreign soldiers he would "classify as the fiercest fighters," Clarke responded without pause: "The best ... I had among the foreign troops were the Commonwealth Division; British and Canadians, Australians, New Zealanders, they were good troops. They're stolid but they're steady."[1] Admired by allies and enemies alike, the officers and men of the division were well known for their discipline and professionalism. While everything seemed to work against them, they held the line in exceptionally fierce periods of fighting. When they first arrived in Korea, most units had not completed their training, and as the war dragged on they faced declining public support.[2] For instance, a 1951 poll of New Zealanders found that "nearly half of those questioned [were] unable to describe Korea's geographical location," and "few could list its neighbours."[3] Nevertheless, Commonwealth troops were motivated and worked well together. Without exception, annual reports highlighted the division's high morale and senior and junior officers regularly corroborated these findings.

Morale plays a crucial role in protecting military personnel from the onset of psychological problems. This is a fact that the military became increasingly cognizant of during the twentieth century. Soldiers and civilian commentators have struggled to understand the concept of morale. The term is difficult to define accurately but mainly refers to the collective attitude of a group. Scholars have recognized that it is "a powerful variable in a military force or unit, which has a substantial effect on operational effectiveness."[4] Measuring morale is problematic because it is not directly quantifiable. However, Australian Major General H.J. Coates has pointed out:

> While accepting that it is hard to quantify, we have ... given it dimensions. We regard morale along with firepower and manoeuvre, as an essential element of combat power. Firepower and manoeuvre are the physical elements of manpower, weapons and equipment; morale is developed from the psychological state of man.[5]

According to historian and psychotherapist Edgar Jones, "most authors are agreed that [military] units which perform efficiently ... manifest good morale."[6]

In a 1968 article, Professor Ernest Andrade Jr. aptly described morale as "a rope of many strands."[7] This was the case in Korea, where several key factors contributed to promoting and maintaining morale within the Commonwealth Division. These included strong and protective leadership, limited tours of duty, the formulation of policies that encouraged strong group cohesion, and the reliable provision of welfare services.

Leadership

There is disagreement and debate over what personality traits characterize an effective leader. Observers of the military agree, however, that leaders of all varieties are crucially important.[8] Throughout the early 1950s, authors on both sides of the Atlantic were confident that a good leader could affect both the individual soldier's state of mind and morale in general. For example, in a February 1951 piece for the *Journal of the Royal Army Medical Corps*, Major Martin Lewis stressed the importance of leadership or man management in preventing unnecessary psychiatric casualties.[9] Describing American psychiatric practices in Korea, Lieutenant Frank B. Norbury of the US Army Medical Corps similarly cited leadership as one of the "sustaining forces in the maintenance of emotional adjustment in combat."[10]

Lecturer on international relations Dr. Sergio Catignani has described the leader as a "protector" who works on behalf of those under his or her command.[11] There is ample evidence to suggest that this was the role that Commonwealth officers assumed in Korea. Australian historian Robert O'Neill has pointed out that "one of the most important factors in the maintenance of morale of the fighting troops was their commanders' insistence that men's lives must not be wasted."[12] He has argued:

> In their determination to see that casualties were suffered only for a significant result, senior Commonwealth commanders adopted a different approach from their American and South Korean, or, for that matter, their Chinese and North Korean counterparts who continued to conduct operations in which hundreds and thousands of men died in order to hold or gain a small outpost or to capture prisoners.[13]

Informed by the massive losses incurred during the First and Second World Wars and by the considerable limitations of Commonwealth manpower, officers were fiercely protective of the men on the ground in Korea.

Prior to deployment, divisional commander Major General Jim Cassels (see Figure 4) and the "commanders of the three brigades fielded by the Commonwealth [were each] issued with ... instructions which charged them

FIGURE 4   Major General Jim Cassels greets Commander-in-Chief of UN forces
General Mark Clark at Commonwealth Headquarters in May 1952.
Source: Philip Oliver Hobson/Australian War Memorial Photo Collection No. HOBJ3173

with maintaining the safety of their commands."[14] If an officer felt that by accepting orders he would imperil "the safety of [his] troops to a degree exceptional in war," he had the right to "appeal to the Commander-in-Chief of British Commonwealth Forces Korea," Lieutenant General Sir Horace Robertson.[15] In such a situation, Robertson was responsible for presenting the case to the British, Australian, and Canadian chiefs of staff. None of the Commonwealth commanders ever invoked this right, but they frequently used it as a bargaining tool. For example, the 2nd Battalion Princess Patricia's Canadian Light Infantry (2 PPCLI) received orders to join the 27 British Brigade immediately on arriving in theatre in December 1950. However, the Canadian government had furnished battalion commander Lieutenant-Colonel Stone with a similar directive, and he was authorized to refuse orders until such time that he thought his troops prepared for battle. As 2 PPCLI had not completed training, Stone was well placed to employ his directive. 27 Brigade's commanding officer, Brigadier Basil Coad, was eager for the battalion to join his men on active operations, but he understood and allowed the Canadians to complete their training for the sake of good inter-allied relations. As UN forces beat a hasty retreat south and abandoned Seoul for the second time in six months, the Princess Pats methodically completed a series of exercises in the hills surrounding a base at Taegu, approximately ninety kilometres northwest of Busan. When it joined the brigade several months later, in mid-February, 2 PPCLI was ready for action.[16]

Commonwealth officers were quick to defend their troops from the worst excesses of American command. Throughout the war, the division was part of US I Corps, which was headed by Lieutenant General John W. O'Daniel. Coming from different doctrinal and strategic schools of thought, relations between O'Daniel and the division's commanding officer, Major General Cassels, were often tense.[17] In October 1951, Cassels informed his superiors in London that he had seriously considered invoking his directive on five separate occasions over the past three months:

On many occasions I was ordered, without any warning, to do things, which I considered militarily unsound, and for which there was no apparent reason. Eventually, I asked the Corps Commander for an interview where I put all my cards on the table. I pointed out that we worked quite differently to them, and that it was impossible to expect that we could suddenly change our ways to conform with American procedure. I then asked that, in the future, we should be given our task, the reasons for the task, and that we should then be left alone to do it in our own way without interference from Corps Staff. The Corps Commander could not have been more helpful and, since then, things have been much better and both sides are happier.[18]

Within the division, "this process of consultation and compromise" became known as "waving the paper."[19] Communication improved considerably, but Cassels continued to negotiate with the Americans when he considered orders unreasonable. Believing firmly in the deterrent power of his directive, he was not afraid to argue his case, much to the chagrin of O'Daniel and his staff. For instance, in May 1952, O'Daniel "directed Cassels to capture at least one prisoner every three days and instructed him to use up to a battalion in order to reach this target."[20] In a confidential report, Cassels fumed that the "raids have had to go a long way to find the enemy ... [and] have been comparatively costly."[21] They were already well aware of the strength and disposition of the enemy forces opposite the division and there was no need to take unnecessary risks. Shortly thereafter, Cassels ordered the raids temporarily suspended. Patrols eventually recommenced, but they were no longer as frequent or ambitious in scale.[22]

Cassels's successor, Major General Mike West, initially managed to foster a more cordial relationship with his American superior, Lieutenant General Paul Kendall. The latter was "widely recognised as being a very different personality type from his predecessor," and was praised for his abilities by UNC Commander-in-Chief General Mark Clark.[23] However, disagreements were inevitable and West was as eager as Cassels to protect the division's interests. He was prepared to use his directive as a bargaining chip with the Americans in determining how Commonwealth troops were employed in the field. On many occasions, he complained about "the renewed pressured to produce prisoners, and of high level interference in such low level matters as the number of patrols to be sent out by forward battalions."[24] In working diligently to prevent unnecessary casualties, he came into increasing conflict with his American colleagues. This clash of personalities eventually resulted in Kendall's unceremonious dismissal. On April 10, 1953, Lieutenant General Bruce Clarke replaced Kendall after the latter "publicly rebuked West in a divisional commanders' meeting and made a number of disparaging remarks about the British."[25] Both Cassels and West were staunch defenders of those on the sharp end.

Junior officers were not in a position to refuse orders or negotiate with their superiors, but they too were encouraged to take initiative and promote the welfare of their men. Returning from tour, British platoon commander 2nd Lieutenant M.F. Reynolds outlined for posterity what he considered to be the main responsibilities of an officer:

> A man's welfare is your primary duty. Never neglect a foot, body or weapon inspection and most important of all ... the time your men want you with them is not only when the sun is shining and when there's no danger, but when everything is at its worst and you feel like looking after yourself first.[26]

The experience and quality of officers varied, but Commonwealth troops were generally well led. Many of the non-commissioned officers (NCOs) were battle-hardened Second World War veterans who helped their younger counterparts cope with front-line service. They also enforced a strict code of discipline and fostered an atmosphere of determination.[27] As peace negotiations dragged on relentlessly, both senior and junior officers demonstrated a remarkable commitment to service. For example, in *Army, Empire and Cold War*, military historian David French points out that "in the 1st Black Watch the commanding officer (CO) helped to integrate every newly joined soldier by introducing himself and speaking to each of them individually."[28] Decades later, Black Watch veteran R.J. Carriage recalled that "there was a great love of our Colonel. We used to call him Colonel Davey and he was everywhere and his concern was the Jocks. Look after the Jocks."[29] Captain Reg Saunders of the 3rd Battalion Royal Australian Regiment (3 RAR) received similarly high praise for his skills in commanding a rifle company. He "quickly established himself and won wide respect for his abilities as a platoon commander, particularly his determination when leading patrols far from the battalion's main position."[30] Men like Davey and Saunders inspired loyalty and were a source of support for the men under their watch. Good leadership at platoon, battalion, and division level played a pivotal role in boosting morale throughout the war.

Tours of Duty

When the Commonwealth Division was formed in July 1951, its member nations agreed to implement a series of measures to ensure that units functioned as efficiently as possible. Without hesitation, they all agreed to set limited tours of duty. Throughout the Korean War, infantrymen spent a minimum of twelve months and a maximum of eighteen months in the Far East. Artillery and support troops were relieved after a year and a half on duty.[31] No matter the unit, no man was allowed to stay in Korea for more than seventeen weeks of winter, defined as the period from December 1 to March 31. Battalions spent three months at a time at the front and the subsequent month and a half in reserve. Servicemen were granted five days of leave for every four months of service, which they could choose to spend at a rest centre in Incheon, at divisional headquarters in Kure, or in Tokyo.[32]

The establishment of limited tours of duty was a significant development and was crucial in maintaining morale for a number of reasons. First and foremost, the aims of the war were ambiguous at best, and for the average soldier there was little ideological motivation to fight. A survey conducted late in 1950 found that "US troops ... repeatedly raised two questions about the war: 'Why are we here?' and 'What are we fighting for?'"[33] Servicemen from Britain, Canada, Australia, and New Zealand were often equally perplexed as to the reasons for their deployment. In a 2009 interview, British veteran Alex Easton recalled: "The thing about it was Korea ... I mean bloody Korea. Where's Korea? I'd never even heard of it."[34] On assuming command of the US Eighth Army in January 1951, General Matthew Ridgway felt compelled to issue a statement. Writing to all the formations under his command, he briefly answered the question of why Western troops were there:

> The real issues are whether the power of Western civilization ... shall defy and defeat Communism; whether the rule of men who shoot their prisoners, enslave

their citizens, and deride the dignity of man, shall displace the rule of those to whom the individual and individual rights are sacred ... The sacrifices we have made, and those we shall yet support, are not offered vicariously for others, but in our own direct defense. In the final analysis, the issue now joined right here in Korea is whether communism or individual freedom shall prevail.[35]

In spite of Ridgway's efforts to clarify the matter, the objectives of the Korean campaign remained vague. Following Ridgway's appointment as Commander-in-Chief of UN forces in April 1951, General James Van Fleet was installed as the new commander of the Eighth Army. At his first press conference, Van Fleet was asked by an American correspondent, "General, what is our goal in Korea?" Disconcertingly, he simply replied, "I don't know."[36]

Considering Van Fleet's answer, it is not surprising that many servicemen continued to be frustrated and confused about their role in the war. This was compounded by the disrespect in which most Koreans were held. Samuel Fuller's 1951 film about Korea, *The Steel Helmet,* includes a key scene where a US soldier asks his compatriot, "How do you tell a North Korean from a South Korean?" His fellow soldier responds, "If he's running with you he's South Korean. If he's running after you he's a North Korean."[37] Intended to be humorous, this scene reflects how American and Commonwealth troops saw Koreans and underlines how commonplace casual racism was at the time. According to Hugh Deane, a British cabinet member visiting the "strife ridden" prisoner-of-war camps on the island of Koje-do characterized the Koreans as "prone to violence."[38] President Truman described the people of Korea "as the inheritors of Genghis Khan and Tamerlane, the greatest murderers in the history of the world."[39] As peace negotiations dragged on from 1951 to 1953, there was little to motivate those on the ground. During the static phase of the war, Commonwealth troops were "required to risk their lives constantly, not to win the war or even gain any significant advance on the ground, but simply to maintain pressure on the Chinese and North Korean Governments so they might modify their negotiating position."[40] Consequently, limited tours of duty provided Commonwealth soldiers with a point of reference and something to which they could look forward. While the war might continue unabated, they would return home after a set period time.

Climate was the second reason the Commonwealth countries agreed to limited tours. The brutality of Korean winters has been well documented by both veterans and historians. Temperatures habitually dropped below $-30°C$ and vehicles and equipment regularly broke down. Hands froze to weapons and it was almost impossible to stay warm. There were even reports that medics were forced to tuck plasma and morphine ampoules under their armpits or in their mouths to keep their contents fluid.[41] US Marine surgeon Captain Hering observed that "the only way you could tell the dead from the living was whether their eyes moved. They were all frozen stiff as boards."[42] No man could be expected to march through deep drifts of snow and endure the long hours of darkness and icy wind for more than a season. The one-winter policy was thus a prudent and humane measure.

Hard-won experience also informed the division's stance on tours of duty and rotation. British studies conducted during the Second World War suggested that infantry soldiers were combat-effective for an average of four hundred aggregate combat days. Past this, they began experiencing greater levels of anxiety and were more prone to psychiatric breakdown.[43] The Americans, who rested their troops less regularly, arrived at lower estimates of between two hundred and two hundred and forty days.[44] They disagreed as to how long the average soldier could continue fighting, but both British and American experts agreed that there were clear limits to endurance. In a 1949 article for the *Bulletin of the US Army Medical Corps*, Major Raymond Sobel referred to this problem as "old sergeant syndrome."[45] He explained that "a fairly consistent constellation of attitudes occurred in well-motivated, previously efficient soldiers as a result of the chronic and progressive breakdown of their normal defenses against anxiety in long periods of combat." Sobel highlighted the fact that "a large number [of the men in question] have received citations, awards, and medals for outstanding conduct and devotion to duty."[46] This research factored heavily into the division's decision to set time limits to tours in the Far East.

Group Cohesion

Policies that promoted strong group cohesion were another vital building block in fostering morale. The meaning of the term "cohesion" is debatable, but it can be generally defined as "the bonding together of members of an organization/unit in such a way as to sustain their will and commitment to each other, their unit and the mission."[47] Eminent Israeli clinical and social psychologist Reuven Gal has observed that "the strength of unit cohesion has been shown, time and again, to be a key factor in soldiers' level of morale and combat effectiveness."[48] He has concluded that "it has been shown to play an unequivocal role in the onset and extent of psychiatric reactions during combat."[49] Since the Second World War, the British and American literature on the subject has focused on the importance of fostering loyalty between men rather than to a particular political or ideological cause.[50] As distinguished historian Professor Hew Strachan has emphasized, "the core assumption concerning morale in the British Army is that soldiers fight less for their country and more for their comrades."[51] This was especially important in Korea, where operational aims were constantly in flux.

The Commonwealth Division promoted cohesion primarily by keeping fighting units intact as they moved in and out of theatre. Rotated in battalion-sized groups, servicemen bonded with other members of their unit through a shared combat experience. For well over a year, they lived, trained, and fought together. 3 RAR was the only group to operate using an individual replacement system. During his tenure, Captain Rutherford of the Royal Australian Army Medical Corps repeatedly complained about the quality of reinforcements dispatched to join the unit. Early in May 1953, he lamented that "the overall effect is to place a heavy burden on the trained few, to their detriment, and ultimately to the battalion as a whole."[52] In light of 3 RAR's experience, the Australian Army chose to discontinue individual rotation in the middle of the war.[53] The Americans, who also adhered to an individual replacement system, experienced similar difficulties in nurturing and strengthening group cohesion at the battalion level. As they approached their rotation date, soldiers grew increasingly risk-averse and the other members of the unit attempted to spare the man in question. "Short timer syndrome" plagued the US Army in Korea and continued to do so during the subsequent war in Vietnam. For the Commonwealth, the Australian and American experience confirmed the wisdom and value of group rotation.[54]

Over the last decade, historians and commentators have questioned and debated the value of the regimental system. Commonwealth officers believed firmly in its power as an organizational construct and source of support. By identifying with the group, individual soldiers develop a sense of belonging and understand their own service within the context of regimental history. Numerous authors have described the regiment as a "family" or "tribe," and in the early 1950s it was still seen as one of the best ways to cultivate morale.[55] In October 1951, the British Director General of Military Training even issued a public statement characterizing the regimental system as the "cornerstone of good morale."[56] It was not an abstract concept but an essential feature of military life to the officers of the Commonwealth Division. Late in January 1951, Lieutenant General Robertson suggested temporarily combining undermanned battalions of the Middlesex and Argyll and Sutherland Highlander regiments to "form one strong British battalion."[57] Brigadier Coad and Chief of the Imperial General Staff Field Marshal Sir William Slim roundly rejected the plan because they felt that it would "strike hard at the strong regimental spirit in each battalion."[58] Although "such ... amalgamations had taken place for short periods in past wars following extraordinary losses," they refused to countenance such a measure.[59] The integrity of the regiment was more important than alleviating manpower shortages. For the remainder of the war, officers continued to use the regiment as an organizational tool to foster a sense of pride and military professionalism. They actively nurtured a friendly sprit of competition between units to boost morale.

Welfare Services

The role of welfare services in promoting morale has received relatively little attention from historians. However, it plays a central role in sustaining the fighting spirit of those in uniform during a protracted campaign. Originally organizing themselves on an ad hoc basis, each of the Commonwealth countries provided its own troops with basic amenities (e.g., clothing, rations, postal services). There are few surviving records from the period prior to the formation of the division. Existing documentary evidence suggests that little was available in terms of recreation, spiritual activity, education, or social services during the mobile phase of the war. The Commonwealth countries worked independently of one another and lacked the necessary manpower and resources to provide effective support.

During the first year of the war, the Canadians were the envy of the division in terms of winter clothing. The 1949 Canadian Arctic parka and windproof trousers were well suited to the climate and could fetch "upwards of $100 on the Korean black market."[60] Attempts to improve the quality of the winter combat suit were unsuccessful. Parkas issued from 1951 to 1952 were made of nylon that was neither water-resistant nor windproof. Commonwealth troops soon came to prefer the American pattern of clothing on offer.[61] The British also experienced difficulties in providing soldiers with appropriate winter weather gear. For example, the War Office failed to supply the British contingent with a sufficient number of coats during the winter of 1952. Many of the coats were far too small and better suited to dry European weather than the damp cold of Korea. On January 6, 1952, the headline "Korea Scandal: Report That Will Shock You!" screamed out from the front page of the *Sunday Dispatch*.[62] A brief article blasted the government for failing to provision troops suitably for cold-weather combat. Although the allegations were greatly exaggerated, officials in the War Office eventually discovered that "the Quartermaster General's staff had showed some want of urgency in pressing procurement from the previous summer and were negligent in supplying the sizes required."[63] The situation was remedied after further criticism and the intense pressure of public scrutiny. In light of the variations in the quality of clothing available, many soldiers became adept at re-equipping themselves for the weather.[64]

In terms of rations, the Canadians enjoyed a very close relationship with the Americans and drew heavily from US stores in order to supplement their own resources. The members of the Canadian Army Special Force were regularly supplied with both American hard and fresh rations. An average American C7 ration pack was generous and included "several varieties of main course, for example, ham and lima beans, pork and beans, frankfurter chunks and beans, meatballs and corned beef hash ... There were tins of fruit, salted crackers, biscuits, chocolate, chewing gum, cigarettes, coffee and dried milk, toilet paper and a tiny tin opener."[65] They also included items like chicken noodles, pork chops, turkey, steak, and the occasional fruit cocktail. The British, Australians, and New Zealanders all survived on a slightly less exotic combination of American and Commonwealth provisions.[66] As veteran Les Peate recalled, they largely ate "US C rations in the line ... Australian and locally purchased fresh rations and British compo rations in reserve."[67] British packs typically consisted of a dull combination of "tinned bully beef, steak and kidney or frankfurters, tinned potatoes and hardtack biscuits."[68] Regardless of one's nationality, cooking in Korea required a hefty dose of creativity and perseverance. In *The Call Up: A History of National Service,* writer and journalist Tom Hickman points out that "whatever was cooked in winter froze as it left the frying pans ... [and] could be almost inedible."[69] Having said that, the quality of food had little impact on the overall state of divisional morale. Most soldiers appear to have accepted unappetizing rations as a regrettable but unavoidable part of service life.

Besides providing clothing and rations, each national contingent was responsible for organizing its own independent postal system. The Canadians, British, Australians, and New Zealanders were all well served by prompt mail delivery. Surface mail was shipped via troop or freight carrier and took approximately six to eight weeks to arrive. Air shipments were usually processed within a week to nine days. From 1951 to 1953, the division relied on the services of both military aircraft and a number of commercial couriers, such as the British Overseas Airways Corporation, Canadian Pacific, and Qantas Empire Airlines to deliver the mail. Letters and parcels from North America and Australasia arrived three times a week and post from the United Kingdom was delivered biweekly.[70] Because of the boost to morale that they provided, Christmas greeting cards and gifts could be sent to the Far East at no cost to the sender. While Commonwealth troops were universally issued twenty cigarettes a day and could buy up to eight hundred a month, packs of cigarettes remained a popular gift for family and friends to send overseas at any time of the year. Shipped free of charge, there was no limit to the number that could be posted, and charitable organizations and private companies were encouraged to purchase cigarettes as an expression of support. Throughout the war, the Canadian Legion, the Red Cross, and the province of Ontario all sent bulk shipments to Korea.[71]

FIGURE 5   Australian soldiers Private Bob Parker and Private Vin O'Brien leaf through the mail from home. During the Korean War, letters and parcels were a vital means of communication and provided soldiers with an invaluable connection to their friends and family back home.

Source: Philip Oliver Hobson/Australian War Memorial Photo Collection No. HOBJ4562

Magazines were another item commonly donated by charities. Although the division subscribed to a number of periodicals, such as *Newsweek, Time, Reader's Digest, Maclean's, Atlantic Monthly,* and *Harpers,* donations were always welcome. Arriving around two months after publication, magazines were purchased from the US Special Services in packs of twenty for groups of around eighty men.[72] Reliable postal delivery was a constant and vital source of support for the members of the division. Serving far away from home, soldiers kept in touch with loved ones through the regular exchange of correspondence and gifts (see Figure 5). Letters remained "the sole means of international communication" in the early 1950s.[73] As Lindsey Koren of the Smithsonian Institute has observed, "mail call is a moment when the front line and the home front connect. Letters, news and packages from home unite families, boost morale and in wartime, elevate the ordinary to the extraordinary."[74]

Adjutant General (A) Branch

The system for supplying basic amenities remained unchanged throughout the war, but the delivery of other welfare services was systematically reorganized after the division was created in the summer of 1951. Working in concert with officers from the other Commonwealth countries, the British Adjutant General (A) Branch took the lead in providing troops with recreational facilities, entertainment, and social services such as chaplaincy, counselling, and education. For the purposes of organization, the Korean/Japanese theatre was divided into three distinct geographic zones: subareas north, south, and Tokyo. Welfare officers were appointed to each sector to coordinate and administer activities in that area.[75] Historically, military welfare work has been the purview of charitable organizations like the Red Cross, the Royal Legion, and the Knights of Columbus. During both world wars, these groups operated successfully in Europe and a number of other theatres.[76] There was, however, a degree of "overlapping, competition and waste of effort and scarce materials,"[77] and beginning in the late 1940s, the British Army took greater control of coordination.

Recreation

Canteens have been a staple of military life since the early twentieth century, and they were a common sight in Korea. From 1951 to 1953, the Navy, Army and Air Force Institute (NAAFI) ran the majority of canteens that divisional personnel frequented. Originally established in 1921, NAAFI was first created to provide British soldiers with fairly priced goods while they served overseas. Prior to its creation, canteens were primarily managed by private companies and were notorious for charging extortionate prices. At the height of the Korean War, NAAFI's operations were extensive and the organization employed over four hundred staff members in theatre, who were commissioned members of either the Royal Army Service Corps or the Women's Royal Army Corps.[78]

A series of NAAFI canteens were built in quick succession at Seoul, Tokchon, and Teal Bridge in 1951.[79] Located close to the front lines, they sold everything from basic groceries, cigarettes, beer, and hard liquor to recreational items like cameras, darts, and cards.[80] The staff even managed to set up a "flourishing gift and sports shop."[81] Housed in vans, fourteen mobile units also operated throughout the country because of the difficulties associated with securing building materials and experienced labour. NAAFI's central depot in Kure provided both

FIGURE 6   A group of Commonwealth soldiers wait to be served by staff at a Navy, Army and Air Force Institute (NAAFI) mobile canteen. Mobile canteen drivers were particularly admired for their intrepid spirit and determination to reach front-line troops under difficult and dangerous circumstances.

Source: Ian Robertson/Australian War Memorial Photo Collection No. P01813.741

the canteens and mobile units with supplies. The staff included over a hundred military personnel and Japanese civilians who regularly processed a huge volume of goods, shipping, for example, nearly ten thousand cases of beer from Japan to Korea every week.[82]

NAAFI's main purpose was to ensure that "little luxuries [were] available at low cost, right up the line."[83] Unlike during both world wars, NAAFI did not have to cope with wartime austerity measures or prolonged shipping disruptions. Goods were easily accessible and reasonably priced, and NAAFI was widely praised for its dependability and customer service.[84] The greatest admiration was reserved for mobile canteen drivers. Writing home in 1951, NAAFI employee Robin McKechney recalled:

A few weeks ago, one of our mobile vans approached a forward unit from the front, and, being in full view for two miles as it lumbered down the road, it narrowly escaped being shot at by a section of Canadian tanks until someone, through binoculars, recognised the name on the front. When he arrived, the mobile driver coolly explained that he had come round the front way because the road surface was better and he did not want to bounce his stock about.[85]

Praised for their intrepid if somewhat foolhardy spirit, drivers frequently put themselves at significant risk to deliver shipments to the front.

Besides canteens, NAAFI set up and ran a series of clubs or roadhouses. First developed during the Western Desert campaign (1941–43), roadhouses included rest areas, games rooms, and small restaurants or cafes. Located along the division's main line of communications, the Newmarket, Newcastle, Northlands, and Ship Inn were all built in a "picturesque old world pub style, and had timbered ceilings, thatched roofs (rice straw from the local paddy fields), brick and tiled fireplaces – a welcome change from the smelly oil stoves that heated the tents – gaily planted window frames and doors. [They] were surrounded by vehicles and gardens where, in summer, brightly coloured umbrellas stood among the seats."[86] Roadhouses were a popular destination for Commonwealth troops and were also frequented by personnel from the other UN contingents.[87]

Throughout the war, there was a lack of basic infrastructure and there were few buildings in which to shelter. Periodic flooding during the summer months exacerbated the logistical challenges. As author Lieutenant Colonel Howard Cole described:

No worse terrain could be imagined for a fast moving mechanised army, the roads ... were little better than ditches of glutinous mud, which later dried into long ribbons of thick dust which, as convoys moved, billowed up in clouds as dark as London "pea soup fog." So dark, it was, on occasions that drivers were ordered to keep their headlights on even in the middle of the day.[88]

NAAFI's accomplishments seem all the more extraordinary given the hazards that they encountered and the difficulties of operating in Korea.

In Japan, the Australian Army Canteen Service (AACS) operated most of the canteens and clubs that Commonwealth soldiers visited on leave. Originally deployed as part of the British Commonwealth Occupation Force, the AACS

FIGURE 7   British soldiers pose with a sailor in front of the Australian Army Canteen Service's Kookabura Club in Tokyo in June 1951.
Source: Harold Vaughan Dunkley/Australian War Memorial Photo Collection No. DUKJ4425

ran the Anzac Club in Kure, the Empire Club in nearby Hiro, and the Kookaburra Club in Tokyo (see Figure 7), and also owned and operated the Ebisu Leave Centre. Located in a leafy and quiet suburb of Tokyo, Ebisu was the most convenient place where soldiers could find accommodations,[89] and was the preferred destination of Brits, Australians, and New Zealanders.

Although they were more than welcome at Ebisu, Canadian troops frequently chose to make alternative arrangements. As one soldier confessed in an interview with author Brent Byron-Watson in 1997, they had little desire to spend their leave "eating mutton and listening to how great the British and Australians thought they were."[90]

Historian David J. Bercuson has argued that "for much of the Korean War, the Canadian army was not prepared to take care of its men's morale or their physical or spiritual well being behind the front."[91] While the men were generally well supported in Korea, the arrangements made for Canadians visiting Japan did leave something to be desired. The Canadian Red Cross managed to remedy the problem only in 1953, when a dedicated leave centre, christened the Maple Leaf Club, was opened to great acclaim in Tokyo.[92] Boasting a lounge, writing and reading rooms, snack bars, a canteen, and a games room, it also included an information desk where the staff could direct soldiers towards "good restaurant and theatre locations, the best place to shop, and even where to swim, fish or get oneself tattooed."[93] Both the Canadian and Australian clubs took great pains to employ female staffers. Prohibited from working in Korea, they acted as a reminder of home and provided a welcome contrast to life in a combat zone.[94]

By any measure, living standards in Korea were exceptionally harsh for civilians and soldiers alike. Infantrymen commonly lived in makeshift trenches and bunkers that could fill with smoke from the improvised stoves that they constructed during the winter months.[95] Exposed to the elements, servicemen often went for weeks without washing and shared their quarters with countless rodents and mites. Describing one such encounter with the local wildlife, veteran Rex Sheppard recalled:

> We had several nasty lodgers. They were the most enormous rats, which had been attracted by, probably food or dead bodies or whatever. The most horrific experience, I was laying in a bunker one night on a bed. During the night, I was conscious that there was a weight on my chest and I gingerly looked down and the biggest damn rat that I'd ever seen was laying inside my sleeping bag. It had got in there for warmth. My reaction, as I can remember it now, was I just ripped the sleeping bag open and threw the whole thing away.[96]

Sheppard's experience was common. Former ambulance orderly Bill Trevett remembers diligently checking his boots for rats in the winter and snakes and spiders in the summer.[97] It is easy to imagine how eagerly soldiers anticipated a visit to the canteen or a roadhouse, or the opportunity to visit Japan.

Entertainment

In a 2012 study titled "Morale, Psychological Wellbeing of UK Armed Forces and Entertainment," Professor Edgar Jones of King's College London explores the place of entertainment in military life. Reviewing the events of the past century, Jones concludes that "evidence gathered from both World Wars ... show[s] that entertainment is a morale sustaining factor."[98] This was true in Korea, where entertainment was critical in supporting Commonwealth morale. From July 1951 to July 1953, the fighting was characterized by long, monotonous patrols punctuated by terrifying nighttime assaults by North Korean and Chinese forces. Throughout the long stalemate, the officers of A Branch worked diligently to entertain and divert soldiers. The four most common types of entertainment in Korea were sports, radio, film, and live concerts.

Easy to organize and stage, sporting competitions were widespread. For British soldiers in particular, the popularity of sport was at fever pitch during the National Service years (1946–63), and troops competed in rugby, cricket, and football on a regular basis.[99] Living up to their national reputation, the Canadians converted frozen sections of the River Imjin into a rink for ice hockey tournaments in the winter.[100] The river was also an ideal place to race iceboats. First developed by a group of enterprising British officers, the small craft were equipped with blades and fitted with large sails. During the colder months, aspiring sailors challenged one another to contests. Attracting large and boisterous crowds, these games gave servicemen an opportunity to socialize and cheer on their favourites.[101] Participation in physical recreation helped foster a healthy spirit of rivalry between the opposing teams and further fostered group cohesion at the battalion level.

The division's front line snaked across the Korean landscape for over nine miles. Units were separated from one another by steep hills, deep ravines, and heavily wooded areas. As a result, radio was another crucial way to communicate and entertain. Early in 1951, units were equipped with radios that could receive signals from US stations in Japan and a number of overseas commercial providers, such as the Canadian Broadcasting Corporation.[102] Opened in March 1952, the divisional station Crown Radio was staffed by members of the Royal Australian Educational Corps (RAEC) and aired news and variety shows every evening (see Figure 9).[103]

Moviegoing was popular, and A Branch organized a divisional film library. Run by the Army Kinema Corps, it included an extensive range of Hollywood pictures and a smaller selection of British, Canadian, and Australian productions. Screened outdoors during the summer months and in hutted theatres in the winter, films could draw crowds of 300 to 400 men at one time. Cinema attendance figures were always high. For example, the film library issued over seven

FIGURE 8 Brigadier John Rockingham drops the puck at a championship game between 2nd Battalion Royal 22e Régiment and 1st Battalion Princess Patricia's Canadian Light Infantry.
Source: Stephens/Canada Department of National Defence PA-128859

FIGURE 9 Two soldiers from the Royal Australian Educational Corps set up projectors for a screening of *The Daughter of Rosie O'Grady* on St. Patrick's Day, 1951.
Source: Harold Vaughan Dunkley/Australian War Memorial Photo Collection No. DUKJ4020

hundred movies a month with an average attendance figure of 120,300 from April to August 1953 alone.[104] Like their friends and families back home, soldiers enjoyed escaping the world outside and immersing themselves in the world onscreen.

Live concerts and performances have always had their own distinct allure. In contrast to other forms of entertainment, "the live show brings direct human contact and spontaneity."[105] During the Second World War, famous performers such as British singers Vera Lynn and Gracie Fields travelled extensively to entertain and amuse servicemen. This tradition continued in Korea. On average, each of the Commonwealth countries dispatched four concert parties to the Far East every year. Sponsored by private companies, concert parties were lively variety shows that typically featured six different performers. For several months at a time, a small band of comedians, singers, and vaudeville acts would visit Commonwealth units across Korea and Japan.[106] From 1950 to 1953, the division played host to the likes of British comedian Frankie Howerd, Australian actor Al Thomas, Canadian comedy duo Wayne and Shuster, and famed American variety performers such as Danny Kaye and Jack Benny.[107] Many years later, British singer and radio host Carole Carr remembered how appreciative the troops were of live performers. Of her 1952 visit, she recalled:

> One of my most vivid memories is the show I did for the Welch Regiment in a rainstorm. They were getting soaked, so I asked them if they wanted me to carry on. They yelled YES, but they had the last laugh. Suddenly the canvas roof over the stage caved in and I was drenched ... to a wave of cheers and whistles.[108]

Social Services

While the officers of A Branch were responsible for providing entertainment, they also fulfilled a more serious function. The Royal Army Chaplain's Department (RAChD), counselling services, and the Royal Army Educational Corps all fell under the control of the Adjutant General. Chaplains, personnel officers, and teachers were a key point of contact for soldiers in distress and those seeking further education and professional opportunities.

Following the Second World War, compulsory church parades were largely abandoned and the number of military chaplains greatly reduced.[109] However, religion remained an important and active force during the Korean War. Religious radio programs were among the most popular shows broadcast by Crown Radio, and many units took it upon themselves to build small chapels along the front. In addition, the number of soldiers who attended church on a weekly basis grew significantly from 1950 to 1953.[110] Writing to the Adjutant General in December 1953, Deputy Assistant Chaplain General M.S. James reported that "confirmation services held both in battalion positions and in Seoul Cathedral and elsewhere were attended by large numbers of troops of every nation."[111] The RAChD organized, "courses of religious instruction" and spiritual retreats for groups of up to the thirty men at the Divisional Rest Centre in Incheon.[112] Maintaining a warm relationship with its American counterparts, it helped host "many joint conferences for study and worship" at the headquarters of the US Eighth Army.[113] Chaplains were regular visitors at all of the division's major medical units, including 25 Canadian Field Dressing Station. According to a historical review of pastoral work in Korea, "as is traditional, the relationship between Chaplains and doctors was at all times close. Visitation of the sick through Medical Evacuation Channels often proved arduous and lengthy but repaid every effort."[114] In comforting the sick and wounded, chaplains were seen as trusted and welcome advisers by patients and staff. Psychiatrists were still regarded with a degree of suspicion by many men. Consequently, chaplains offered an acceptable alternative outlet for expressing grievances or distress.

Chaplains provided spiritual counsel and succour. Personnel officers (POs) were primarily trained to address domestic problems and issues surrounding resettlement. POs could contact families or arrange to send someone home in extreme circumstances. Resettlement counselling was designed to help soldiers negotiate future career options, and was mandatory for those entering their last six months on tour. Personnel officers also organized over ninety different pre-release courses to help servicemen train as qualified tradesmen.[115]

In addition to these vocational courses of instruction, the Royal Army Educational Corps coordinated an array of secondary- and postsecondary-level modules. It was possible to learn Japanese, Russian, French, and various other languages. One could take correspondence courses from Oxford, Cambridge, the City and Guilds Institute, the Institute of Civil Bankers, the University of Melbourne, or the Institute of Bankers in Scotland. Based in Kure, the RAEC headquarters were equipped with classrooms, a darkroom, and equipment for handicrafts such as woodworking, model making, and leatherwork. Course reading materials and other pertinent literature were available at 41 Command Library. Opened in August 1952, it held 4,762 books. Mostly donated by the public, the collection included fiction and nonfiction books that were available to troops through a mail order borrowing service. On average, 41 Command Library issued around 72 books per day and regularly dispatched mobile libraries to the front.[116]

Reflections

Morale is a difficult concept to pin down, and professional debate continues over how to define it and establish its parameters. Since the 1950s, the way that we fight has continued to evolve with the introduction of new technologies and strategies. However, morale remains critically important. Levels of morale can have a dramatic impact on combat-effectiveness, resilience, rates of psychiatric breakdown, and the ability to withstand extreme stress. Leadership, tours of duty, and policies fostering group cohesion and welfare services all played a part in raising morale during the Korean War. These factors helped soldiers survive and thrive in dire circumstances. Nevertheless, war always comes with a cost. The best preventative measures cannot protect everyone against psychiatric illness and trauma. It is to these men that we now turn our attention.

4
Weathering the Storm
Psychiatrists and Soldiers in the Field, 1950–53

JOHN WAS ONLY nineteen years old when he was sent to Korea. An intelligent and optimistic young man, National Service represented an adventure and his first foray into the wider world. With experience of first aid, he was quickly dispatched to Keogh Barracks to train as a nursing orderly with the Royal Army Medical Corps. As the Korean War escalated, he was assigned to a field ambulance to care for wounded soldiers in the field. During his time in the Far East, he cheerfully endured the vagaries of a life in uniform and the dangers of front-line service alongside the other members of his unit. Several months before he was due to return home, however, they found themselves the target of heavy and sustained shelling. Under the cover of darkness, the enemy launched an attack that lasted for hours. As John later recalled, "the war was almost always at night."[1] That evening, he was caring for a patient who appeared to be stable and in relatively good condition. In the bustle of attending to others, John and his fellow orderlies put the man to one side but soon noticed that he was rapidly deteriorating. Rushing him to the main field ambulance, they discovered that the soldier had been struck in the back with a piece of shrapnel that cut all the nerve endings to his stomach and shredded his arteries. There was nothing they could do.

That night John lost the second of only two patients that he would lose in Korea. Many years later, he remembered that "once it had quieted down, I went into my little dugout, where we sleep and suddenly burst into tears and just couldn't stop crying."[2] Inconsolable, John was hurriedly evacuated from the front lines and diagnosed with battle exhaustion. Given that he was nearing the end of his tour, his doctors decided to keep him removed from the fighting and occupied at the field ambulance. Shortly thereafter, he was put on a troopship back to Britain. Safely aboard, he continued to recuperate slowly from his experiences overseas. He quickly adjusted to life back home, eventually married, and had a successful career, but Korea had a lasting impact on his life. Over the years, he would occasionally dive for cover on hearing a loud sound. This sometimes proved embarrassing, but there were other deeper and more devastating changes. Most importantly, he remembered, "I was a bit depressed ... I could never get myself in gear again."[3] As he bravely confided, "I was never the same bright character" again.[4]

John is not alone. In a war zone, psychological scars are as inevitable as those left by bullets, bombs, and shrapnel, and the Korean War was no different from any other campaign. Moreover, it seemed to be a theatre primed for disaster. The Commonwealth troops deployed to the Far East in the summer of 1950 were not prepared for what they would encounter, their training was incomplete, and they knew little of the enemy they were expected to defeat.[5] Since 1945, the Royal Canadian Army Medical Corps (RCAMC) and the Royal Army Medical Corps (RAMC) had also experienced severe cuts to manpower and a massive loss of organizational knowledge. Consequently, there were relatively few doctors on hand to provide vital medical support.[6] Psychiatric casualties were also exceptionally high during the early months of the war. In July 1950, the US Army categorized 50 men per 1,000 as neuropsychiatric cases, and this figure had skyrocketed to 158 per 1,000 by the following month. Reports indicated that from July to December 1950, the 8054th Evacuation Hospital managed to return only 15 percent of cases back to duty.[7] At the time, contemporary observers derisively referred to this period of the war as the "great bug out."[8] When Commonwealth troops and medics first arrived, they faced an uphill battle (see Figure 10).[9]

FIGURE 10   An American serviceman comforts a fellow soldier who saw one of his friends killed in action in August 1950. American physical and psychiatric casualties were high during the early mobile phase of the war.

Source: Sergeant First Class Al Chang/US National Archives and Records Administration 111-SC-347803.

Organizing for War

Prior to the formation of the division in the summer of 1951, the Commonwealth countries worked together in a loose grouping. As new units landed in Busan, they were attached to either 27 British Commonwealth Infantry Brigade or 29th Independent Infantry Brigade Group.[10] During these early months, no psychiatric personnel were deployed to Korea. Anticipating that the war would be over soon and considering their limited resources, the Commonwealth countries chose to maintain a policy of evacuating all psychiatric casualties for treatment in Japan throughout late 1950 and early 1951. Most of the patients were dispatched to No. 29 British General Hospital at headquarters in the port city of Kure.[11] Opened in November 1950, the hospital included a small psychiatric ward of thirty beds commanded by the well-respected Captain J.J. Flood of the Royal Army Medical Corps. The remaining casualties were funnelled through the American evacuation system for treatment at 361 Station Hospital in the Japanese capital of Tokyo. Large and well equipped, it was widely considered to be the hub of American neuropsychiatric activity in the Far East and boasted a staff of psychiatrists, neurologists, psychologists, and social work assistants.[12]

As the largest contingent in the theatre, the Americans were infinitely better equipped than their Commonwealth counterparts to meet the challenges posed by the Korean campaign. The US Army Medical Corps was well funded and could afford to invest heavily in the development of psychiatric programs. Under the guidance of Second World War veteran Colonel Albert J. Glass, "US divisional psychiatry became operational within eight weeks of the beginning of hostilities and by December 1950 a three tier system of treatment (forward psychiatry, hospitals in Korea, and two convalescent units in Japan) was in place."[13] In contrast, the US Army took over two years to implement similar measures during the Second World War.[14] Despite these improvements, Glass complained that the "steps to prevent and salvage psychiatric casualties were taken after the need [had become] glaringly apparent."[15] Due to lack of available bed space in Korea, the Americans initially evacuated neuropsychiatric patients to Japan. As Commonwealth doctors similarly discovered, this was an ill-conceived decision. Studies conducted during the two world wars suggested that the further back a soldier was evacuated from the front lines for treatment, the less likely he was to return to duty. With this policy in force, "only 50% of [American] psychiatric patients were salvaged" for either combat or non-combat duty from July to September 1950.[16]

When the Commonwealth Division finally became operational on July 28, 1951, a divisional psychiatrist was immediately appointed in order to staunch the flow of psychiatric evacuees from Korea. The job entailed organizing and overseeing all psychiatric care in theatre, supervising field/hospital-based treatment, and advising officers on matters of discipline and morale. Based at 25 Canadian Field Dressing Station (25 FDS), the divisional psychiatrist oversaw a ward of forty-four beds and a small team of staff, including an assisting clinical officer and several specially trained nurses.[17] British officers "with psychiatric qualifications were [generally] not deployed to Korea but kept in Germany, the UK and other long term postings."[18] Therefore, the position of divisional psychiatrist was primarily a Canadian appointment from 1951 to 1953. Majors R.J.A. Robitaille, F.C.R. Chalke, and J.L. Johnston were all career officers in the Royal Canadian Army Medical Corps as well as Second World War veterans.[19] With widespread commitments elsewhere, the RAMC only took responsibility for the role when Major Johnston was forced to return home unexpectedly in May 1953. By that time, it was already clear that the worst of the fighting was over and the war was coming to a close. Johnston's replacement, Captain N.G. Fraser, was a National Service officer who had worked as his assistant over the preceding months. A recent graduate of the University of Aberdeen, Fraser was young and relatively inexperienced when he was first appointed, as was his successor, fellow Aberdeen classmate and friend Lieutenant Leslie Bartlet, who took the reins in November.[20]

While Commonwealth resources were concentrated in one key location, the Americans fielded multiple psychiatric units in Korea. Major medical centres like 121 Evacuation Hospital included dedicated neuropsychiatric sections. The US Army Medical Corps also created travelling psychiatric detachments or KO teams to augment existing services.[21] Positioned in areas with the greatest number of casualties, KO teams were "100 percent mobile with trucks, jeeps, and enough tents for ... staff and a few patients."[22] Equipped with the latest diagnostic technology, the units typically included a psychiatrist, a psychologist, and social workers who had around one or two years of "professional training in their speciality."[23] According to James A. Martin, Linette R. Sparacino, and Gregory Belenky, KO teams, "could roll into a medical clearing company to give it expertise in battle fatigue restoration or reconditioning, and perhaps even take it over and make the medical clearing company into ... a neuropsychiatry centre."[24] Considering the extent of their resources, the Americans would prove to be a crucial ally for the Commonwealth over the next few years.

Screening and Rotation

In light of the American "bug out," Commonwealth officials initially anticipated a high level of psychiatric casualties. Although the numbers ultimately failed to materialize, there were significant problems with the first troops deployed to Korea. Poor recruit screening was largely to blame. For example, many of the first Canadians sent to Korea presented with previously undiscovered conditions such as "chronic bronchitis, flat feet, atrophy of the leg muscles, cardiac palpitations [and] hypertension" on arriving in the Far East.[25] In the first six months, nearly 20 percent were also repatriated because of "disciplinary, attitudinal, and psychiatric problems."[26] Recruitment of the Canadian Army Special Force was hastily carried out throughout the summer and autumn of 1950. Overwhelmed by the sheer number of new recruits, medical officers conducted cursory examinations and failed to spot numerous physical and psychological complaints. Military historians Brent Byron-Watson and David J. Bercuson have also argued that the members of Special Force did not receive proper training before deployment.[27] The "training syllabi were virtually the same as those used by the Canadian Army during the Second World War, modified only slightly to meet what was known about the special circumstances of geography, climate, and the enemy's tactics in Korea."[28] Furthermore, the tempo of training was too slow. Believing that the war would be over soon, Canadian authorities failed to institute an appropriate training schedule. As a result, they were caught off guard when China entered the war in November 1950.[29]

For the remainder of the war, greater care was taken in screening servicemen bound for Korea. Problems periodically arose with the arrival of new troops in theatre. For instance, the fresh 1st Battalion Royal Australian Regiment (1 RAR), 1st Battalion Royal Canadian Regiment (1 RCR), and 1st Battalion Royal 22é Régiment (1 R22er) landed in Korea from April to June 1952. During this period, psychiatric admissions to 25 Canadian Field Dressing Station nearly tripled over the previous few months. Reporting to his superiors, divisional psychiatrist Major F.C.R. Chalke indicated that most of his patients were members of the recently rotated units and that figures would improve as they adjusted to front-line service. Over the following months, Chalke's predictions proved correct.[30]

Infantry soldiers who arrived in theatre as individual replacements were considered to be at an elevated risk of psychiatric breakdown. It was therefore divisional policy to rotate troops in battalion-sized groups of between six hundred and eight hundred men.[31] This was not the case for members of the 3rd Battalion Royal Australian Regiment (3 RAR). Unlike the other Australian units, the officers and men of 3 RAR were replaced individually as circumstance dictated.[32] According to noted historian Robert J. O'Neill, this system presented many drawbacks and was the reason that "army headquarters in Melbourne ... decided it was preferable to replace whole units after twelve months service in Korea."[33] The failures suffered in Korea contributed to Australia's decision to abandon individual rotation altogether, "in later commitments such as the Malayan Emergency, the Indonesian Confrontation and the Vietnam War."[34] The arrival of untried strangers disrupted the group dynamic of units and could have a negative impact on combat effectiveness. There were numerous "complaints from the battalion [3 RAR] about the suitability of some of the soldiers selected for reinforcement drafts."[35] It was also apparent that "some of these men would not have been accepted for war service by a unit training as a whole to go to Korea, because their weakness would have been revealed in exercises before embarkation."[36] In his May 1953 report, Captain Rutherford of 3 RAR pointed out the increase in the number of soldiers on sick parade presenting with psychosomatic and purely psychological complaints. He was quick to identify the root of the problem, stating that "the battalion suffers to some degree from the results of inadequate screening, physical and psychological, of the reinforcements which it receives under the system of individual replacement."[37]

The US Army encountered similar difficulties. In common with the Australians, American soldiers were rotated as individuals using a points-based system rather than as members of a particular unit or group. Problems arose when new soldiers arrived in theatre or as experienced men approached the end of their tour. Reviewing American policy shortly after the war, Colonel Glass contended that "the most pertinent defect of rotation ... arises from the disruption of group identification which occurs when the combat soldier is notified or becomes aware that soon he will go home."[38] Glass further argued that

> the increase of tension that follows as the [soldier] shifts his feelings for the group to concern for himself often makes battle fear unbearable. In some cases there is inability to function, with temporary breakdown. For most individuals, anxiety is noticeably increased in the last days of combat, as if it were now more dangerous to tempt fate.[39]

Like the rest of the Commonwealth Division, the British experienced elevated levels of psychiatric illness during periods of rotation. Logic suggests that young and inexperienced National Servicemen would be at greatest risk. After all, "just over half [of British troops] were national servicemen – nearly three quarters in the final year" of the war.[40] This was not the case, however. In his monthly report in January 1953, psychiatrist Major Johnston recorded that 26 out of 30 British patients were Regulars and emphasized that this "large preponderance ... [was] consistent with findings of previous months."[41] There are several pivotal reasons why events took shape this way. First, the British government was forced to recall the "A and B sections of the Regular Reserve" to meet the emergency in the Far East. These men "had served through the Second World War, and many had only a short period of reserve left when they were recalled."[42] As Jeffrey Grey has pointed out, "they were by definition likely to be settled family men with jobs or businesses to run, and their resentment at this disruption to their lives can be imagined."[43] Re-enlisted men were willing participants, but they too presented problems. In a January 1950 article for the *Journal of the Royal Army Medical Corps*, Lieutenant Colonel Harry Pozner revealed that there was a "high and increasing incidence of psychiatric breakdown among re-enlisted personnel."[44] He postulated that they were prompted to rejoin the army because of a failure to cope effectively with civilian life following demobilization. Pozner argued that veterans hoped to regain a sense of stability in the forces and recapture the camaraderie of their previous service, but were frequently disappointed by what they found.[45]

Psychiatric Casualties

While untried recruits and newly rotated troops were more susceptible to psychiatric breakdown, everyone in theatre was at risk, and the patient population represented a broad spectrum of the division, from young conscripts to officers. Casualties were at their highest during the first year of the war, when hostilities were mobile and UN forces suffered the greatest number of battle casualties.[46] From December 1950 to November 1951, Captain Flood recorded that among the British contingent around 35 men per 1,000 were admitted for mental health problems.[47] Similarly, American rates hovered between 32 and 36 men per 1,000 from July to October 1951.[48] These figures are comparable with "many theaters of World War Two."[49] As the front line stabilized and the division suffered fewer casualties, admissions declined correspondingly. Throughout 1952 and 1953, psychiatric admissions to medical units commonly ranged from 5 to 9 percent of the total patient population.[50] American rates also fell "as the battle lines stabilized" and "medical support for ... UN forces became more uniformly and systematically applied with less of the improvised procedures that were made necessary by the previous erratic tactical situation."[51] Commonwealth soldiers suffered from a wide range of mental health problems, but most fit into one of three diagnostic categories: psychoneurosis, character disorder, or battle exhaustion.

Over 50 percent of Commonwealth psychiatric patients were diagnosed as psychoneurotic. Since the early twentieth century, Army psychiatrists have commonly used the word as a generic term denoting an anxiety condition, and they continued to do so in Korea.[52] As a diagnostic label, it was applicable to a variety of patients, and contemporary RAMC and RCAMC teaching manuals broadly defined psychoneurosis as an illness "resulting from the exclusion from consciousness of powerful emotional charges."[53] Distinguished British psychiatrists Sir David K. Henderson and Dr. Robert D. Gillespie were equally vague in their description. The 1950 edition of Henderson and Gillespie's seminal *Textbook of Psychiatry for Students and Practitioners* simply refers to psychoneurosis as "an indication of mental conflict" and one of the "commonest modes of faulty response to the stresses of life."[54] The condition was primarily characterized by, "anxiety ... either free floating and unbound or directly felt and expressed."[55]

Roughly 10 to 17 percent of the division's psychiatric casualties were admitted for character-related disorders.[56] In contrast to psychoneurosis, problems of this nature were not distinguished by "mental or emotional symptoms," but rather behavioural difficulties.[57] Writing to Canadian medical officers in September 1947, the acting Director of Army Medical Services, Colonel Stanley Shier, pointed out that "such disorders are characterised by developmental defects or pathological personality structure, with minimal subjective anxiety, and little or no sense of distress."[58] He also stated that "in most instances, the disorder is manifested by a life-long pattern of action or behaviour (acting out)."[59] As a result, alcoholics, drug addicts, the habitual troublemaker, and those who manifested immature personality traits were typical patients. The number of admissions for character or behavioural problems invariably increased when the division was in reserve. American medics also noted that cases were "predominantly characteriological" during "quiescent periods with less artillery fire."[60]

Divisional policy dictated that men presenting with behavioural problems be dealt with administratively. This was an arduous, time-consuming, and highly bureaucratic process, however. Doctors at 25 FDS regularly complained that officers attempted to dispose of troublemakers through medical channels. In July 1953, Captain N.G. Fraser reported that "it would appear that the principal reason for this [was] that administrative modes of disposal [were] so ponderous, or knowledge of them so lacking that it [was] thought simpler and quicker to present men as psychiatric cases."[61] When routine examination revealed the ruse, the man was sent back to his unit. This was rarely the end of the matter, however. Corresponding with the author, former divisional psychiatrist Dr. Leslie Bartlet described what frequently happened in such situations: "The units would be disappointed. They would simply love to get rid of them and would often protest, 'How can you say this guy is normal?'"[62] Bartlet recalled that some officers insisted on sending men back for further examination, which helped fuel a vicious cycle that wasted both time and resources. The divisional psychiatrist could only respond by doggedly enforcing the rules and rejecting cases that should be disposed of administratively. American doctors had to be similarly vigilant in addressing abuses, and psychiatrist Hyam Bolocan reminded his colleagues that "busy and harassed officers are likely to [take advantage of medical channels] ... if encouraged by lax medical discipline."[63]

Throughout the twentieth century, battle exhaustion has been the source of "considerable losses of effective manpower among Commonwealth and US troops."[64] Since the First World War, it has been known by many names, including shell shock and combat fatigue.[65] Psychiatrists and soldiers alike have struggled to adequately define, understand, and label this condition. When the Korean War began in the summer of 1950, it was generally regarded as an anxiety disorder stemming from direct combat exposure, with symptoms including "weariness, apathy, jumpiness [and] disinterest."[66] While the division failed to maintain detailed records about the early phases of the war, "only 37 cases [of battle exhaustion] were reported in the context of 2,026 casualties" from May 1952 to July 1953.[67] In reviewing the Korean campaign, members of the Canadian Defence Medical and Dental Advisory Board later concluded that this was largely because "battles were of short duration and the fatigue factor was not operative."[68] Moreover, the division suffered a relatively low level of casualties in the static phase of the war (July 1951 to July 1953). Subsequent academic studies indicate that levels of battle exhaustion are directly tied to the number of killed and wounded.[69] For example, the British Second Army recorded rates as high as 200 per 1,000 at the height of the Normandy campaign from July to September 1944.[70] During the Korean War, casualties were more manageable and rose only in periods of heavy combat. For instance, from October 2–5, 1951 Commonwealth troops "advanced some 6,000 yards to capture and establish a new line north of the River Imjin" as part of Operation Commando.[71] Later that month, Chinese and North Korean forces attempted to recover the ground they had lost. Meanwhile, psychiatric admissions increased measurably. Around 240 men were admitted to 25 FDS for treatment during the operation, a 60 percent increase in admissions over the previous two months. In his report of November 1952, Major J.L. Johnston clearly linked the rising number of casualties to the division's participation in Commando (see Figure 11).[72]

The American experience of battle exhaustion closely mirrored that of the 1st Commonwealth Division. For example, the US 7th Infantry Division participated in Operation Showdown from October 14 to November 25, 1952. In attempting to gain control of a critical hilltop position, it suffered heavy casualties. Neuropsychiatrist Captain Robert J. Lavin reported prior to Showdown, that rates of battle exhaustion were negligible and admissions were confined to cases of anxiety and character and behavioural problems. During the operation, however, over 50 percent of psychiatric admissions were cases of exhaustion. As the tempo of operations increased, so did the number of beleaguered and exhausted soldiers.[73]

In addition to psychoneurosis, character disorder, and battle exhaustion, "post-combat syndromes typified by unexplained medical symptoms were a feature of the Korean War."[74] From April 1952 to June 1953, "the chief causes of admission to the base hospital were respiratory (10%), gastrointestinal (2.7%) and skin reactions (10.3%)."[75] The commanding officer of the Canadian section of the

FIGURE 11   This photo of Private Heath Matthews of the Royal Canadian Regiment has become one of the most famous of the Korean War. The image of Matthews waiting to be seen by a medical officer is an iconic representation of the grim and exhausting nature of combat.
Source: Paul Tomelin/Library and Archives Canada PA 128850.

British Commonwealth General Hospital, Lieutenant-Colonel N.H. McNally, reported in June 1952 that "the manpower wastage ... due to evacuation of such patients has been enormous."[76] While he concluded that the majority of cases displayed clear physical signs of disease, McNally also recognized that "psychological factors" were at play.[77] On being interviewed, many patients revealed that the onset of their illness coincided with domestic difficulties and other personal problems.[78] Several months later, Assistant Director of Medical Services Colonel Morgan Smith issued Administrative Instruction Serial No. 12, in which he called on medical officers to be wary of evacuating patients with unexplained physical symptoms. Morgan Smith reminded his colleagues that these conditions were often "bodily responses to anxiety, resentment or low morale."[79] They (the medical authorities) theorized that somatic reactions were a way to relieve this anxiety, "by channelling the originating impulses through the autonomic nervous system into visceral organ symptoms and complaints."[80] British and Canadian records do not indicate the number of patients who fell into this category, but a study of US Army orthopedic patients reported in the *American Journal of Psychiatry* in January 1951 concluded that "psychiatric symptoms were present in ... 56% of patients."[81] It is plausible that the division's figures were comparable given that American and Commonwealth troops worked closely together, endured similar privations, and were exposed to the same environmental hazards.

Throughout the winter of 1950–51, over eight thousand UN servicemen were treated for cold-weather injuries such as frostbite, trench foot, and immersion foot. Like its allies, the division quickly found itself severely challenged by the extremes of the Korean climate.[82] A correspondent for the *British Medical Journal* reported that "the number of [British troops admitted] to hospital for the period November 1950 to February 1951 was 120, of which 66 were diagnosed as frostbite, 37 as trench foot, and 22 as exposure conditions."[83] Investigating the problem, the ADMS and his staff became convinced that cold injuries, like other medically unexplained disorders, were not the result of chance mishap or particularly severe conditions alone. They had good reason to come to this conclusion. In a study of American servicemen in Korea titled "Cold Injury in Man," H.E. Hanson and R.F. Goldman "estimated that the number of cases reported during combat was greater than would have been predicted based solely on temperature or wind-chill."[84] They believed that it was necessary to consider psychological motivation. Commonwealth medics also took this into account. There were even concerns that some cases were "self inflicted by men who had removed their boots or neglected to take proper precautions."[85]

Both the British and the Americans dispatched research teams to the Far East in the winter of 1951–52 to investigate what "had given rise to the incidence of cold injury in the military operations of the previous winter."[86] British Physiologist Major J.M. Adam and Senior Medical Research Officer W.S.S. Ladell arrived in Korea in January 1952. Over the next two months, they studied 700 front-line troops from the Commonwealth Division to gauge how they responded to cold weather. They compared the control group against men who were hospitalized for cold injuries at either the British Commonwealth General Hospital or one of several American hospitals. Their findings highlighted the role of stress, morale, and the individual's mental state in the incidence of cold injury.[87] Samuel C. Bullock, Luther L. Mays, and Albert N. Berenberg of the US Army Medical Research Laboratory came to the same conclusion. Comparing 110 frostbitten American soldiers with 20 other troops who were hospitalized for unrelated conditions, they argued that the frostbitten men "had a lower drive for prestige, took fewer precautions against the cold and exhibited a greater range of hypochondriacal beliefs."[88] As historian and psychotherapist Edgar Jones has argued, physical injuries like frostbite "served as a defence against psychiatric disorders in situations of intolerable stress."[89]

Thenceforth, commanders went to great lengths to prevent further cold injuries, and only thirty-five admissions were reported from the Commonwealth Division in the winter of 1952–53. Several key factors contributed to this development. First, the division secured kit and clothing better suited to requirements. Second, a strict inspection regime was put in place to ensure that units adhered to hygienic practices and complied with other preventative measures. Servicemen were also more consistently and rigorously briefed about the dangers of cold weather and how best to prevent injury. Finally, the division took a more punitive stance on the treatment and disposition of future cold injuries.[90] Early in the season, the Assistant Director of Medical Services announced that "the division has reached a stage when one should treat every case of cold injury within our lines as a self-inflicted wound."[91]

Throughout the twentieth century, the military severely punished soldiers presenting with self-inflicted wounds (SIWs), and the Korean campaign was no exception. As they had done in the past, the Commonwealth countries took a hard line on the issue. Servicemen treated for SIWs were not seen as psychiatric casualties or victims but as offenders deserving of punishment.[92] In light of this consideration, the authorities were alarmed to discover that medical units were admitting an increasing number of accidentally wounded soldiers throughout 1951. The Americans also experienced an increase in the number of patients who required treatment for accidental burns and gunshot wounds (GSWs). Events came to a head in February 1952, when the British Director General of Army Medical Services, Sir Neil Cantlie, toured the Commonwealth General Hospital in Kure. During his visit, Cantlie was distressed to learn that twenty-four out of eighty-three patients admitted that day were being treated for accidental GSWs. On examining the men, he became convinced that they had injured themselves, and he contacted his superiors back in Britain.[93] Shortly thereafter, Chief of the Imperial General Staff Field Marshal Sir William Slim wrote to the division's commanding officer, Major General Cassels. On March 19, 1952, Cassels responded to Slim's inquiries and was quick to reassure him. While acknowledging that "a great number of ... accidental wound cases ... were self inflicted," he also felt it necessary to explain that the division had suffered "a number of genuine accidental wounds."[94] Although it was difficult to prove whether or not a wound was self-inflicted, Cassels informed Slim that suspicious cases were investigated thoroughly:

It is standard procedure in all contingents in the division that any accidental wound is immediately investigated ... All medical officers understand that they must report, to the unit commanding officer (CO), any case of accidental wounding. If there is a shred of evidence that it was self-inflicted all COs are only too keen to court-martial the man and I am completely certain that no CO in this division would try or wish to hide any case. In many cases where self-infliction cannot be proved the man is charged with negligence and punished as far as possible.[95]

Cassels was positive about how Commonwealth troops were coping with the campaign and noted that the number of accidents had not affected morale. He remarked that "when one remembers the very wide front we are holding and the extreme cold at night it puts a very great strain on the individual and, in my view, it says a very great deal for the soldiers as a whole that they have performed so well and have kept in such good spirits."[96]

Despite Cassels's reassurances, Field Marshal Slim sent the Commander-in-Chief of Far Eastern Land Forces, General Sir Charles Keightley, to make further inquiries. Touring divisional medical units, Keightley reported to Slim on April 22, 1952, that while "there are certainly a surprisingly large number of accidental wounds in hospital at present," he did not "believe that the problem was really as serious as it appears."[97] Keightley believed that most of the accidents were genuine and listed several contributing factors. Accidents could be the result of:

- the intense cold, which makes fingers slip
- the inherent unreliability of Stens [submachine guns]
- jumpiness in night fighting against Chinese who are apt to appear in any direction
- lack of practice in handling weapons with so many National Service men seeing war for the first time.[98]

Although some accidents were undoubtedly self-inflicted, there was no need for alarm. Keightley agreed with Cassels that "morale was uniformly good and the bearing of men smart and alert."[99] He noted that this was "especially creditable in view of the very difficult time battalions are having; static wars are always such a test in this way."[100] While reports of SIWs declined, the division monitored the situation and carefully investigated accidents. Cassels was determined that any soldier who was discovered to have wounded himself would meet with punishment rather than medical care. In a letter to Slim, he referred to such men as "weaklings who [had] taken the easy way out."[101] He promised that "if and when we ... catch one he will certainly be dealt with most severely." However, despite his zeal to prosecute SIW cases, it appears that Cassels had little opportunity to punish offenders. Given the difficulty of gathering evidence, only a handful of Commonwealth soldiers were ever charged.[102]

For the remainder of the war, psychiatric casualties remained relatively low and manageable. There was a noticeable increase in admissions immediately prior to the armistice in July 1953. Beginning in May, divisional psychiatrist Captain Fraser reported a dramatic increase in the number of hysteric patients. While only a handful of servicemen had been diagnosed with this condition since the beginning of the war, hysterics now comprised an astonishing 39 percent of the division's caseload. By June, this figure had risen to 43 percent.[103] Classified as a conversion reaction, hysteria occurs when an "impulse causing anxiety ... is converted into functional symptoms in organs or parts of the body, mainly under voluntary control."[104] Symptoms can include anything from partial paralysis and tremors to functional blindness and deafness.[105] Knowing that Chinese, North Korean, and UN representatives were on the verge of a peace agreement, Fraser was not concerned about the rise in hysteria. Roughly a month later, he was vindicated when there was a corresponding drop in the number of patients. In his monthly report for August 1953, Fraser explained:

> Although fighting on many sectors of the front was very fierce just before the cessation of hostilities, the Commonwealth front was relatively quiet. Correlating the increased front line psychiatric casualties with the decreased activity we can assume that tension in the minds of the men must have been higher and the fear of being killed just at the last moment greater.[106]

Following the armistice, the division slowly became an occupation force. This transition presented new and unexpected challenges. In early August 1953, a condition called "truce exhaustion" began to appear among infantry soldiers in "sufficient numbers to be regarded as a specific clinical entity."[107] Captain Fraser reported that the disorder usually affected those with "several months Korea service," and that a typical case, "complain[ed] of gradually increasing irritability – felt the country itself was getting him down – that he could no longer tolerate the boredom (or its opposite – excessive drilling) – that if he was allowed to go on 'something inside will give' and he would not be responsible for his actions."[108] Patients were "often of the roving mildly psychopathic type, show past histories of inability to settle down to one occupation and have thinly veiled or moderately controlled aggressive tendencies with low frustration tolerance."[109] During the war, they were able to channel this aggression. As Fraser explained, "combat activity or [the] persistent prospect of combat was sufficient to hold in check or allow canalisation of underlying aggressive energy into useful channels in front line work."[110] After the armistice, this was no longer possible. Associated with behavioural problems, cases of truce exhaustion escalated rapidly and could lead to "actual physical violence against superiors."[111] This was alarming, but truce exhaustion was a short-lived phenomenon and had disappeared by December 1953. A possible explanation may lie in the area of welfare provision. Throughout the autumn, there was a substantial increase in the number of canteens, roadhouses, and other entertainment facilities for soldiers based in Korea and Japan. In addition, the division went to great pains to screen films and hold concerts. These changes undoubtedly helped maintain and boost divisional morale.[112]

Care and Convalescence

Addressing his colleagues at a conference following the Korean War, American psychiatrist Dr. Hyam Bolocan stated that "the major function of the Division and Army psychiatrist is the conservation of manpower."[113] Bolocan's words still ring true. An army psychiatrist may have personal reservations about returning a man to duty, but he is obligated to send as many soldiers as possible back into the field. In the article "Ethical Challenges for the Psychiatrist during the Vietnam Conflict," Dr. Norman Camp explained:

> The combat psychiatrist's foremost military responsibility is that of stemming the flow of individuals who manifest a psychological incapacity or reluctance to soldier, he may be obligated to deny a psychologically traumatized soldier's expectation of medical exemption from further exposure to combat ... to conform to the military's expectation that the soldier be returned to the environment.[114]

Since the early twentieth century, military psychiatric treatment has been guided by manpower considerations, and this was true in Korea. In keeping with the principles of forward psychiatry developed during the First World War, psychologically traumatized soldiers were treated as quickly and close to the front lines as possible. Hard-won experience indicated that patients only worsened if treatment was delayed or delivered at a rear-echelon medical unit. It was also critical to treat patients like soldiers who were required to return to duty rather than as victims. Doctors avoided the suggestion that men were seriously ill or would benefit in any way from their condition.[115]

The Regimental Medical Officer was the first port of call for servicemen who required medical attention. Equipped to provide first aid and pain relief, RMOs were generally ill prepared to deliver the most basic psychiatric care. In contrast to their American counterparts, who were issued with a guide to combat psychiatry and additional reading materials, Commonwealth medics received no guidance on the subject. Furthermore, over 50 percent of British RMOs were National Servicemen. As recently qualified doctors, they had relatively little clinical or psychiatric experience. However, the Regimental Aid Post (RAP) was a refuge for anxious and exhausted troops who were expected to recover within twenty-four hours (see Figure 12). Within the confines of the RAP, soldiers were sedated and provided with a respite from the strain of the front lines.[116] Patients presenting with more severe or protracted symptoms were evacuated by forward sections of the field ambulance back to headquarters. Visiting each field ambulance once a week, the divisional psychiatrist assessed patients and decided whether they needed to be transported to 25 Canadian Field Dressing Station for further treatment. These visits served an important purpose, enabling the psychiatrist to "obtain first-hand information of combat psychological problems."[117] Consequently, "his recommendations then display[ed] a more practical appreciation of the difficulties involved in combat adaptation."[118] It was also crucial that the divisional psychiatrist gain the trust of his colleagues and

FIGURE 12   The 3rd Battalion Royal Australian Regimental Aid Post (RAP) as photographed during the Korean War. Regimental aid posts provided a much-needed respite for fatigued soldiers and those struggling with psychological distress.

Source: Claude Rudolph Holzheimer/Australian War Memorial Photo Collection No. 147776

the soldiers. As American psychiatric consultant Colonel Albert Glass recognized, "the divisional psychiatrist who remains in the rear is resented as one who fears to share their [front-line soldiers'] hardships, even briefly, and is therefore an impractical, theoretical person who does not belong in their world of deprivation and trauma."[119]

Psychiatric patients sent to 25 Canadian Field Dressing Station were typically sedated on admission to the unit with a barbiturate such as sodium amytal.[120] Throughout the early twentieth century, barbiturates were the "most widely used of all sedative drugs." Developed by Eli Lilly and Company in the 1920s, sodium amytal was first used by psychiatrists to help calm psychotic patients.[121] During the Second World War, doctors used it to sedate soldiers and help them communicate more freely. For example, noted British psychiatrists William Sargant and Eliot Slater used sodium amytal to treat servicemen evacuated from Dunkirk following the fall of France in June 1940.[122] Sargant and Slater believed that by quickly sedating patients, it was possible to stop "neurotic pattern[s] of thought or behaviour from remaining fixed in a patient's brain."[123] Commonwealth psychiatrists adhered to the same theory during the Korean War, using the drug to enable anxious patients to rest for a day or two and regain their composure.[124]

Following a period of sedation, service patients faced a thorough physical and psychiatric examination. In the absence of a clear and definitive diagnosis, they were occasionally sent to 123 American Holding Company in Seoul for additional tests. During the war, Commonwealth medics developed a close and friendly rapport with their counterparts in the US Army Medical Corps.[125] Early in 1951, a group of American MOs founded the 38th Parallel Medical Society, which many Canadian and British officers joined. Hosting fortnightly conferences on subjects of relevance to the Korean/Japanese theatre, the events provided Commonwealth officers with an opportunity to socialize and consult with their US Army colleagues.[126] These relationships proved invaluable when the Americans subsequently encouraged Commonwealth doctors to make use of their resources. Divisional psychiatrist Captain Fraser commented on the beneficial nature of the arrangement in a July 1953 letter to his mother and brother. He acknowledged that "it is very ... useful to know them [US Army psychiatrists] as they have the facilities for doing all sorts of mental tests on patients that we don't have."[127]

Once a diagnosis was confirmed, Commonwealth patients were generally required to attend several brief sessions of psychotherapy. These appointments presented an opportunity for the divisional psychiatrist to further evaluate his patients and to assess whether or not they could be returned to duty. Despite addressing the reasons behind the patient's admission, the sessions were primarily designed to reassure the man that he would recover, rather than to uncover deeper emotional distress.[128] As Colonel Glass of the US Army explained in his 1954 article "Psychotherapy in the Combat Zone":

> Any therapy ... that sought to uncover basic emotional conflicts or attempted to relate current behavior and symptoms with past personality patterns seemingly provided patients with logical reasons for their combat failure. The insights obtained by even such mild depth therapy readily convinced the patient and often his therapist, that the limit of combat endurance had been reached as proved by vulnerable personality traits. Patients were obligingly cooperative in supplying details of their neurotic childhood, previous emotional difficulties, lack of aggressiveness and other dependency traits, or any information that displaced onus for the current combat breakdown to events over which they had no control and therefore could not be held responsible.[129]

Patients who developed such a "defeatist and fatalistic attitude" were difficult to return to their original units or to duty of any kind.[130] The central goal of therapy was to relieve symptoms that interfered with the soldier's ability to function safely and effectively.[131]

Divisional war diaries reveal that over 50 percent of Commonwealth psychiatric casualties were returned to some form of duty, and return to unit (RTU) rates peaked at a high of 83 percent in the months preceding the armistice. The Americans similarly estimated that from 65 to 90 percent of patients returned to duty from 1952 to 1953.[132] The Commonwealth Division did not keep a record of the number of men who relapsed, but US Army returns from 1951 to 1952 suggest that "5 to 10% were 'Neuropsychiatric Repeaters.'"[133] In a 1954 article penned for the *Journal of the Royal Army Medical Corps*, Captain Flood claimed that the nature of Korean combat accounted for this level of success. During the war, there was a "distinct absence of enemy shell fire and aerial bombing," which contributed to greater recovery rates.[134] Furthermore, battles were short. Flood's arguments are legitimate, but RTU rates should be treated with a degree of caution. Throughout the First and Second World Wars, psychiatrists struggled to obtain the professional respect and acceptance of their colleagues in the armed forces.[135] In the early 1950s, military psychiatrists continued to face stigma as well as cuts to funding. They were therefore under pressure to produce results in Korea. Discussing American sources, author Ben Shephard has pointed out that "the literature on Korea ... was written by ... professionals with records to protect."[136] This is equally true of the Commonwealth Division and doctors may have exaggerated their results to some degree. Nonetheless, the existing documentary evidence indicates that only 5–10 percent of evacuations to the British Commonwealth General Hospital in Japan were psychiatric.[137]

In the event that a psychiatric casualty could not return to his original unit, this did not necessarily signal evacuation. Whenever feasible, troops were re-employed along the division's main line of communications in Korea or in more "sheltered conditions" in Japan.[138] After a rash of unnecessary evacuations, the Americans adopted the same policy in early 1951. Both the US Army and the Commonwealth Division saw manpower as a precious commodity given that it could take weeks or months for replacements to reach theatre. Therefore, it was critical to employ any man who could still be useful.[139] The Australians were the only contingent to which this policy did not apply. If an Australian soldier was not passed fit for combat following treatment, he was immediately repatri-ated. In September 1952, clinical officer of psychiatry Captain R.G. Godfrey expressed his frustration over this decision, noting that most of his Australian patients "could have been employed in less exposed positions in the Division, and their evacuation rendered unnecessary, were it possible to downgrade them in Korea in a similar manner" to the rest of the division.[140]

Evacuation was a daunting prospect. Korea's harsh terrain and climate made transporting casualties from the front lines to the British Commonwealth General Hospital in Kure a hellish and complex operation. As a rule, the most severely injured were evacuated by helicopter and airlifted to Japan by the Royal Australian Air Force (RAAF). Located in the small village of Iwakuni, the RAAF base was a short drive from the hospital. Less urgent cases were moved by rail or jeep ambulance to the coast. Despite the best efforts of the Royal Engineers, Korea had little established infrastructure and only the most rudimentary of road networks. Journeys were long and arduous.[141] One RAMC ambulance orderly recalled that in many cases "you had to tie the patients on [to the stretch-ers]. If they were unconscious you had to strap them in. They would just roll out of stretchers because the ambulance went all over the place sometimes."[142]

Arriving in Busan, patients were loaded on hospital ships bound for Japan. Former troop carriers like the *Maine* were refitted to serve as hospital ships during the Korean War. Sailing back and forth between Busan and Kure, His Majesty's Hospital Ship (HMHS) *Maine* was staffed by "one principal medical officer, four [subordinate] medical officers, one matron, four nursing sisters, six naval [members of the] Volunteer Aid Detachment, one wardmaster, and thirty-six sick berth staff" (see Figure 13).[143] For patients, the conditions on-board were oppressive. As retired Queen Alexandra's Royal Naval Nursing Service Matron Ruth Stone described:

The water line Wards required that the portholes be secured when at sea and as the temperature there registered 90–116°F since these wards were actually situated over the main generators and ... did not have either air conditioning or washing facilities, you can imagine the resemblance to Dante's Inferno as we descended the ramp to cope with some 80–100 battle soiled and dehydrated walking wounded. But in spite of the lack of normal, basic nursing conditions, the wounded were so grateful just to be able to lie down in comparative safety and sleep. Numerous large jugs of water and lime juice were placed in strategic positions and all ... battle-fatigued patients were sedated to spite the noise of the all too near ship's engines below.[144]

The British Commonwealth General Hospital's ward 17 was assigned the task of treating the division's most serious and protracted psychiatric cases. Roughly 5 percent of BCGH patients were admitted for mental health problems that included everything from unexplained somatic conditions to schizophrenia, alcoholism, drug addiction, epilepsy, and a range of other illnesses.[145] Many suffered from complex and comorbid disorders that required prolonged treatment.[146] Staffed by a psychiatrist and a small team of nurses, the ward served as a dedicated inpatient facility. The unit's first director was Captain J.J. Flood of the RAMC. Acting as an administrator and clinician, Flood held the position from November 1950 to the early months of 1952, when he was replaced by his

FIGURE 13   The hospital ship *Maine* sits in dry dock at Commonwealth headquarters in Kure, Japan, in 1951.

Source: Harold Vaughan Dunkley/Australian War Memorial Photo Collection No. DUKJ4089

colleague and countryman Major R.G. Davies as the hospital's resident psychiatrist. For the remainder of the war, the post alternated between several key officers: Major J.L. Johnston, Major J.J. McGrath, Captain N.G. Fraser, and Lieutenant Leslie Bartlet. Each man alternated between working in the hospital and out in the field.[147]

Whether physically or mentally ill, patients typically spent very little time in hospital. For example, in February 1953 the average serviceman spent only eleven days at BCGH before being discharged or transferred to another unit. Patient turnover was exceptionally high. Troops who required more time to recuperate were dispatched to one of several convalescent facilities in the area.[148] Opened in 1951, No. 6 Convalescent Depot could accommodate nearly three hundred men and was only a short walk from the division's hospital.[149] In the unit war diary, commanding officer Major R. Fuller (RAMC) emphasized that "the aim of the Convalescent Depot [was] to bridge the gap between the period of Hospital inpatient treatment and the return to full duty of the individual soldier who may

FIGURE 14   A group of Commonwealth soldiers demonstrate their exercise regime for visitors at No. 6 Convalescent Depot in Japan. Physical exercise and drill were seen as key components in helping wounded and sick servicemen recuperate and rejoin their units quickly.

Source: Philip Oliver Hobson/Australian War Memorial Photo Collection No. HOBJ304

have been admitted to Hospital for a variety of reasons."[150] Through a daily regime of drill and exercise, Fuller and his team worked to transform the wounded and ill back into fit and capable soldiers (see Figure 14). When the depot was full or over capacity, servicemen were sent to a smaller unit on the nearby island of Miyajima (Itsukushima).[151] The US Army ran a series of convalescent camps throughout Korea and Japan where soldiers were required to wear fatigues and "participated in an active daily program of calisthenics, supervised athletics and other training activities."[152] A psychiatrist was attached to each of the American camps in order to address emergencies and guide struggling patients. This was not the case in Kure or Miyajima, where resources were not available. The division did not have the money or the manpower to make similar arrangements. Consequently, psychiatrists and mental health nurses were concentrated in locations where they would be of the greatest use to the division as a whole.

Medical evacuations took place once a month, and in order to "qualify for repatriation, a wounded man had to be incapable of returning to duty within 120 days."[153] Former operating theatre technician Dr. David Oates recalled that "ambulances transported patients to Kure railway station (5 minutes from the hospital) and then by ambulance train to Iwakuni."[154] Accompanied by a nursing sister, patients were carefully loaded onto waiting planes and secured for the subsequent flight. In *Salute to the Air Force Medical Branch*, Harold M. Wright explains that

> the aircraft in use at the time was the Douglas C-54 Skymaster, a four-engine passenger cargo plane that could take twenty-eight patients, and the Douglas C-57 Liftmaster, a larger four-engine troop cargo carrier that could accommodate as many as sixty-nine patients. Patients were accommodated on canvas stretchers stacked along the side walls of the fuselage and five high along the centre of the cargo bay. The centre stacks were two deep, requiring nursing staff on both sides ... Regardless of their degree of mobility, all casualties had to be on litters because of the duration of the flight and the limited walking space around the plane's interior.[155]

Regardless of the destination, the journey home was a lengthy process. For instance, flights from Tokyo to North America stopped at the "Kwajalein Atoll in the Marshall Islands, Wake Island, and Midway" before landing at Hickam Air Force Base in Hawaii.[156] After refuelling, the flight continued on to Los Angeles. Once on the mainland, patients were reloaded onto planes bound for other American and Canadian cities.[157]

When they landed, patients were funnelled into an extensive service medical system that had grown exponentially during the Second World War. During the Korean War, many of these hospitals remained in operation, but only a select few were designed for the treatment of the mentally ill.[158] All British psychiatric cases were sent to the Royal Victoria Hospital Netley just outside the city of Southampton in Hampshire. Netley was first equipped for the treatment of psychiatric cases in the late nineteenth century. Throughout the 1950s, the hospital admitted around a thousand servicemen each year as part of its inpatient program. P Wing was a closed ward for the care of psychosis, while E Wing was an open ward designated for the treatment of psychoneurosis.[159] A 1956 Board of Control report characterized the Hampshire facility as a "progressive and active unit," where patients could benefit from advanced physical treatment methods such as deep insulin, modified insulin coma, continuous narcosis, and electroshock.[160] Moreover, patients were required to participate in individual and group therapy sessions while in residence. Men awaiting discharge could avail themselves of vocational guidance. On average, soldiers spent four to six weeks in treatment at Netley. Roughly 70 percent of those treated for psychoneurosis returned to their units without further treatment, and only 8 percent of total admissions were certified.[161]

Acting in the same capacity as Netley, Ste-Anne-de-Bellevue in Quebec provided returning Canadian servicemen with psychiatric treatment. Founded in 1917, the hospital was considered a leader in the field of mental healthcare by the

FIGURE 15   An aerial view of the military and veterans' hospital in Ste-Anne-de-Bellevue, Quebec.

Source: Northern Affairs/Library and Archives Canada PA-037489

time of the Korean War.[162] Staff and patients alike benefited from a close and collegial relationship with the faculty at McGill University and the wider medical community in nearby Montreal. In 1954, around half of the hospital's 1,078 patients were admitted for a psychiatric disorder.[163] It is not certain where troops from Australia and New Zealand were sent for treatment on their return home, but it is clear that options were limited. As in the Britain and Canada, specialist inpatient facilities were available at only a select number of hospitals.[164]

Reflections

Throughout the Korean War, medical officers continued to adhere to the principles of military psychiatry as developed during the two world wars. In keeping with this philosophy, manpower considerations were paramount, and the soldier's ability to function was prioritized over restoring his previous state of mental health.[165] Canadian MO Dr. John Beswick best summed up the pragmatic tenor of Korean medical policy when he argued that "people get squirrelly in war. There is nothing the matter with the guy who draws ducks on the wall. However, when he starts to feed them, you have trouble."[166]

In one of his numerous reports, Assistant Director of Medical Services Colonel Morgan Smith concluded that the division was "well served with a good psychiatric service."[167] Although critical of other units, he had nothing but admiration and praise for the divisional psychiatrist and his staff.[168] Indeed, over 50 percent of troops were returned to some form of active duty or re-employed in a support capacity. This was largely because of the static nature of the Korean War, where battles were brief and casualties never overwhelmed the division. Moreover, MOs were generally familiar with the common psychiatric illnesses encountered in Korea, such as psychoneurosis, character disorder, and battle exhaustion.

5
Forever Changed
The Korean War, Veterans, and the Pensions System

DURING THE KOREAN WAR, most psychologically traumatized servicemen recovered and returned to duty quickly. The Commonwealth Division regularly recorded return to unit (RTU) rates of over 50 percent.[1] Once in the hands of medical professionals, the majority of soldiers responded well to a treatment regime of sedation and brief psychotherapy. This was not the case for a minority, however. For them, the field medical unit was the first step in a long journey home. While comparable figures are not available for the other Commonwealth countries, an average of only 7 percent of British troops were evacuated from the Korean/Japanese theatre to the United Kingdom between 1950 and 1953 for psychiatric reasons.[2] Following repatriation, patients strove to deal with the psychological consequences of war and to recover sufficiently to rejoin their comrades. As veterans, they faced new but equally great challenges. This chapter looks at what was available to Korean War veterans in terms of pensions, allowances, and medical care. On discharge, to what were they entitled? How were a new generation of disabled men treated compared with their predecessors from the First and Second World Wars? Since the 1950s, the pensions system has evolved in response to social, political, and economic change. The chapter concludes with a discussion of what effect these changes have had on Korean War veterans, and of the current state of veterans' affairs.

Veterans' Rights
Across the Commonwealth, Korean War veterans were entitled to the same pensions and medical care as their Second World War counterparts.[3] Pensions were seen as a material recognition of the sacrifices that soldiers had made in defence of their respective countries.[4] Over the previous fifty years, entire government departments were established and developed to attend to veterans' affairs. Generally, there were two types of pensions available to applicants. Service pensions were awarded to men who had served overseas in an active conflict, but they were means-tested and granted only to those in financial need.[5] The amount of the award was based on the length of service and the rank attained while in uniform.[6] Disability pensions were granted to ex-servicemen whose impairment resulted "from injury or disease or aggravation thereof incurred during military service."[7] In a 1950s study of Canadian pension and

rehabilitation schemes, the word "disability" was broadly defined as "the loss or the lessening of the power to will and do any normal mental or physical act."[8] The level of compensation depended on the severity of the handicap and how it impinged on the veteran's earning capacity.[9] One's degree of disability could range anywhere from 5 percent to 100 percent.[10] With this system in mind, it was often very difficult to assess psychiatric cases. While physical problems can be measured, the impact of poor mental health is not directly or easily quantifiable.[11] In each country, disability pensions were adjusted for the cost of living and issued regularly rather than in a lump sum.[12] Veterans in the United Kingdom and New Zealand were paid weekly. Australians received their pensions on a fortnightly basis and Canadians were compensated monthly.[13]

In addition to service and disability pensions, a number of other compensation schemes were open to ex-servicemen. Due to their loss of earning capacity, severely disabled veterans (100 percent disabled) were entitled to unemployment, marriage, and child benefits. They could receive constant attendance allowance for any home nursing care they required.[14] Other payments available to veterans were designed to help them re-enter the job market or adjust to civilian life. Education and vocational training was offered in all the Commonwealth countries, although the schemes varied widely in their generosity.[15] Former British servicemen were entitled to only six months of free vocational training through the Ministry of Labour and National Service.[16] Canadians could spend as many months in training as they had spent in the military, and if they decided to attend university, they were eligible for limited government funding.[17] New Zealand and Australia had the most liberal policies. New Zealanders could spend up to three years in vocational training.[18] Under the Commonwealth Rehabilitation Scheme, former Australian soldiers could receive "university education, or technical and apprenticeship training, with the aid of generous scholarships, sustenance, and training allowances" for a maximum of two years.[19] Ex-servicemen in each country also qualified for home and business loans. Land settlement programs were popular in the rural areas of Canada, Australia, and New Zealand.[20] Self-sufficiency was the order of the day. Government planners believed that those capable of working should be actively employed, and allowances and benefits were designed with this ethos of independence in mind.[21] The centrality of work is made clear in an Australian poem of 1919. In "The Wounded Man Speaks," an anonymous veteran proclaims:

They busted me up like a mangled pup
But – THEY DID NOT BUST MY NERVE
And no pussy footing sissy
Shall grab my one good hand ...

Just to make himself feel grand
For I'm damned if I'll be a hero
And I ain't a helpless slob
After what I've stood, what is left is good
And all I want is – A JOB.[22]

Written in the aftermath of the First World War, the poem is equally applicable to veterans of the Second World War and the Korean War. Pensions and other forms of compensation were not meant to encourage reliance on government funds. Fit and capable disabled men were expected to support themselves if possible. As citizens, they had an economic duty to contribute rather than act as a drain on public resources.[23]

The process of applying for a disability pension or benefits began either by post or at a local government office.[24] Once a claim was filed, service medical records were gathered and a panel of physicians assembled to examine the applicant in question.[25] A war pensions committee (WPC) was assigned to assess the veteran's claim. WPCs varied in size and composition from country to country but typically consisted of three to four appointed persons. Committee members were usually prominent members of the community, and in Australia they were required to be veterans themselves.[26] In New Zealand, one position was always reserved for a member of the medical profession.[27] When all the required documentation had been gathered, a meeting was convened in order to consider and decide on the petition. Veterans who were denied compensation had the right to appeal. Pensions appeal tribunals could review cases several times before they were finally dismissed.[28] All appellants were given the benefit of the doubt, and the burden of proving that a disability did not relate to service rested with the government.[29] There was no time limit for applications made in Canada, Australia, or New Zealand. British veterans were required to apply within seven years of discharge, after which time the burden of proof switched to the veteran and greater evidence was necessary to make a successful claim.[30] By the mid-1950s, all four Commonwealth countries were paying out close to two million pensions to veterans of the First World War, Second World War, and several other conflicts.[31] As Britain and Canada were responsible for over 80 percent of Commonwealth Division strength, they also had the largest proportion of Korean War veterans.[32] However, only a small number of these men were receiving compensation during this period. In 1956, only 3 percent of Britons and Canadians who had served in Korea were collecting a service or disability pension.[33]

War pensions committees encountered many challenges in assessing disability claims. Chief among these was a lack of medical expertise. While committees in New Zealand always included a physician, this was not the case in the other Commonwealth countries. Appointees were welcome to seek medical opinion but were themselves drawn from a range of professions.[34] Despite this, they were asked to evaluate complex conditions and understand a bewildering range of disabilities.[35] In a December 1957 letter to a colleague, a Ministry of Pensions and National Insurance (MPNI) official in the United Kingdom remarked that "it is exceedingly doubtful whether the War Pensions Committees as they are constituted are really competent to judge the medical issues in the cases which now come before them."[36] Although well intentioned, many WPC members lacked the basic medical education that they needed in order to judge applications fairly.

The imprecise nature of pension legislation was another major shortcoming of the application process. Throughout the Commonwealth, "the central criterion for entitlement to a war disability pension was an incapacity arising out of, or aggravated by, active service in war."[37] Australian author Stephen Garton has rightly noted that "the terms *arising* and *aggravated* are vague,"[38] and that while "it seems clear that legislators intended that pensions should be for those conditions that were a 'direct' consequence of service ... the ambiguity in the terms they used to frame the legislation points to the difficulty in any such determination."[39] For war pensions committees, it was particularly difficult to establish the origins of a psychiatric disorder. Who was deserving of compensation? Could those men with a long-term history of mental health problems blame their current condition on war service? Canadian authorities doubted that WPCs could answer these questions effectively. They were also convinced that regular pension payments were harmful and would encourage veterans to prolong their symptoms.[40] Therefore, policy dictated that "unless positive proof of definite exaggeration of symptoms during service exists, the illness is termed, 'pre-enlistment in origin,' and compensation is refused."[41] Patients suffering from conditions termed "purely functional or hysterical"[42] were also denied. Funds were awarded only if the serviceman in question underwent psychiatric care at a recognized institution and treatment subsequently failed.[43] Within the pensions system, veterans with a psychological disability were at a distinct disadvantage. Physical wounds are visible, but psychological problems are hidden and can arise for multiple reasons. The Canadian example underlines the problems inherent in the pensions process and the stigma that was still attached to mental illness.

For the veteran population as a whole, applying for a pension was an equally rewarding and infuriating process. By its very nature, the pensions system was "adversarial."[44] Governments have to balance the needs of veterans with the limitations of public spending. Ex-servicemen were often very grateful for the help they received but could also encounter resistance to their requests for compensation. For instance, the Australian "Repatriation Department received numerous letters of gratitude,"[45] but it also came in for its fair share of complaints. Many veterans felt that "they were treated as 'criminals' and 'malingerers,' and sometimes openly abused as 'drongos' and 'hypochondriacs' by officers of the department."[46] Representing the Korea Veterans Association of Australia, Ivan Patrick Ryan recalled that applying for and appealing a pension could be a "complicated [and] demeaning" process.[47] Across the Commonwealth, bureaucrats and veterans worked together and opposed one another. Individual experiences varied greatly depending on the nature of the veteran's disability and the pensions officials he encountered.

Veterans' Medical Care

Disability pensioners were universally entitled to free hospital treatment for any health problem related to service. Under legislation, veterans were considered to be priority patients.[48] Although ex-servicemen could be admitted to either military or civilian hospitals, they were increasingly the responsibility of the public healthcare system. In the 1950s, governments across the Commonwealth slowly began to close military hospitals. Budgetary restrictions in the 1960s and the 1970s helped accelerate this process.[49] The smaller, professional armies of the Cold War did not require the large and dedicated network of medical facilities that had been developed during the Second World War.

Psychologically traumatized veterans were treated in a range of institutions that included private care homes, general hospitals, and asylums. Outpatient care was becoming more widespread, but inpatient treatment was still common.[50] The majority of veterans were admitted as service patients. Service patient programs were first developed following the First World War and were designed to ensure that veterans received a higher standard of care than was generally available for psychiatric patients at the time. There was a stigma surrounding the mentally ill and the hospitals that treated them. It was untenable that former soldiers should be treated in the same fashion.[51] If admitted to a hospital or an asylum, veterans were treated on separate wards, wore distinctive clothing, and received pocket money.[52] In the United Kingdom, rank played an additional role in determining the quality of care that an individual could expect. As a rule, former officers were admitted to private homes and other ranks were sent to public institutions. Ex-officers were allowed to handle their own finances with the approval of the attending physician. No matter how stable they proved, patients from other ranks were not trusted with their own money.[53]

Vocational and industrial rehabilitation schemes were established to help patients re-engage with the working world following their release from hospital.[54]

However, the system was not specifically designed to address mental health. In accommodating for the physically impaired, rehabilitation projects often failed to adequately address the needs of recovering psychiatric patients.[55] Specialized programs were exceedingly rare. The British Ex-Services Mental Welfare Society was one of the few organizations that catered solely to psychiatric pensioners.[56] It ran a small residential scheme in Surrey, where men were hired to "[assemble] cardboard boxes for blankets made by [company] Thermega Limited."[57] Charity employees were housed in a nearby hostel for the duration of their stay. Despite the value of the society's work, there were limits to the number of patients it could accept.[58] In the battle to recover, many veterans were left to their own devices.

There are no reliable statistics on the number of Korean War veterans who were discharged from the military for mental health problems. Pension and welfare records often include the Korean War in the same category as the Second World War and post-1945 conflicts such as Malaya, and individual medical files remain closed to the public. Consequently, it is difficult to establish how many men applied for compensation or received medical treatment. Nonetheless, anecdotal evidence suggests that Korean War veterans were generally ill informed about their healthcare options.[59] Canadian author Ted Barris has argued that the continued stigma of mental illness deterred the majority of ex-servicemen from stepping forward. Like previous generations, men were encouraged to address their problems privately with the support of family and friends.[60] While many veterans managed to recover and thrive, others struggled to leave the war behind. Private Arthur Marion served as a reinforcement with the 2nd Battalion of the Princess Patricia's Canadian Light Infantry (PPCLI) during the Korean War.[61] Prior to deployment, he was neither a "public smoker or drinker," but when he returned from the Far East he was a "changed man."[62] Decades later, he remembered, "I was a nervous wreck ... If Mom dropped a spoon on the floor I was down under the table in a second."[63] He began smoking and drinking heavily in order to quell his nerves. In subsequent years, Marion never approached a doctor or psychiatrist for help. As an elderly man, he confessed that "I still wake up at night, moaning and groaning. I'm still fighting that war."[64] Other veterans suffered from similar problems with depression, anxiety, and substance abuse. Mary McLeod's husband, Keith, served with the Royal Australian Air Force in Korea and Japan. She noted that the war had a "profound and long lasting" impact on him.[65] In an interview, she recalled that "he was never the same again ... if you take a gentle man and make him kill, he'll never be the same again."[66]

Organizations like the Royal Legion and the Australian Returned and Services League (RSL) have long offered an alternative source of support to ex-servicemen. Throughout the twentieth century, they have campaigned tirelessly on behalf of veterans, and have served as a network for old comrades and a venue in which to relive old memories and vent present frustrations. Korean War veterans were equally entitled to membership in and the benefits of such an association,[67] but local branches were not universally welcoming. Don Flieger of the Royal Canadian Army Service Corps (RCASC) was evacuated from Korea in February 1952 after contracting epidemic hemorrhagic fever. When he was released from hospital, he returned to his home depot in Fredericton, New Brunswick.[68] He later recalled: "That night, I went to the Legion. I was in my uniform. But they wouldn't let me in. Said I wasn't a veteran. I told them my story, but they said, 'That doesn't cut it here.'"[69] Flieger's experience may appear extreme, but it was not unique. Other veterans recall meeting with similar hostility. In conversation with the author, members of the Korea Veterans Association of Australia recalled that the Returned and Services League was generally unsupportive of their membership.[70] The opposition they encountered was largely the result of public perception. During the 1950s, the Korean War was characterized as a relatively minor "police action." The troops deployed to the Far East were primarily volunteers and served limited tours of duty. The scale of public involvement was limited in comparison with previous conflicts. Veterans' organizations like the Royal Legion and the RSL were chiefly composed of men who had fought in either the First or Second World War. Events in Korea contrasted sharply with their own experiences of war and how they understood the term "veteran."

Adapting to Change

Over the past six decades, the pensions system has changed and adapted in response to the needs of its clientele. Governments have had to allow for the rising cost of living and an aging veteran population.[71] The clinical practice of psychiatry has been similarly transformed. Custodial care and closed wards have been largely replaced with outpatient treatment and community-based programs. Psychotropic drugs are now commonly prescribed to treat disorders such as depression, anxiety, and schizophrenia.[72] At the time of the Korean War, there were few treatment options for the mentally ill and physicians could offer little in terms of prevention or cure. Since the nineteenth century, psychiatric patients had been primarily housed and cared for in large public asylums.[73] The 1950s were a period of medical innovation and the beginning of a revolution. Antibiotics, better blood transfusions, and new surgical techniques were all pioneered over the course of the decade.[74] Comparable developments were made in psychiatry. In the wake of the Second World War, progressive ideas about open wards, community care, and prevention became increasingly popular and entered the mainstream medical discourse. As medicine advanced, doctors were optimistic that they could combat mental illness. Legislation around the world began to reflect the new zeitgeist.[75] For example, the 1959 British Mental Health Act supported the closure of large asylums in favour of outpatient programs. It also encouraged the mentally ill to seek voluntary treatment at an early stage.[76] Exciting developments in psychopharmacology fuelled a growing sense of confidence.

Early in 1951, French army surgeon Henri Laborit was looking for a way to counter surgical shock. He began experimenting with the drug chlorpromazine, which had been developed as an antihistamine by the chemical and pharmaceutical company Rhône-Poulenc.[77] He discovered that it was a highly effective sedative and immediately recognized the psychiatric value of such a drug.[78] Over the following months, Laborit pressed colleagues to prescribe chlorpromazine for their psychotic patients. He eventually convinced psychiatrists Jean Delay and Pierre Deniker to trial the drug at St. Anne's Hospital in Paris. The results were astounding. For the first time, violent and uncontrollable patients were calm and could communicate clearly with their doctors.[79]

Chlorpromazine was the first effective antipsychotic and transformed the lives of patients and psychiatrists alike.[80] Doctors across Europe and North America quickly replicated Delay and Deniker's results.[81] By 1954, nearly two million patients were prescribed the drug in the United States alone.[82] The success of chlorpromazine encouraged the development of other antipsychotics and psychopharmaceuticals. Antidepressants such as the monoamine oxidase inhibitors (MAOIs) and tricyclic antidepressants (TCAs) were tested and developed in the late 1950s and early 1960s. Their arrival on the market was greeted enthusiastically.[83] In the manner of other medical specialists, psychiatrists could now offer targeted treatments for specific disorders.[84] As Dr. Thomas A. Ban noted, the emergence of these drugs "turned psychiatrists from caregivers to full-fledged physicians who [could] help their patients and not only listen to their problems."[85]

Like other psychiatric patients, psychologically traumatized veterans benefited from advances in drug treatment and the liberalization of public attitudes.[86] Since the First World War, British legislation had discriminated against ex-servicemen with psychological problems. When a single man was admitted to hospital for a pensionable psychiatric illness, his pension was revoked and replaced by an allowance. Further deductions were made from this allowance if he remained in hospital for more than five years.[87] The deductions in question were more "severe than those made for any other type of patient in receipt of treatment allowance."[88] In addition, the quality of treatment varied depending on rank. Former officers were entitled to significantly better facilities and treatment options. When the Ministry of Pensions and National Insurance reviewed its existing procedures in 1971, it was clear that policy did not meet modern standards, nor was it in line with public sentiment.[89] Civil servant Mr. R. Windsor lamented that the situation was "acutely embarrassing," and that "there [was] little internal consistency and some of our practices in terms of contemporary standards [were] not merely indefensible but positively offensive."[90] MPNI practices were no longer politically viable in the social climate of the 1970s. Distinctions that were previously regarded as natural were quickly and quietly eliminated. Other Commonwealth governments responded in similar fashion to public feeling and veterans benefited accordingly.[91] The greatest changes were yet to come, however.

The Vietnam War (1961–75) was one of the most controversial and politically contentious conflicts of the twentieth century. It has also been cited as a key turning point in the history of military psychiatry.[92] With regard to mental healthcare, Vietnam was initially considered to be a success story. US Army "psychiatric casualties were reported as being ten times lower than in World War Two, and three times lower than in Korea, smaller than 'any recorded in previous conflicts.'"[93] These unparalleled results were "commonly ascribed to the widespread use of forward psychiatry" as well as "the less intense nature of the fighting ... shorter tours of duty and the better links with home."[94] Soon thereafter, however, a different picture began to emerge.

On returning home, many American veterans struggled to adjust to civilian life. They suffered from long-term psychological problems, which they linked to service in Vietnam. Groups like Vietnam Veterans Against the War (VVAW) and the National Veterans Resource Project (NVRP) began campaigning vigorously on behalf of traumatized ex-servicemen, convinced that "the war had left a psychological scar on all who fought in it."[95] In the charged atmosphere of the late 1970s, a spark was lit. Post-Traumatic Stress Disorder (PTSD) was first recognized as a distinct diagnostic entity in the 1980 edition of the *Diagnostic and Statistical Manual of Mental Disorders (DSM-III)* of the American Psychiatric Association (APA).[96] The *DSM* is widely employed by doctors as a clinical tool for the classification of psychiatric conditions.[97] When PTSD appeared in *DSM-III*, little clinical research had been conducted on the condition. In contrast to other disorders, PTSD was included largely as the result of heavy pressure from the veterans' lobby and its allies in the psychiatric profession, such as Dr. Robert J. Lifton.

Before 1980, veterans rarely succeeded in obtaining pensions for cases of trauma with a delayed presentation. It was nearly impossible to link mental health problems directly to earlier war service. Moreover, pensions officials could argue that a veteran had a prior history of psychiatric illness. By including Post-Traumatic Stress Disorder in *DSM-III*, the APA established an important precedent, acknowledging that patients could present with symptoms of trauma many years after the precipitating events. Moreover, PTSD is the only condition included in the *DSM* that identifies the etiology of the disorder in question. The traumatic event itself is to blame, as opposed to the patient's pre-enlistment history and early psychological development. Consequently, the possibilities for compensation are significantly broadened. For veterans, this was a paradigm shift.[98]

Roughly sixty thousand Australian soldiers were deployed to Southeast Asia throughout the 1960s and 1970s.[99] As in the United States, the war in Vietnam was highly controversial in Australia and veterans were similarly politicized by events.[100] The government was sharply criticized for the way it treated ex-servicemen, and demand grew for better and more accessible care options. The Vietnam Veterans Counselling Service (VVCS) opened in 1982 with offices in Canberra, each of the state capitals, and the cities of Albury, Launceston, and Townsville.[101] For the first time, serving personnel, veterans, and their families could access long-term counselling. They could attend both individual and group therapy sessions with trained psychiatrists and clinical psychologists.[102] Since 1982, the Australian Department of Veterans' Affairs (DVA) has continued to expand its mental health programing.[103] The Australian Centre for Posttraumatic Mental Health (ACPMH) (recently renamed Phoenix Australia [2015]) was established in 1995 with the aid of DVA funding. In partnership with the department and the University of Melbourne, the ACPMH (Phoenix Australia) conducts specialized research into PTSD and other forms of trauma.[104] DVA officials have also collaborated with scholars at Monash University to examine the long-term health consequences of service life. As of 2008, 18 percent of the department's clients were being treated for psychiatric problems every year. Spread across the country, they represent an important segment of Australia's veteran population.[105]

Australia was the first Commonwealth country to appreciate the importance of PTSD and its implications for the pensions system. Events in Vietnam acted as a catalyst for change. Other major Commonwealth countries – New Zealand, Canada, and the United Kingdom – were much slower to respond. From 1964 to 1972, over three thousand members of the New Zealand Defence Force were sent to Vietnam, but the New Zealand government failed to develop a comparable counselling service until the early 1990s. With a much smaller veteran population, there was no public demand. Canadian and British policy began moving in the same direction as New Zealand and Australia in the late 1990s and early 2000s. Although both countries recognized PTSD and related disorders, mental healthcare provisions were far from systematic. Neither country deployed forces to the war in Vietnam or experienced the resulting political upheaval. Subsequent events would change their perspective.

The 1990s saw an increased operational tempo for both Canadian and British troops. In 1991, each country contributed ground forces to the Gulf War. Following their return from the Middle East, veterans began to present with a variety of health problems ranging from fatigue and headaches to cancer. While the etiology of Gulf War Syndrome has never been properly explained, it drew significant public attention to matters of military health. It also highlighted the shortcomings of existing pensions legislation and how veterans were treated for mental health problems. The cracks in the system were becoming increasingly obvious.[106] By the late 1990s, events in Canada had reached a critical point. In 1999, the government established the Croatia Board of Inquiry (Sharpe Inquiry) to investigate claims that Canadian soldiers had been exposed to environmental toxins during their deployment to the Balkans. A large number of veterans were exhibiting health problems similar to those experienced by their Gulf War counterparts. Air Force Colonel Joe Sharpe's mandate was soon expanded to look at how troops with medically unexplained symptoms were treated by the military and by Veterans Affairs Canada (VAC).[107] The problems inherent in the Canadian system were further underlined in 2000 when Lieutenant-General Roméo Dallaire's suicide attempt shocked the country and helped galvanize public opinion in favour of reform.[108]

With the deployment of troops to Iraq and Afghanistan, the Canadian public has become increasingly aware of the role that military personnel play and the health risks that they can run in the execution of their duty. Over the past fifteen years, the government has invested heavily in developing healthcare programs attuned to the needs of returning veterans. There has been a particular emphasis on the development of mental healthcare resources. For example, Veterans Affairs Canada established a network of operational stress injury (OSI) clinics across the country.[109] Modelled on Australia's Vietnam Veterans Counselling Service, these clinics are "staffed by multidisciplinary teams of psychiatrists, psychologists, mental health nurses, social workers, chaplains and addiction specialists."[110] According to a North Atlantic Treaty Organization (NATO) report on operational stress injuries, the clinics "are responsible for providing assessment and treatment of [veterans] who present with psychiatric symptoms related to military operations."[111] Veterans who cannot attend an OSI clinic are eligible for care through an Operational Trauma and Stress Support Centre (OTSSC). OTSSCs are designed to address the needs of serving personnel and are similarly distributed throughout the country. In addition, veterans can seek treatment with one of over nine hundred private mental health professionals approved by the department.[112]

The Canadian government has also made sweeping changes to the existing pensions system. Reforms include the enactment in 2007 of a Veterans Bill of Rights that outlines the basic standard of treatment to which all veterans are entitled.[113] Most importantly, the House of Commons unanimously passed the

New Veterans Charter (NVC) in 2005. When it came into effect in 2006, the NVC was praised as "the most sweeping change to Veterans' services and benefits in the past 60 years."[114] At the time, Senator Roméo Dallaire described the legislation as "a new social contract between the people of Canada and the new generation of veterans of the Canadian Forces."[115] Characterized as a "living charter," the NVC was intended to change over time rather than remain a static document.[116] In the decade since its passage, over 145 amendments have been made to the NVC. Most of these changes are encompassed in the Enhanced NVC, or Bill C-55 as enacted in October 2011.[117]

Despite early optimism among legislators and ex-service personnel, the NVC has drawn extensive criticism from both commentators and the veteran community alike. The bill's detractors have principally focused on the decision to eliminate lifetime disability pensions for injured servicemen and women in favour of lump sum awards.[118] This matter has proved so contentious that a group of six veterans launched a class action lawsuit against the federal government. While former Veterans Affairs minister Erin O'Toole brokered a temporary agreement between both parties, the matter was never satisfactorily resolved and litigation is presently pending at the British Columbia Court of Appeal.[119] The plaintiffs in the *Equitas* case argue that the NVC denies veterans access to the same level of compensation that they were entitled to under the old Pensions Act, and does not meet the standards set in civil court for "accidents or personal injury."[120] They contend that this is unconstitutional and the NVC should be repealed.[121]

The Office of the Veterans Ombudsman (OVO) was created in 2007 to independently assess the activities of Veterans Affairs Canada. Commissioned to evaluate the NVC, the ombudsman published a series of reports throughout 2013 and 2014.[122] Although concluding that veterans would receive less financial compensation under the terms of the NVC, the ombudsman ultimately did not recommend parity between the two regimes.[123] Instead, he recommended that changes be made to ensure that "economic support is sufficient to enable Veterans to meet their needs during transition to civilian life, or until end of life, if required, with minimal reduction in the standard of living," and that "Canadian Forces Veterans receive non-economic compensation for pain and suffering resulting from a service related injury or illness that is at least equivalent to the max amount (currently $342,000) that is awarded ... by Canadian courts for pain and suffering."[124] Although the government has expressed a willingness to accept the ombudsman's recommendations, these changes have yet to be enacted.

Over the past few years, Veterans Affairs Canada has also come under fire for failing to process disability claims efficiently and effectively.[125] The Office of the Auditor General of Canada issued a report reviewing the speed at which VAC

processed claims between April 2006 and August 2014. It praised the department for its efficiency in helping new veterans access rehabilitation programs
on leaving the Canadian Forces.[126] However, the authors noted that "access to
the Disability Benefits Program – the program through which most veterans
access mental health services – is slow, and the application process is complex."[127]
During the 2013–14 fiscal year, VAC failed to meet its target of processing 80
percent of applicants within sixteen weeks. The majority of veterans found that
it took an average of nearly thirty-two weeks to receive a decision with regard
to eligibility.[128] The Auditor General also criticized the lengthy and bureaucratic
nature of the appeal process.[129] In early January 2015, Veterans Affairs Minister
Julian Fantino was dismissed and replaced largely as a result of the controversy
surrounding the problems identified by the Auditor General.[130] Moreover,
Veterans Affairs was subjected to a series of budget cuts throughout this period.
Like other government departments, it has struggled to secure sufficient funds
since the global financial crisis of 2008. In 2015, this led to the closure of nine
out of thirty-two Veterans Affairs offices across the country and provoked further
criticism from the veteran community.[131]

It is clear that Veterans Affairs Canada has faced significant challenges over
the last few years. The system is far from perfect. Nevertheless, there is a much
greater awareness of veterans, their medical needs, and the necessity of robust
mental health programing. The Auditor General's review of 2014 highlights this
issue, noting that

> veterans with mental health conditions represent an increasing proportion of
> [VAC] clients, up from less than 2 per cent in 2002 to almost 12 per cent in 2014.
> The number of veterans with identified mental health conditions is expected to
> continue to increase as those with service in Afghanistan return to civilian life,
> and as awareness and recognition of mental health conditions increase. In the
> 2012–13 fiscal year, the Department estimated its total mental health expendi-
> tures at $508 million for military veterans.[132]

Across the Atlantic, extended deployments to the Middle East have also served
to raise the profile of veterans in the United Kingdom. The introduction of the
Military Covenant in 2000 formally outlined the "mutual obligations and
expectations that bind the British nation (described as the government and the
electorate), the Army and the individual soldier together" for the very first time.[133]
In 2003, the High Court of England and Wales also "handed down judgment in
what has come to be known as the Ministry of Defence (MoD) post-traumatic
stress disorder case."[134] A group of over two thousand ex-service personnel sued
the MoD for compensation and claimed that the ministry was "negligent in

failing to take measures to prevent, detect, or treat the development of psychiatric illness in general and PTSD in particular."[135] The claimants lost the case but succeeded in attracting intense media scrutiny. Since 2003, public interest in the long-term health and well-being of veterans has continued to grow.

Media reports suggest the existence of an alarming number of British veterans experiencing service-related psychological problems. Commentators argue that a growing pool of ex-servicemen and women are falling through the cracks. As operations in Afghanistan have come to a close, numerous authors have expressed the fear that a record number of veterans will present with mental health problems such as PTSD in the near future.[136] This does not appear to be the case, however. According to a 2014 study conducted by researchers at the King's Centre for Military Health Research, "contrary to many people's expectations, deployment to Iraq and Afghanistan has not led to an overall increase in mental health problems among UK personnel."[137] The authors estimated that only around 1.3–4.8 percent of UK Regulars returning from deployment exhibited symptoms of probable PTSD. Recent studies also indicate that rates of suicide are lower within the military than in the civilian population.[138]

At present, the National Health Service (NHS) is the primary care provider for these veterans. They can be assessed for service-related psychological problems under the Veterans and Reserves Mental Health Programme (VRMHP). The VRMHP is "available to veterans who have deployed since 1982 and are experiencing mental health challenges as a result of military service."[139] Under the program, "a full mental health assessment [is conducted] by a Consultant Psychiatrist with accompanying guidance on care and treatment for the veteran's local [NHS] clinical team."[140] Outside of the NHS, veterans have many options. The charitable sector has exploded with the growth of organizations such as Combat Stress, Help for Heroes, PTSD Resolution, and the like. While this can be seen as a positive development, the sector remains largely unregulated. There is no governing body to monitor the quality of these organizations or the treatments they offer clients. In the absence of such a body, ill veterans are forced to navigate a bewildering variety of choices with little guidance.[141]

Pensions and access to treatment remain contentious issues in all of the Commonwealth countries considered in this book. Both government officials and the relevant stakeholders have struggled to establish who is entitled to care and the extent of the resources to which they should have access. In general, they have adopted a broad definition of the word "veteran."[142] The British government has embraced the most inclusive understanding of this term, defining a veteran as anyone "who has performed military service for at least one day and drawn a day's pay."[143] Academic research suggests that early service leavers (those who leave within four years of their initial enlistment) encounter more problems with mental health than their counterparts who remain in the armed forces for extended periods of time. By adopting a broad understanding of the term "veteran," officials hope to ensure that the most vulnerable receive the attention they require.[144]

The younger generation of veterans have been the main beneficiaries of the improving pensions and care system, but traditional veterans (e.g., Second World War and Korea) have also felt their impact. Significant funds have been invested in designing specialized services for the elderly.[145] Canada's Gerontological Advisory Council (GAC) was founded in October 1997 "to advise ... on policies, programs, services and trends impacting Canada's aging veteran population."[146] The GAC's flagship project is the Veterans Independence Program (VIP). First established in 1981, VIP is designed to keep older veterans self-sufficient by providing homecare services. Both Australia and New Zealand have made similar provisions.[147] Funding is available for "domestic assistance, personal care, safety related home and garden maintenance, respite care and social assistance."[148]

In Australia and Canada, older veterans have also been actively encouraged to seek compensation and treatment for long-term psychiatric conditions such as PTSD.[149] Ste-Anne-de-Bellevue Hospital in Montreal acts as a hub for psychiatric research and care. Specializing in geriatrics and psychogeriatrics, it attracts experts from across North America and around the world.[150] The Older Veterans Psychiatric Unit at Heidelberg Hospital in Melbourne serves the same purpose. According to the Korea Veterans Association of Australia, at Heidelberg:

> Every effort is aimed at tender, loving care and home care, whenever possible. The younger doctors and nurses are better educated in their field, than in the past. Assistance is available – physiotherapy, gymnasium/swimming pool for physical activity, occupational therapy, hydrotherapy, as well as socialisation sessions during mental health treatments.[151]

In 2007, the Government of Canada estimated that two thousand traditional veterans die every month. Great strides have been made in improving the health of those who remain, but there are limits to what can be done for the surviving veterans of the Korean War.[152] The elderly are often unaware of how they can benefit from legislative developments and changes to the care system. Governments can more easily engage with younger veterans through the Internet, and are investing heavily in improving online resources. For example, the Government of Canada recently pledged to invest $2.1 million into upgrading its online portal, "My VAC Account."[153] However, this is of little consequence to many older veterans, who either do not engage online or make only limited use of the Internet. Furthermore, magazine and newspaper advertisements can reach only a minority of subscribers and regular readers.[154] Korean War veterans are also part of a generation for whom mental illness remains a taboo subject. Despite the liberalization of public attitudes, many prefer to address psychological health problems privately. In an interview with historian Tom Hickman, British veteran Smyttan Common noted that it was better to "keep the demons under lock and key."[155] If veterans choose to claim compensation, they often present with complex and chronic psychiatric conditions that have worsened over time.[156] A Monash University study conducted in 2005 surveyed 81 percent of Australia's remaining Korean War veterans.[157] The authors concluded that they were "five to six times more likely to meet the criteria for PTSD" than men of a similar age, and "one and a half times more likely to meet the criteria for current hazardous alcohol consumption."[158] Comparable studies have not been carried out in any of the other Commonwealth countries.[159] Nevertheless, the Australian example is telling.

Reflections

Throughout the twentieth century, mentally ill servicemen have faced significant challenges, and Korean War veterans are no exception. While few men were evacuated from the Korean/Japanese theatre for psychiatric reasons, many more came home with lasting problems. As veterans, they had the right to seek compensation and medical treatment. However, the pensions/care system was not designed for the psychologically traumatized and was inherently antagonistic. Pension rates were calculated on the basis of physical disability and loss of earning capacity, and legislation was framed for the same purpose. Neither government nor pensions committees could easily come to grips with war-related trauma. In terms of medical care, little could be done at the time of the Korean War, and the stigma of mental illness loomed large. Furthermore, ex-servicemen were denied many of the traditional forms of support on which their predecessors had relied. Veterans' organizations did not welcome the new generation with open arms. Korea was not a popular conflict but a distant war with vague aims. In short, it lived in the shadow of the Second World War.

The intervening decades have witnessed steady changes and improvements to the pensions/care system. From the late 1950s to the 1970s, psychiatry matured as a medical specialty and was revolutionized by the introduction of new psychopharmaceuticals and by progressively tolerant attitudes. However, further experiences of war (e.g., Vietnam, the Gulf War) have had the greatest impact on how mentally ill veterans are treated. The state's "duty of care" has become a subject of passionate public discussion and debate. As the military professionalized, a younger generation has come to expect more. Although Korean

War veterans have largely missed out on these developments, they have finally achieved a degree of public recognition. Since 1996, Korean War memorials have appeared in all four of the countries from which the members of the Commonwealth Division were drawn. Significant anniversaries have caught the attention of the media and the public at large.[160] The Canadian government declared 2013 the year of the Korean War veteran, and in late 2014, the United Kingdom became the last UN country to unveil a public memorial in its capital city.[161] Situated on the banks of the Thames close to the Ministry of Defence, the six-metre memorial is made of Portland Stone and features a bronze statue of a British soldier.[162] Of those veterans who remain, over three hundred endured wind and rain to attend an unveiling ceremony. Guests included the Duke of Gloucester, the Republic of Korea's Minister of Foreign Affairs, and British Defence Secretary Michael Fallon.[163] In his remarks, Fallon was quick to address the mistakes of the past, stressing that "we must never allow the notion of a 'forgotten war' to take hold. When Britain's armed forces put their lives on the line for their country, they must be commemorated, and in the right way."[164] His words were reinforced by Queen Elizabeth II, whose congratulatory message read: "The memorial is a fitting tribute to the veterans of that fierce conflict and will ensure that they, and their fallen comrades, are never forgotten."[165]

Conclusion
Korea and Its Legacy

One woman asked my Mum, "Where's John?" "In Korea," she answered. The woman replied, "Oh, on holidays." I'll say no more.

– AUSTRALIAN VETERAN JOHN BUSHY BURKE

FIGHTING ON BEHALF of four different nations, the troops of the 1st British Commonwealth Division lived and worked side by side during the Korean War (1950–53). They were a unique, close-knit group. While arguments could arise out of national differences, they succeeded in their goals and were much admired by their allies. The medical team was equally multinational in composition and included Brits, Canadians, Australians, and Indians. I set out to write a history of military psychiatry in Korea, principally as practised by the Commonwealth countries. I did so partly as a tribute to the service and sacrifice of Korean veterans. But as the evidence mounted, the argument for exploring the postwar legacy of Korea became stronger and stronger. So it is that this book includes both a narrative of post-Korea developments in government approaches to the handling of wartime mental trauma as well as reflections on the connection between those developments and the earlier Korean experience.

Like the Vietnam War, Korea was initially a psychiatric success story. The Commonwealth Division had a low rate of psychiatric illness (one in twenty wounded or sick).[1] Despite enduring many privations, the division was well known for combat efficiency and high morale.[2] Medical officers excelled in returning men to active duty, and return to unit (RTU) rates soared from 50 percent to 83 percent from July 1951 to July 1953.[3] However, both Korea and Vietnam were problematic in the long term. Commonwealth officials failed to put support systems in place and have only recently encouraged veterans to seek compensation or psychological counselling. There was no deliberate mistreatment or abuse on the part of government or pensions officials. This failure reflected the medical, cultural, and social realities of the period.

The Korean War took place at a time when psychiatry was still young and effective psychopharmaceuticals were just beginning to arrive on the market.[4] There was also a strong stigma surrounding mental illness and the seeking of treatment. In all of the Commonwealth countries, those who struggled with psychiatric conditions were encouraged to deal with their problems privately. Active employment was the best medicine. The pensions and care system was a product of the era and of a conservative society where rehabilitation and treatment programs centred on returning veterans to work and fostering economic independence. Compensation was believed to have a detrimental rather than salutary effect on the mentally ill. Financial aid only worsened or prolonged symptoms that naturally diminish over time.[5] While the modern observer might perceive this approach as callous, it was seen as benevolent and generous at the time.

In addition, Korean War veterans were denied other forms of support that had proved invaluable in the past. Unlike many of their predecessors, they were not greeted with parades and acclaim, when they returned home nor were they universally welcomed by veterans' organizations like the Royal Legion and the Returned and Services League. Responding to inquiries by the author, Ivan Patrick Ryan of the Korea Veterans Association of Australia expressed disappointment at how veterans were received by these groups.[6] Les Peate of the Korea Veterans Association of Canada had a similar response, and many veterans from Britain and New Zealand faced rejection as well.[7] Korean War memorials did not appear until the late 1990s, and there were no major memorials to highlight the service of those who had fought in the Far East. When the Australian government attempted to secure "royal messages of condolence to the relatives of service personnel killed in Korea," they were told that such letters were not issued "in operations of lesser magnitude than a World War."[8] As Australian historian Richard Trembeth has emphasized, "it appeared that grief, like bravery, was measured in degrees, and some wars, like some acts of courage, only deserve lesser awards."[9]

Neither the Commonwealth governments nor the public at large acknowledged the sacrifices that veterans had made or gave them a public forum in which to grieve. There were a number of reasons for this. The war did not involve the same level of public involvement as the Second World War and a far smaller group of men were sent to Korea. Over 6 million soldiers from Canada, the United Kingdom, Australia, and New Zealand enlisted or were conscripted from 1939 to 1945. In contrast, only 145,000 were deployed from 1950 to 1953.[10] Moreover, they had primarily volunteered for the task. US Presidents Harry S. Truman and Dwight D. Eisenhower both referred to Korea as a "police action." The Commonwealth prime ministers followed suit.[11] They were afraid that the use of provocative terminology would escalate hostilities and refused to label Korea as a war.[12] In downplaying the ferocity of the fighting, they helped perpetuate a misunderstanding. Finally, UN forces neither won nor lost the Korean War. Unlike the Second World War, there was no great victory to celebrate or to help focus commemorative events.

The Korean War raises important questions about why we choose to commemorate one conflict rather than another. No matter how advanced or attentive military medicine may become, how society responds to returning service personnel is crucial to how veterans process their experiences and reconcile themselves to loss. Second World War veterans were feted as heroes and celebrated for their accomplishments. Vietnam veterans were abused and eventually became symbols of an unjust war. Korean War veterans were simply ignored. There is no quantitative way of measuring the impact of this exclusion. Nevertheless, there is more than enough anecdotal evidence to suggest that veterans were negatively affected. For instance, Jean Rayner's husband, Louis, was a driver with the Australian Army during the war. In an interview with author Joy Damousi, she recalled:

One thing that did annoy Lou ... was that people called it a pointless action, not a war. Even when I became a war widow, I was asked point blank, "How come you're a war widow?" ... And they said, "You're not old enough for the Second World War and you are too old for Vietnam." Now I was asked that point blank. And I said there was such a thing as Korea. And anyway [they said] "was that a war?" ... If they hadn't kicked up a stink about Vietnam, would have been the same thing. Put it out of your mind and forget it, it didn't happen.[13]

Jessie Morland, the wife of another Australian veteran, remembered that "it was like they tried to wipe it [the Korean War] off the earth ... no one ever want[ed] to talk about it."[14] When former Canadian medic Don Leier applied for a home loan in the early 1960s, the veterans loan officer refused him, saying, "Korea was no war, just a police action. Here's fifty cents. That's all you're getting."[15]

This widespread lack of public acknowledgment has contributed to the neglect of the Korean War as a subject of scholarly debate and interest over the past six decades. Chronologically, Korea is also positioned between two major wars. As a topic of study, it lacks the scope and scale of the Second World War or the political controversy of the Vietnam War. These conflicts have overshadowed and distorted how both academic and popular writers understand Korea. However, the Korean War is historically important for a variety of reasons. In terms of military psychiatry, it represents the last major deployment of Commonwealth forces before a revolution in psychiatric medicine, and an example of what pragmatic treatment methods can achieve. It was also the first time that limited tours of duty were uniformly enforced for the purpose of boosting morale. Commonwealth and UN operational goals were constantly evolving from 1950 to 1953. Be that as it may, the Commonwealth Division remained combat-effective and morale was high during periods of rest as well as intense fighting.[16] As a campaign, Korea shares many similarities with modern operations in Afghanistan and around the world. Working out of static bases, soldiers are called on to patrol and infiltrate enemy territory on a daily basis. Political necessity dictates the direction of events on the ground, and destroying the enemy is not necessarily the end goal. Soldiers, scholars, and commentators can all learn a great deal about operations of this nature by studying Korea more closely.

This book also shows that the establishment of long-term care and support systems is as important as the development of forward and front-line psychiatric treatment. Since 2001, roughly 145 troops from New Zealand, several thousand Australian soldiers, 40,000 Canadian personnel and 134,780 British servicemen and women have been deployed to Afghanistan alone. Over 2 million Americans have served in either Afghanistan or Iraq.[17] In a March 2013 article for the *Atlantic*, journalist and historian James Wright argued that Americans have already begun to forget the war in Afghanistan. He argues that Americans, preoccupied with other international commitments and domestic woes, are war-weary.[18] Blogging for the *London Review of Books* on July 10, 2013, retired British ambassador Oliver Miles made similar claims about his own country.[19] How the public receives these veterans will have a lasting impact on their lives. Korea underlines important lessons about commemoration and acknowledgment that present-day policymakers ignore at their peril.

Korea is also an example of successful inter-allied cooperation. Over the past several decades, multinational operations have become increasingly common and a hallmark of the new operating environment. Countries commonly work in tandem for reasons of finance, manpower, or politics. For example, the International Security Assistance Force (ISAF) in Afghanistan and the North Atlantic Treaty Organization (NATO) are multinational groups, and recent United Nations peacekeeping missions to Mali and South Sudan have involved soldiers from all corners of the globe. The Commonwealth Division included four countries with competing agendas and objectives. Canada, Australia, and New Zealand were beginning to distance themselves from Britain and to assert their independence, but they were able to compromise for the common good and for the benefit of the troops. Besides the Commonwealth countries, Colombia, Belgium, France, Greece, Ethiopia, the Netherlands, Luxembourg, the Philippines, Turkey, and Thailand all contributed ground troops to the UN Command. There is still much to be discovered as to how these formations worked together and survived. These lessons could benefit those interested in the inner workings of an inter-allied coalition. There are many other stories waiting to be uncovered.

This book is only the beginning and represents a modest contribution to the developing literature on mental health and war. I hope that it will act as a starting point for others who wish to understand the psychological consequences of what happened over sixty years ago, and for those who are passionate about helping veterans today. Although Korea is popularly referred to as the "forgotten war," it still haunts many of the men who fought there. Many decades later, former operating theatre technician Dr. David Oates reminisced about his experiences and wondered: "Looking back on those days it is the comradeship I think about and as the years have gone on I have often thought and wondered how those soldiers who passed through our hands are getting on. The broken bones and scarred tissue will have healed, but what of the emotional trauma that these young men suffered?"[20]

Appendices

Chronology of Events

June 1950 – December 1953

1950

June 25	North Korean People's Army (NKPA) attacks the Republic of Korea.
June 27	United Nations calls on member states to "furnish such assistance to the Republic of Korea as may be necessary to repel armed attack and to restore international peace and security in the area."[1]
June 28	North Korean People's Army captures Seoul.
June 29	United Kingdom, Australia, and New Zealand announce that they will send naval forces to Korea.
July 1	American ground troops arrive in Korea as part of Task Force Smith.
July 7	General Douglas MacArthur is appointed Commander-in-Chief of UN forces in Korea.
July 12	Canadian naval forces dispatched for service in Korea.
July 26	Australia, Britain, and New Zealand announce that ground troops will be sent to Korea.
August	UN forces retreat to a perimeter around Busan on the south coast of Korea.
August 7	The Canadian government announces the recruitment of a Canadian Army Special Force (CASF) for Korea.
August 28	27 British Brigade lands at Busan. They are put under the command of IX Corps, US Eighth Army.
September 5	27 British Brigade becomes operational.
September 15	US X Corps lands at Incheon on the northwest coast of Korea in order to outflank the NKPA.
September 22	US Eighth Army breaks out of the Busan Perimeter.

September 26	UN forces recapture Seoul.
September 28	3rd Battalion Royal Australian Regiment arrives in Korea and joins 27 Brigade.
September 30	Republic of Korea (ROK) troops advance across the 38th parallel.
September-October	UN forces capture the North Korean capital of Pyongyang and advance towards the Yalu River.
October 14	Chinese forces cross the Yalu River.
October 25	Chinese forces launch first-phase offensive.
November	Chinese launch second-phase offensive and UN forces retreat. 29 British Independent Infantry Brigade arrives in theatre. They are supported by 26 British Field Ambulance, 22 Field Surgical Team, 9 Field Transfusion Team, and 223 and 224 Mobile Dental Teams. 29 British General Hospital (29 BGH) opens in Kure, Japan, with 400 beds. A 30-bed psychiatric unit opens under the command of Captain J.J. Flood (Royal Army Medical Corps [RAMC]).
December	60th Indian Parachute Field Ambulance arrives in theatre to support 27 Brigade.
December 18	2nd Battalion Princess Patricia's Canadian Light Infantry (PPCLI) land in Busan.
December-January	Chinese launch third-phase offensive.

1951

January 4	Seoul falls to North Korean and Chinese forces. 27 Brigade acts as rearguard for the withdrawal of UN forces.
January 14	UN front line stabilizes.
January 22	16 New Zealand Field Artillery Regiment arrives in Korea to support 27 Brigade.
February	2nd Battalion PPCLI joins 27 Brigade.
February 14-17	Chinese launch fourth-phase offensive.
February-March	UN forces launch Operation Killer in response to Chinese fourth-phase offensive.
March	UN forces advance across the Han River as part of Operation Ripper.
March 3-15	27 Brigade advances to Kapyong as part of Operation Rugged.

March 18	UN forces recapture Seoul.
Spring	The number of beds available at 29 BGH goes from 400 to 600.
April	On orders from President Harry S. Truman, General Matthew Ridgway takes over command of UN forces from General MacArthur.
	28 British Commonwealth Infantry Brigade relieves 27 Brigade.
	Canadian medical reconnaissance teams tour Korea and Japan in preparation for the arrival of the 25th Canadian Infantry Brigade.
April 22	Chinese launch fifth-phase offensive and push towards Seoul.
April 22–25	Battle of Imjin River.
April 24–25	Battle of Kapyong.
May	Chinese launch offensive.
	Remaining forces of 25 Canadian Infantry Brigade arrive in theatre and the 2nd Battalion PPCLI is integrated. 25 Canadian Field Ambulance accompanies troops.
May 20	Chinese offensive halted by UN forces.
May–June	UN forces advance north.
Summer	An 80-bed Canadian section of 29 British General Hospital is opened.
June–July	Negotiations for a ceasefire begin. UN forces establish a defensive line.
July	Rotation of Australian troops.
July 2	No. 6 Convalescent Depot opens in Kure with 200 beds.
July 21	25 Canadian Field Dressing Station arrives in theatre. Major R.J.A. Robitaille (Royal Canadian Army Medical Corps [RCAMC]) is attached to the field dressing station as a psychiatrist.
July 28	1 Commonwealth Division is officially formed and put under the command of I Corps, US Eighth Army. Major General A.J.H. Cassels is appointed as the General Officer Commanding of the Division. Colonel G. Anderton (RAMC) assumes his appointment as the division's first Assistant Director of Medical Services (ADMS).

	Major Robitaille (RCAMC) becomes divisional psychiatrist.
August 9	25 Canadian Field Dressing Station moves to Seoul. The unit can accommodate 200 patients. The psychiatric wing has room for 44 patients.
October 2–15	Operation Commando.
October-November	Rotation of Canadian troops.
October-December	Rotation of British troops.
December 29	British General Hospital becomes the British Commonwealth General Hospital (BCGH). The hospital expands to a 1,000-bed facility. Brigadier J.E. Snow (RAMC) becomes the hospital's first commandant and Director of Medical Services.

1952

February	British Director General of Army Medical Services (DGAMS) Lieutenant General Sir Neil Cantlie and divisional Deputy Director of Medical Services (DDMS) Brigadier C.W. Nye (Royal Australian Army Medical Corps [RAAMC]) tour medical units in Korea and Japan.
March 18	Psychiatrist Major F.C.R. Chalke (RCAMC) replaces Major Robitaille as divisional psychiatrist.
April-May	Rotation of Canadian troops. Rotation of Australian troops. 37 Canadian Field Ambulance relieves 25 Canadian Field Ambulance.
May	Colonel G.L. Morgan Smith (RCAMC) replaces Colonel Anderton as the Assistant Director of Medical Services. Colonel A.N.T. Meneces (RAMC) arrives in Japan as the officer commanding BCGH.
June-September	Rotation of British troops.
June 18	An 80-bed forward section of 25 Canadian Field Dressing Station opens. A third of the beds are allocated for psychiatric patients. A rear section of the field dressing station continues to operate in Seoul.
August	Colonel A.N.T. Meneces (RAMC) and a party of officers visit Commonwealth medical units in the field

	to assess the feasibility of opening a new composite medical unit in Seoul.
September	The rear section of 25 Canadian Field Dressing Station moves forward to the Tokchon-Uijeongbu area.
September 7	Major General Mike West replaces Major General Cassels as commanding officer of 1 Commonwealth Division.
September 16	The British Commonwealth Communications Zone Medical Unit (BCCZMU) opens in Seoul.
October 3	Major J.L. Johnston (RCAMC) arrives in theatre to replace Major F.C.R. Chalke (RCAMC) as divisional psychiatrist.
December 15	Lieutenant N.G. Fraser (RAMC) is attached to 25 FDS. He serves as a clinical assistant in psychiatry to divisional psychiatrist Major Johnston (RCAMC).

1953

February	Lieutenant N.G. Fraser (RAMC) promoted to rank of Captain.
Spring	Rotation of Canadian troops.
March	Brigadier R.V. Franklin (RAMC) arrives in Japan to replace Brigadier O'Meara as DDMS. Rotation of Australian troops.
April	Major J.S. McCannel (RCAMC) replaces Major G.L. Morgan Smith (RCAMC) as ADMS.
April 20 – May 3	Operation Little Switch (exchange of sick and wounded prisoners of war).
May	Captain Fraser (RAMC) replaces Major J.L. Johnston (RCAMC) as divisional psychiatrist when the latter has to return home unexpectedly.
May 1	38 Canadian Field Ambulance relieves 37 Canadian Field Ambulance.
July	Rotation of British troops.
July 27	Armistice signed.
August 5 – September 6	Operation Big Switch (exchange of remaining prisoners of war.
August 29	60 Indian Field Ambulance is reassigned to the United Nations Custodian Force.
September	Psychiatrist Major J.J. Magrath (RAMC) visits Korea.
October	Psychiatric unit moves to 26 British Field Ambulance.

December 16   38 Canadian Field Ambulance is redesignated 4
                     Canadian Field Ambulance.

Archival Sources
25 Canadian Field Dressing Station War Diaries, 1951–53, Library and Archives
   Canada (LAC): RG 24-C-3, vols. 18395–97; British Commonwealth
   Communications Zone Medical Unit War Diary 1952, The National Archives
   at Kew (TNA): WO 281/898; and Historical Notes: Medical Services, British
   Commonwealth Forces Korea, TNA: WO 308/21.

Prisoners of War

From April 20 to May 3, 1953, the first Commonwealth prisoners of war (POWs) were released from captivity in Operation Little Switch. After protracted discussions, both sides agreed to the exchange of injured and sick prisoners. Several months later, the remaining POWs were released during Operation Big Switch. Roughly 1,036 Commonwealth soldiers were taken prisoner during the course of the Korean War. The majority fell into enemy hands between September 1950 and June 1951.[2] Over the following years, they suffered severe deprivation and poor treatment at the hands of their captors.[3] Throughout the summer of 1953, 25 Canadian Field Dressing Station was temporarily transformed into Camp Britannia for the purposes of Operation Homeward Bound or the repatriation of Commonwealth prisoners.[4] Despite widespread concern over POW physical and mental health, the men were largely in good condition and high spirits. While many were malnourished, few appear to have suffered irreversible damage.[5] Divisional psychiatrist Captain N.G. Fraser assisted during the physical examinations in order to "obtain a general impression of the POW's mental attitude as this was thought to be preferable to a routine 'frankly psychiatric examination interrogation so soon after release.'"[6] Fraser and his colleagues were largely satisfied with the mental stability of the POWs that passed through Camp Britannia. Nevertheless, they recognized that "the sheer joy of release may be covering up any existing psychiatric conditions."[7] Furthermore, during "routine [physical] examination it is possible to detect numerous complaints which are of probable psychogenic aetiology."[8] However, Fraser did not have time to investigate or treat any of the men about whom he might have harboured concerns. Commonwealth POWs were processed and repatriated as quickly as possible.

Notes

Introduction

Epigraph: Richard A. Gabriel, *No More Heroes: Madness and Psychiatry in War* (New York: Hill and Wang, 1967).

1 Sima Kotecha, "Care for UK Military Veterans Is 'Flawed,' Medical Experts Say," *BBC News*, October 29, 2014, http://www.bbc.com/news/uk-29807947; and Max Hastings, "Veterans and Mental Health in Contemporary Britain," *Royal United Services Institute Journal* 159, 6 (December 2014): 36.

2 Richard Whelan, *Drawing the Line: The Korean War, 1950–1953* (London: Faber and Faber, 1990), 373; Max Hastings, *The Korean War*, Pan Grand Strategy Series (London: Pan Macmillan, 2000), 7, 45–48, 438; Lt. Col. Herbert F. Wood, *Strange Battleground: The Operations in Korea and Their Effects on the Defence Policy of Canada* (Ottawa: Queen's Printer and Controller of Stationery, 1966), 10–12, 42; Tim Carew, *The Commonwealth at War* (London: Cassell, 1967), 13, 27, 71; and Jeffrey Grey, *The Commonwealth Armies and the Korean War: An Alliance Study* (Manchester: Manchester University Press, 1988), 172.

3 Brig. Cyril N. Barclay, *The First Commonwealth Division: The Story of British Commonwealth Land Forces in Korea, 1950–1953* (Aldershot: Gale and Polden, 1954), 12, 34, 110; Gen. Sir Anthony Farrar-Hockley, *The British Part in the Korean War*, vol. 1, *A Distant Obligation* (London: Her Majesty's Stationery Office [HMSO], 1990), 136–38; Ian McGibbon, *New Zealand and the Korean War*, vol. 1, *Politics and Diplomacy* (Auckland: Oxford University Press, 1992), 41–47; and Grey, *Commonwealth Armies*, 77, 172.

4 Richard Trembeth, *A Different Sort of War: Australians in Korea 1950–1953* (Melbourne: Australian Scholarly Publishing, 2005), 1; "Commonwealth Forces' Record in Korea: 'A Successful Experiment,'" *Times of London*, July 21, 1953; and Wood, *Strange Battleground*, 257.

5 Paul M. Edwards, *The Korean War*, American Soldiers' Lives: Daily Life through History (Westport, CT: Greenwood, 2006), 92–94; Lt. Col. Howard N. Cole, *NAAFI in Uniform* (London UK: Navy, Army and Air Force Institute, 1982), 175; and Bill Trevett, interview with author, Wiltshire, UK, November 2010.

6 Hastings, *Korean War*, 95.

7 US Army Survey, as quoted in Stanley Sandler, *The Korean War: No Victors, No Vanquished* (Lexington, KY: University of Kentucky Press, 1999), 131–32; and Robert J. O'Neill, *Australia in the Korean War 1950–1953*, vol. 2, *Combat Operations* (Canberra: Australian War Memorial and the Australian Government Publication Service, 1985), 239; and McGibbon, *Politics and Diplomacy*, 301.

8 Capt. J.J. Flood, "Psychiatric Casualties in UK Elements of Korean Force: December 1950 – November 1951," *Journal of the Royal Army Medical Corps (JRAMC)* 100, 1 (January 1954): 41; and 25 Field Dressing Station (25 FDS) War Diaries, 1951–53, Library and Archives of Canada (LAC): RG 24-C-3, vols. 18395–397.

9 25 FDS War Diaries, 1951–53, ibid.

10 Secondary sources that look at American medical/psychiatric practice include: Albert E. Cowdrey, *The Medics' War: The United States Army in Korea* (Washington, DC: US Army Center of Military History, 1987); Col. Albert J. Glass, "Psychiatry in the Korean Campaign: A Historical Review," *US Armed Forces Medical Journal* 4, 10 (October 1953): 1387–1401; Col. Albert J. Glass, "Psychotherapy in the Combat Zone," *American Journal of Psychiatry* 110, 10 (1954): 725–31; and Col. Elspeth C. Ritchie. "Psychiatry in the Korean War: Perils, PIES and Prisoners of War," *Military Medicine* 167, 11 (2002): 898–903.

11 Flood, "Psychiatric Casualties in UK Elements," 40–47.

12 Col. J.E. Andrew and Brig. Ken A. Hunter, "The Royal Canadian Army Medical Corps in the Korean War," *Canadian Medical Association Journal* 72 (February 1, 1955): 178–84.

13 Bill Rawling, *The Myriad Challenges of Peace: Canadian Forces Medical Practitioners since the Second World War* (Ottawa: Canadian Government Publishing, 2004), 45–83; and Bill Rawling, *Death Their Enemy: Canadian Medical Practitioners and War* (Quebec: AGMV Marquis, 2001).

14 Edgar Jones and Ian Palmer, "Army Psychiatry in the Korean War: The Experience of 1 Commonwealth Division," *Military Medicine* 165, 4 (2000): 256–59; Edgar Jones and Simon Wessely, "Psychiatric Battle Casualties: An Intra- and Interwar Comparison," *British Journal of Psychiatry* 178 (March 2001): 242–47; Edgar Jones and Simon Wessely, *Shell Shock to PTSD: Military Psychiatry from 1900 to the Gulf War* (London: Taylor and Francis, 2005), 119–27.

15 Flood, "Psychiatric Casualties in UK Elements," 40–47; Jones and Wessely, *Shell Shock to PTSD*, 121.

16 Jones and Wessely, ibid., 121.

17 Ibid., 121–23.

18 Ibid., 125.

19 Ibid., 127.

20 Ibid., 126.

21 Jones and Palmer, "Army Psychiatry in the Korean War," 256–60; Jones and Wessely, "Psychiatric Battle Casualties," 242–47; and Jones and Wessely, *Shell Shock to PTSD*, 241–69.

22 Examples include: Anthony Babington, *Shell Shock: A History of the Changing Attitudes to War Neurosis* (London: Leo Cooper, 1997); Peter Leese, *Shell Shock: Traumatic Neurosis and the British Soldiers of the First World War* (London: Palgrave Macmillan, 2002); Peter Barham, *Forgotten Lunatics of the Great War* (New Haven, CT: Yale University Press, 2004); Hans Binneveld, *From Shell Shock to Combat Stress: A Comparative History of Military Psychology* (Amsterdam: Amsterdam University Press, 1998); Ben Shephard, *A War of Nerves: Soldiers and Psychiatrists in the Twentieth Century* (Cambridge, MA: Harvard University Press, 2001); Terry Copp and Bill McAndrew, *Battle Exhaustion: Soldiers and Psychiatrists in the Canadian Army 1939–1945* (Montreal and Kingston: McGill-Queen's University Press, 1990); Joy Damousi, *Living with the Aftermath: Trauma, Nostalgia and Grief in Post-War Australia* (Cambridge: Cambridge University Press, 2001); Alison Parr, *Silent Casualties: New Zealand's Unspoken Legacy of the Second World War* (North Shore, NZ: Tandem, 1995); and Terry Copp and Mark O. Humphries, *Combat Stress in the 20th Century: The Commonwealth Perspective* (Kingston: Canadian Defence Academy Press, 2010).

23 Copp and Humphries, ibid., xi.

24 Roger Cooter, "Medicine and the Goodness of War," *Canadian Bulletin of Medical History* 7 (1990): 147.

25 Other major academic publications include: John Melady, *Korea: Canada's Forgotten War* (Toronto: Macmillan of Canada, 1983); David J. Bercuson, *Blood on the Hills: The Canadian Army in the Korean War* (Toronto: University of Toronto Press, 1999); Brent Byron-Watson, *Far Eastern Tour: Canadian Infantry in Korea, 1950-1953* (Montreal and Kingston: McGill-Queen's University Press, 2002); William C. Johnston, *A War of Patrols: Canadian Army Operations in Korea* (Vancouver: UBC Press, 2003); and Trembeth, *A Different Sort of War.*

26 The official histories of the Korean War include: Farrar-Hockley, *A Distant Obligation;* Gen. Sir Anthony Farrar-Hockley, *The British Part in Korean War*, vol. 2, *An Honourable Discharge* (London: HMSO, 1995); McGibbon, *Politics and Diplomacy;* Ian McGibbon, *New Zealand and the Korean War*, vol. 2, *Combat Operations* (Auckland: Oxford University Press, 1996); Robert J. O'Neill, *Australia in the Korean War 1950-1953*, vol. 1, *Strategy and Diplomacy* (Canberra: Australian War Memorial and the Australian Government Publication Service, 1981); and O'Neill, *Combat Operations.*

27 Rawling, *The Myriad Challenges of Peace*, 45-83; Rawling, *Death Their Enemy*, 239-63; Simon C. Gandevia, "An Australian Army Doctor – Bryan Gandevia," in *War Wounds: Medicine and the Trauma of Conflict*, ed. Ashley Ekins and Elizabeth Stewart (Wollombi, NSW: Exisle Publishing, 2011), 110-15.

28 John Tosh, *The Pursuit of History: Aims, Methods and New Directions in the Study of Modern History*, rev. 3rd ed. (London, UK: Longman, 2002), 303-4.

29 Farrar-Hockley, *An Honourable Discharge*, 212; and McGibbon, *Combat Operations*, 158-59.

30 Patrick Mileham, Richard Lane, David Rowland, and Philip Wilkinson, "Panel – Morale in the Armed Forces," *Royal United Services Institute Journal* 146, 2 (2001): 46.

31 McGibbon, *Politics and Diplomacy*, 41-47; and Michael Hickey, *The Korean War: The West Confronts Communism 1950-1953* (London: John Murray, 2000), 92.

Chapter 1: Brave New World

1 Richard Norton-Taylor, "Executed WW1 Soldiers to Be Given Pardons," *Guardian*, August 16, 2006, http://www.theguardian.com/uk/2006/aug/16/military.immigrationpolicy.

2 Ibid.

3 Simon Wessely, "The Life and Death of Private Harry Farr," *Journal of the Royal Society of Medicine* 99 (September 2006): 442.

4 Ibid., 440.

5 Ibid.

6 Ibid., 441.

7 Ben Shephard, *A War of Nerves: Soldiers and Psychiatrists in the Twentieth Century* (Cambridge, MA: Harvard University Press, 2001), 1; and Julian Bogousslavsky and Laurent Tatu, "French Neuropsychiatry in the Great War: Between Moral Support and Electricity," *Journal of the History of the Neurosciences: Basic and Clinical Perspectives* 22, 2 (2013): 144-54.

8 Ibid., 21.

9 Anthony Babington, *Shell Shock: A History of the Changing Attitudes to War Neurosis* (London: Leo Cooper, 1997), 46; and Andrew Scull, *Hysteria: The Disturbing History* (Oxford: Oxford University Press, 2011), 157.

10 Babington, ibid., 43; and Edgar Jones, "Shell Shock," Lecture, King's College London, 2010.

11 Shephard, *War of Nerves*, 54.

12 Peter Leese, *Shell Shock: Traumatic Neurosis and the British Soldiers of the First World War* (London: Palgrave Macmillan, 2002), 60, 94.

13 Fiona Reid, "Distinguishing between Shell-Shocked Veterans and Pauper Lunatics: The Ex-Services' Welfare Society and Mentally Wounded Veterans after the Great War," *War in History* 14, 3 (2007): 354; and Leese, *Shell Shock*, 60, 110.

14 Hans Binneveld, *From Shell Shock to Combat Stress: A Comparative History of Military Psychology* (Amsterdam: Amsterdam University Press, 1998), 107–36; Shepherd, *War of Nerves*, 87–110; Babington, *Shell Shock*, 54; and Leese, ibid., 76.

15 Leese, ibid., 90, 98.

16 Edgar Jones and Simon Wessely, *Shell Shock to PTSD: Military Psychiatry from 1900 to the Gulf War* (London: Taylor and Francis Group, 2005), 28–33, 233; and Babington, *Shell-Shock*, 98.

17 Peter Barham, *Forgotten Lunatics of the Great War* (New Haven, CT: Yale University Press, 2004), 4.

18 E. Ginzberg, J.K. Anderson, S.W. Ginsburg, and J.L. Herma, *The Lost Divisions* (New York: Columbia University Press, 1959); and Jones and Wessely, *Shell Shock to PTSD*, 106.

19 Shephard, *War of Nerves*, 205–27, 257–77.

20 Simon Wessely, "War and Psychiatry: A Story in Three Acts," Lecture, Global History Seminar, London Centre of the University of Notre Dame, March 27, 2013.

21 Col. C.P. Stacey, "Development of the Canadian Army," *Canadian Army Journal* 6, 4 (July 1952): 19; Rex Pope, "British Demobilisation after the Second World War," *Journal of Contemporary History (JCH)* 30, 1 (January 1995): 67–71; Dean F. Oliver, "Awaiting Return: Life in the Canadian Army's Overseas Repatriation Depots, 1945–1946," in *The Veteran's Charter and Post World War II Canada*, ed. J.L. Granatstein and Peter Neary (Montreal and Kingston: McGill-Queen's University Press, 1998), 36–38; and Historical Section of Army HQ, "Army HQ Report No. 97: A Study on Demobilization and Rehabilitation of Canadian Armed Forces in the Second World War, 1939–1945," Library and Archives of Canada (LAC): RG 24, vol. 22327, file HQS-9072-2-6, 17.

22 Jeffrey R. Rivard, "Bringing the Boys Home: A Study of the Canadian Demobilization Policy after the First and Second World Wars" (MA thesis, University of New Brunswick, 1999), 168.

23 Pope, "British Demobilisation," 67.

24 Alan Allport, *Demobbed: Coming Home after the Second World War* (New Haven, CT: Yale University Press, 2009), 32; J.L. Granatstein, *Canada's War: The Politics of the Mackenzie King Government, 1939–1945* (Toronto: University of Toronto Press, 1990), 412; and Historical Section of Army HQ, "Army HQ Report No. 97," 17.

25 Susan Howson, "The Origins of Cheaper Money, 1945–7," *Economic History Review*, New Series 40, 3 (August 1987): 433.

26 L.V. Scott, *Conscription and the Attlee Governments: The Politics and Policy of National Service 1945–1951* (Oxford: Oxford University Press, 1993), 15; and Allport, *Demobbed*, 30.

27 "Editorial Comments: A Health Survey of Canada," *CMAJ* 50, 4 (April 1944): 364; and Central Medical War Committee, Demobilisation of Doctors 2/1943–1944, October 8, 1943, The National Archives at Kew (TNA): MH 79/547.

28 G.H. Agnew, "The Shortage of Hospital Beds," *CMAJ* 46, 4 (April 1942): 373.

29 H.E.M., "Editorial Comments: Nursing Service Problems in Hospitals," *CMAJ* 47, 2 (August 1942): 157.

30 J.P. Wetenhall to Sir William Jowitt, KC, November 3, 1943, TNA: MH 79/547; and Thomas S. Legg, Marie-Louise Legg, "Jowitt, William Allen, Earl Jowitt (1885–1957)," in *Oxford Dictionary of National Biography* (Oxford: Oxford University Press, 2004), http://www.oxforddnb.com/view/article/34246.

31 "Editorial Comments: A Health Survey of Canada," *CMAJ* 50, 4 (April 1944): 364; Central Medical War Committee, Demobilisation of Doctors: Memo 2/1943–1944, October 8, 1943, TNA: MH 79/547; and Offices of Cabinet and Minister of Defence, Meeting Concerning Demob of Doctors, September 2, 1945, TNA: MH 79/547.

32 Offices of the Cabinet and Minister of Defence, Meeting Concerning Demob of Doctors, September 2, 1945, TNA: MH 79/547.

33 Ibid.

34 Terry Copp and Bill McAndrew, *Battle Exhaustion: Soldiers and Psychiatrists in the Canadian Army, 1939–1945* (Montreal and Kingston: McGill-Queen's University Press, 1990), 5–10, 149–59; Jones and Wessely, *Shell Shock to PTSD*, 67–69, 78–79, 89–97, 103–5; Lt. Col. J.N. Crawford to DGMS, December 10, 1948, LAC: RG 24, vol. 19, 466, file C-3848-1; and Shephard, *War of Nerves*, 325–38.

35 Jones and Wessely, ibid., 115.

36 W.R. Feasby, *Official History of the Canadian Medical Services, 1939–1945*, vol. 2, *Clinical Subjects* (Ottawa: Queen's Printer and Controller of Stationery, 1953), 57; John Farley, *Brock Chisholm, the World Health Organization, and the Cold War* (Vancouver: UBC Press, 2008), 1–3; Terry Copp and Mark Osborne Humphries, *Combat Stress in the 20th Century: The Commonwealth Perspective"* (Kingston, ON: Canadian Defence Academy Press, 2010), 135; J.A. MacFarlane, Speech to Canadian Medical Association, June 18, 1954, LAC, Directorate of History and Heritage, vol. 2, file 325.009 (D315); Canadian Psychiatric Association, "In Memoriam," *Canadian Psychiatric Journal* (January 2010); Copp and McAndrew, *Battle Exhaustion*, xx–xxi, 93–94; Canadian Mental Health Association, Ontario Branch, "Remembering & Celebrating a Good Life: The Jack Griffin Education and Research Endowment Fund" (Canadian Mental Health Association, n.d.), http://ontario.cmha.ca/files/2013/04/jack_griffin_brochure.pdf.

37 Army Psychiatric Advisory Committee, Committee Minutes, February 16, 1946, January 2, 1947, December 10, 1948, April 1, 1949, TNA: WO 32/13462; ACS to DGAMS, July 8, 1948, TNA: WO 32/13462; Brig. Sandiford to ACS, February 16, 1946, TNA: WO 32/13462; Anon. to DGAMS, July 8, 1946, TNA: WO 32/13462; and Jones and Wessely, *Shell Shock to PTSD*, 76.

38 Jones and Wessely, ibid., 117.

39 A career medical officer, Brigadier Rosie joined the RAMC in the 1920s. During the Second World War, he worked as a psychiatrist at the Royal Victoria Hospital Netley and at Northfield Hospital. From 1948 until his retirement in 1954, he served as Director of Army Psychiatry. Prof. Anthony J. Rosie, email to author, June 2010.

40 Defence Medical and Dental Services Advisory Board to Minister of National Defence, November 28, 1950, LAC: RG 24, acc. 1983-1984/215, vol. 3, file C-1225-M1.

41 Working Party on Revised Establishment of MOs: Memo by AMD1, 1953, TNA: WO 32/10383.

42 Mr. Morrison to Dept. of Labour, October 27, 1950, LAC: RG 24, acc. 1983-1984/216 GAD, vol. 1, box 2491, file 801-M90, ATIP A2010-0042.

43 Ibid.

44 Col. R.H. Robinson, "Future Medical Officers for the Army," *JRAMC* 96, 2 (February 1951): 131; Col. R.H. Robinson, "Future Medical Officers for the Army Part III: Some Suggestions," *JRAMC* 96, 3 (March 1951): 183.

45 ISMC, September 4, 1946, Minutes of Meeting, LAC: RG 24, acc. 1983-1984/167, box 7717, 20-1-1, pt. 1.

46 Chair Ad Hoc Committee to Secretary of Personnel Member's Committee, May 9, 1951, LAC: RG 24, acc. 1983-1984/167, box 7717, 20-1-1, pt. 3, A/C F.G.

47 DGAMS, RAMC – Rates of Pay: Review Consequent on Danckwerts Award, 1952, TNA: WO 32/15673.

48 MoD, Appendix A, to ACS/B/3224, April 10, 1950, TNA: WO 32/13369; Standing Committee of Service Ministers, Increases of Pay for MOs, April 25, 1950, TNA: WO 32/13369.

49 "Forty Million Pounds," *BMJ* 1, 4760 (March 29, 1952): 697–98; 40th Parliament, *Debates,* House of Commons (5th Series) (October 30, 1952), vol. 505, 2109–15; and DGAMS, RAMC Officers – Rates of Pay: Review Consequent on Danckwerts Award, Minute Sheet, August 21, 1952, 1, TNA: WO 32/15673.

50 Bill Rawling, *The Myriad Challenges of Peace: Canadian Forces Medical Practitioners since the Second World War* (Ottawa: Canadian Government Publishing, 2004), 31.

51 *Report on Health of Army 1949–1950,* March 27, 1953, TNA: WO 279/610; Army Medical Advisory Board, Meetings July 1, 1949–54: and Deficiency of MOs in the RAMC, July 1, 1952, TNA: WO 32/13465.

52 Harold M. Wright, *Salute to the Air Force Medical Branch on the 75th Anniversary, Royal Canadian Air Force* (Ottawa, 1999), 195; Paul Sneath, Report of Five Year (1954–59) Survey of Sources of Supply, Professional Attainments and Wastage MOs of Canadian Forces, 1960, LAC: MG31-J7, vol. 1; *Report on Health of Army 1949–1950,* ibid.; Army Medical Advisory Board, ibid.

53 Sir John Crocker, Deficiency of MOs in the RAMC: Paper for Consideration by Army Council, April 17, 1953, TNA: WO 32/13465.

54 Army Medical Advisory Board, Minutes of Meetings, July 1, 1949 – September 1954, May 19, 1950, TNA: WO 32/13465.

55 Specialties with the greatest deficiencies (1950)

	May 1950		Establishment on July 1, 1950	
	No.	%	No.	%
Anesthetists	17	37.7	22	48.8
Otologists	19	50	11	61.1
Radiologists	13	54.1	13	54.1
Psychiatrists	12	34.2	17	48.5
Surgeons	24	34.2	30	42.8

Note: The statistics in this table are based on the Army's minimum requirements for medical consultants as opposed to trainee and graded specialists.

Source: Army Medical Advisory Board, Minutes of Meeting, May 19, 1950, TNA: WO 32/13465.

56 Army Medical Advisory Board, Minutes of Meeting, May 19, 1950, TNA: WO 32/13465; and Standing Committee of Service Ministers, Specialists in RAMC, Annex A to ACS/B/3023 Requirements of Specialists for Army, July 26, 1949, TNA: WO 32/13369.

57 Standing Committee of Service Ministers, ibid.

58 Secretary of State for War, Shortage of Specialists RAMC: Extract from Minutes of 8th (50) Meeting of Standing Committee of Service Ministers, May 16, 1950, TNA: WO 32/13369.

59 Brig. C.S. Thompson to Dr. G.H. Hutton, September 23, 1946, LAC: RG 24, vol. 19, 466.

60 W.R. Feasby, *Official History of the Canadian Medical Services, 1939–1945,* vol. 2, *Clinical Subjects* (Ottawa: Queen's Printer and Controller of Stationery, 1953), 53.

61 Brig. C.S. Thompson to Dr. G.H. Hutton, September 23, 1946, LAC: RG 24, vol. 19, 466.
62 Maj. F.C.R. Chalke to Senior Consultant, November 20, 1952, LAC: RG 24, vol. 19, 466, file C-3848-1; and Lt. Col. J.N. Crawford to DGMS, December 10, 1948, LAC: RG 24, vol. 19, 466, file C-3848-1; and DGMS Brig. W.L. Coke to MOs, HQ Central Command, December 4, 1951, LAC: RG 24, vol. 19, 466, file C-3848-1.
63 Copp and McAndrew, Battle Exhaustion, 159; and DGMS Brig. W.L. Coke to MOs, HQ Central Command, December 1951, LAC: RG 24, vol. 19, 466, file C-3848-1.
64 Assistant Director of Organization Lt.-Col. G.D. Dailly, "Memo on Psychiatry in the Canadian Army," March 20, 1948, LAC: RG 24, vol. 19, 466, file C-3848-1.
65 Copp and McAndrew, Battle Exhaustion, 159; and ISMC to Dr. C.W. MacCharles, Medical Section of Defence Research Board, November 20, 1952, LAC: RG 24, vol. 19, 466, file C-3848-1.
66 Born in 1916, F.C.R. Chalke grew up in Winnipeg. He studied for his medical degree at the University of Manitoba and obtained a Master of Science from Queen's University. Chalke joined the RCAMC in 1940 and served as a medical officer throughout the Second World War. Qualifying as a psychiatrist after the war, he continued to serve in the RCAMC during the 1950s. After his retirement from the army, he opened a private practice in Ottawa. During the remaining years of his career, Chalke became a highly influential figure, helping to found the Royal Ottawa Psychiatric Hospital and serving as the president of the Canadian Psychiatric Association. Douglas Chalke, email message to author, November 3, 2011.
67 Army Psychiatric Advisory Committee, Minutes, July 31, 1946, TNA: WO 32/13462.
68 Brig. H.A. Sandiford to DGAMS Maj. Gen. Alexander Hood, July 5, 1945, TNA: WO 32/13462; and Joint Secretary of ACS, Register No. 24, September 1945, TNA: WO 32/13462.
69 Army Psychiatric Advisory Committee, Minutes, July 31, 1946, TNA: WO 32/13462.
70 Ibid.
71 Army Psychiatric Advisory Committee, Minutes, December 15, 1956, TNA: WO 32/13462.
72 ADA Psych Lt. Col. N. Copeland, Post-War Army Schools, March 20, 1945, TNA: WO 32/11971.
73 Ibid.; ADA Psych Lt. Col. J.C. Penton to the DDGAMS, School of Army Psychiatry, June 14, 1947, TNA: WO 32/11971; Sir James Steele, Medical Schools and Training Establishments in Post-War Army: and Memo by AG for Consideration by ECAC in a Future Meeting, August 6, 1947, TNA: WO 32/11971.
74 ADA Psych Lt. Col. J.C. Penton to the DDGAMS, ibid.
75 ECAC, Minutes, June 6, 1947, TNA: WO 32/11971.
76 Ibid.
77 Ibid.
78 Ibid.
79 Ibid.
80 DGAMS Maj. Gen. Alexander Hood to Sir Richard O'Connor, Work of Psychologists and Psychiatrists in the Services, December 4, 1946, TNA: WO 32/11974; ACS, Brief for Secretary of State: Prepared by ACS in Consultation with AG and PUS, March 31, 1945, TNA: WO 32/11974; and ACS, Ministerial Committee on Work of Psychologists and Psychiatrists in the Services: Report of Expert Committee, TNA: WO 32/11974.
81 DGAMS Maj. Gen. Alexander Hood to Sir Richard O'Connor, ibid.
82 Advisory Committee of Psychologists, Record of a Meeting, November 9, 1946, TNA: WO 32/11974.
83 Ibid.

84 Sir Richard O'Connor to ACS, December 5, 1946, TNA: WO 32/11974.
85 Advisory Committee of Psychologists, Record of a Meeting, November 9, 1946, TNA: WO 32/11974.
86 Ibid.
87 ADA Psych Lt. Col. N. Copeland, Post-War Army Schools, March 20, 1945, TNA: WO 32/11971; D Psych Brig. H.A. Sandiford, Minutes of PAC, July 5, 1945, TNA: WO 32/13462; and Army Medical Advisory Board, Minutes, May 19, 1950, TNA: WO 32/13465.
88 The British Army used a modified version of the PULHEMS system called PULHEEMS. Eyesight was measured and scored for the left and right eyes independently. While the British first began to use this system in 1944, they also employed a number of other testing and screening methods. In 1947, they decided to apply PULHEEMS universally. Pulheems – Army Admin Pamphlet, September 30, 1946, TNA: WO 32/10957; Lt. Col. Robert J. Rosie, Comments for Interdepartmental Committee on Standardization of Medical Categories for Fighting Services, June 14, 1948, TNA: WO 32/10957; Maj. R.G. Fletcher, Loose Minute: Pulheems Examinations, December 23, 1947, TNA: WO 32/10957; and ADA Army Health Maj. R.G. Fletcher, Loose Minute: Army Publications – British Army System of Medical Categorisation, May 8, 1947, TNA: WO 32/10957.
89 Standing Committee of Service Ministers, Specialists in RAMC, Annex A to ACS/B/3023, July 26, 1949, TNA: WO 32/13369.
90 Ibid.
91 *Report on Health of Army 1949-1950*, March 27, 1953, TNA: WO 279/610.
92 Ibid.
93 Ibid.
94 Ibid.

Chapter 2: Together We Stand

1 "Commonwealth Forces' Record in Korea: A Successful Experiment," *Times of London*, July 21, 1953.
2 Max Hastings, *The Korean War* (London: Pan Macmillan, 2000), 286; Robert J. O'Neill, *Australia in the Korean War 1950-1953*, vol. 2, *Combat Operations* (Canberra: Australian War Memorial and the Australian Government Publication Service, 1985), 173–74, 239; and Maj. P. Devine, "La Belle Alliance – Lessons for Coalition Warfare from the Korean War 1950-1953," *Australian Defence Force Journal (ADFJ)* 118 (May/June 1996): 56.
3 Ted Barris, *Deadlock in Korea: Canadians at War 1950-1953* (Toronto: Macmillan of Canada, 1999), 110; Eric Linklater, *Our Men in Korea* (London: HMSO, 1952), 66; Lt. Col. Herbert Fairlie-Wood, *Strange Battleground: The Operations in Korea and Their Effects on the Defence Policy of Canada* (Ottawa: Queen's Printer and Controller of Stationery, 1966), 258–59; and 25 Field Dressing Station (25 FDS) War Diaries, 1951–53, Library and Archives of Canada (LAC): RG 24-C-3, vols. 18395–397.
4 Gen. Sir Anthony Farrar-Hockley, *The British Part in the Korean War*, vol. 1, *A Distant Obligation* (London: HMSO, 1990), 210–11; Hastings, *Korean War*, 45–48; and Fairlie-Wood, ibid., 10–12.
5 83 (1950), Resolution of June 27, 1950 [S/1511] as quoted in Evan Luard, *A History of the United Nations*, vol. 2, *The Years of Western Domination 1945-55* (London: Macmillan, 1982), 241–42.
6 Tim Carew, *The Commonwealth at War* (London: Cassell, 1967), 13, 27; Jeffrey Grey, *The Commonwealth Armies and the Korean War: An Alliance Study* (Manchester: Manchester University Press, 1988), 27; David Smurthwaite and Linda Washington, *Project Korea: The British Soldier in Korea, 1950-1953* (London: National Army Museum, 1988), 14; and Hastings, *The Korean War*, 7, 438.

7   Robert J. O'Neill, *Australia in the Korean War 1950-1953*, vol. 1, *Strategy and Diplomacy* (Canberra: Australian War Memorial and the Australian Government Publication Service, 1981), xv-xvi.

8   Australian War Memorial, "War at Sea: The Royal Australian Navy in Korea," http://www.awm.gov.au/exhibitions/korea/ausinkorea/navy/; and Gen. Sir Anthony Farrar-Hockley, *The British Part in Korean War*, vol. 2, *An Honourable Discharge* (London: HMSO, 1995), 295-329.

9   Carew, *Commonwealth at War*, 27, 71; Fairlie-Wood, *Strange Battleground*, 42; and Hastings, *Korean War*, 96-115.

10 Lee Jong-Seok, "Struggling through Times of Darkness and Despair: Korean Communists from the Anti-Japanese Resistance to the Chinese Civil War," in *Foreigners and Foreign Institutions in Republican China*, ed. Anne-Marie Brady and Douglas Brown (New York: Routledge, 2013), 263.

11 "Australian Force to Go to Korea," *West Australian*, July 27, 1950.

12 Ibid.

13 Fairlie-Wood, *Strange Battleground*, 22.

14 Franklin B. Cooling, "Allied Interoperability in the Korean War," *Military Review* 63, 6 (June 1983): 28; Smurthwaite and Washington, *Project Korea*, 14; and Brig. Cyril N. Barclay, *The First Commonwealth Division: The Story of British Commonwealth Land Forces in Korea, 1950-1953* (Aldershot: Gale and Polden, 1954), 12.

15 Farrar-Hockley, *A Distant Obligation*, 125.

16 Ibid., 126.

17 Ibid., 126-27.

18 Carew, *Commonwealth at War*, 43.

19 Michael Hickey, *The Korean War: The West Confronts Communism 1950-1953* (London: John Murray, 2000), 65; Smurthwaite and Washington, *Project Korea*, 9; Farrar-Hockley, *A Distant Obligation*, 116, 126, 128-29; and Grey, *Commonwealth Armies*, 34-35.

20 Farrar-Hockley, ibid., 116.

21 Richard Trembeth, *A Different Sort of War: Australians in Korea 1950-1953* (Melbourne: Australian Scholarly Publishing, 2005), 19; Malcolm van Gelder and Michael J. Eley, "Anzacs, Chockos, and Diggers: A Portrait of the Australian Enlisted Man," in *Life in the Rank and File: Enlisted Men and Women in the Armed Forces of the United States, Australia, Canada, and the United Kingdom*, ed. David R. Segal and H. Wallace Sinaiko (Washington, DC): Pergamon-Brassey's International, 1986), 17; Fairlie-Wood, *Strange Battleground*, 16-17; Grey, *Commonwealth Armies*, 90; and O'Neill, *Strategy and Diplomacy*, 31.

22 Brent Byron-Watson, *Far Eastern Tour: Canadian Infantry in Korea, 1950-1953* (Montreal and Kingston: McGill-Queen's University Press, 2002), 27; O'Neill, *Combat Operations*, 18; and Ian McGibbon, *New Zealand and the Korean War*, vol. 1, *Politics and Diplomacy* (Auckland: Oxford University Press, 1992), 41-44.

23 McGibbon, ibid., 41.

24 Trembeth, *A Different Sort of War*, 91, 94; Fairlie-Wood, *Strange Battleground*, 32; and McGibbon, ibid., 45.

25 Grey, *Commonwealth Armies*, 67, 73; O'Neill, *Combat Operations*, 101, 105; and Fairlie-Wood, *Strange Battleground*, 47-48, 53.

26 McGibbon, *Politics and Diplomacy*, 41-47; and Grey, ibid., 77.

27 Eiji Takemae, *The Allied Occupation of Japan* (New York: Continuum, 2003), 131-37.

28 Fairlie-Wood, *Strange Battleground*, 134.

29 Darryl McIntyre, "Australian Army Medical Services in Korea," in *Australia in the Korean War 1950-1953*, vol. 2, *Combat Operations*, by Robert J. O'Neill (Canberra:

Australian War Memorial and the Australian Government Publication Service, 1985), 570–71; Simon C. Gandevia, "An Australian Army Doctor – Bryan Gandevia," in *War Wounds: Medicine and the Trauma of Conflict*, ed. Ashley Ekins and Elizabeth Stewart (Wollombi, New South Wales: Exisle, 2011), 110–15; Historical Notes: Medical Services, BCFK, The National Archives at Kew (TNA): WO 308/21; O'Neill, *Combat Operations*, 237; McGibbon, *Politics and Diplomacy*, 76; and Farrar-Hockley, *An Honourable Discharge*, 427.

30 The Indian government did not dedicate ground troops to the war in Korea to preserve peaceful relations with China. William W. Stueck, *The Korean War: An International History* (Princeton, NJ: Princeton University Press, 1995), 156, 196; and Historical Notes: Medical Services, BCFK, TNA: WO 308/21.

31 The buildings had been in use as a Japanese naval hospital since the late nineteenth century. Located in a mountainous region, the hospital was built on large rollers to allow for earthquake tremors. Kenneth Davison, interview by author, Newcastle upon Tyne, November 17, 2010; and David Oates, "Memories of Kure Japan: A Personal Experience," Memories of Kure: A Medic in the Korean War, http://www.kurememories.com/page4.htm.

32 J.C. Watt, *Surgeon at War* (London: Allen and Unwin, 1955), 147; and "Discussion on Military Medical Problems in Korea," *Proceedings of the Royal Society of Medicine* 46 (June 10, 1953): 1037.

33 McIntyre, "Australian Army Medical Services in Korea," 571.

34 Ibid.

35 Ibid.

36 Albert E. Cowdrey, *The Medic's War: The United States Army in Korea* (Washington, DC: Center of Military History, 1987), 150–250; Col. Geoffrey Anderton, "The Birth of the British Commonwealth Division Korea," *Journal of the Royal Army Medical Corps (JRAMC)* 99, 2 (January 1953): 47; Lt. Col. Bernard L.P. Brosseau, "Notes from Korea: Medical Services," *Canadian Army Journal* 8, 1 (April 1953): 119; Barclay, *First Commonwealth Division*, 87; McGibbon, *Politics and Diplomacy*, 76; and Hickey, *Korean War*, 92.

37 Grey, *Commonwealth Armies*, 172.

38 Minutes of Conference at BCOF HQ, August 15, 1950, Australian War Memorial (AWM): file 417/20/32, part 1: Medical Policy; Anderton, "The Birth of the British Commonwealth Division," 47; and McIntyre, "Australian Army Medical Services," 572.

39 O'Neill, *Strategy and Diplomacy*, 78, 224.

40 Grey, *Commonwealth Armies*, 92.

41 Ibid.

42 Directorate of History and Heritage, Department of National Defence, *Canada and the Korean War* (Ottawa: Art Global, 2002), 38.

43 David Reynolds, "From World War to Cold War: The Wartime Alliance and the Post-War Transitions, 1941–1947," *Historical Journal* 45, 1 (March 2002): 212–15; John Darwin, "Imperial Twilight, or When Did the Empire End," in *Canada and the End of Empire*, ed. Philip Buckner (Vancouver: UBC Press, 2005), 21; and John Hilliker and Greg Donaghy, "Canadian Relations with the UK at the End of Empire, 1956–1973," in *Canada and the End of Empire*, ibid., 26.

44 J.N. Hitsman, Report No. 90: Canada's Post-War Defence Policy, 1945–1950, 1961, LAC: RG 24-C-6-0, vol. 6928, file 90.

45 Barclay, *First Commonwealth Division*, 3; and Farrar-Hockley, *A Distant Obligation*, 269, 273, 276.

46 Australian War Memorial, "Korean War, 1950–1953," https://www.awm.gov.au/atwar/korea/.

47 Callum MacDonald, *Britain and the Korean War* (Oxford: Blackwell, 1990), 38; and Peter Lowe, "An Ally and a Recalcitrant General: Great Britain, Douglas MacArthur and the Korean War, 1950–1951," *English Historical Review* 105, 416 (July 1990): 635.

48 Lt. Gen. Sir Horace Robertson to CGS Melbourne, CGS Wellington, CIGS London, Cipher Message, November 15, 1950, National Archives of Australia (NAA): CRS A5954, box 1661, file 4.

49 Ibid.

50 Formation of Division for Korea, c 1950, TNA: WO 216/341; O'Neill, *Strategy and Diplomacy*, 93; and Grey, *Commonwealth Armies*, 100–1.

51 Farrar-Hockley, *An Honourable Discharge*, 64.

52 CIGS to Robertson, March 12, 1951, TNA: DEFE 11/209.

53 Farrar-Hockley, *An Honourable Discharge*, 214.

54 Barclay, *First Commonwealth Division*, 86.

55 Anderton, "The Birth of the British Commonwealth Division," 44; Historical Notes: Medical Services, BCFK, TNA: WO 308/21; Col. J.S. McCannel, Study on Commonwealth Medical Services in Korea, June 12, 1954, Directorate of History and Heritage (DHH), Department of National Defence (DND), 681.013 (D48); and Hastings, *Korean War*, 104.

56 Historical Notes: Medical Services, BCFK, TNA: WO 308/21.

57 "High US Honor for Australian," *Barrier Miner*, March 28, 1951.

58 Ibid.

59 ADMS War Diary, 1951–53, TNA: WO 281/886-888; Maj. Gen. R.D. Cameron, "The British Army Divisional Medical Organisation," *JRAMC* 96, 3 (March 1951): 237–41; and Col. G.L. Morgan Smith, Monthly Liaison Letter Serial 14 – July 1952, TNA: WO 281/887.

60 Col. J.S. McCannel, Study on Commonwealth Medical Services in Korea, June 12, 1954, DHH, DND: 681.013 (D48).

61 25 FDS War Diary, August 1951, LAC: RG 24-C-3, vol. 18395; McCannel, Study on Commonwealth Medical Services, ibid.; 25 FDS War Diaries, 1953, LAC: RG 24-C-3, vol. 18397; ADMS War Diaries, 1951–53, TNA: WO 281/886-888; and Bill Rawling, *Death Their Enemy: Canadian Medical Practitioners and War* (Quebec: AGMV, 2001), 68, 240, 250–51.

62 G.W.L. Nicholson, *Canada's Nursing Sisters* (Toronto: Samuel Stevens, 1975), 217; 25 FDS War Diaries, 1951–53, LAC: RG 24-C-3, vols. 18395–97; Cameron, "The British Army Divisional Medical Organisation," 241; and Maj. W.R. Dalziel, Monthly Progress Report August 1951, September 1, 1951, LAC: RG 24-C-3, vol. 18395.

63 ADMS War Diary, 1951–53, TNA: WO 281/886-888; N.G. Fraser to Mrs. C.C. Fraser and Mr. Rupert Fraser, January 22, 1953 and March 1953, Personal Letters of N.G. Fraser, Glasgow, UK; Col. Byron L. Steger, "Medical Societies in Korea," *Medical Bulletin of the United States Army Far East* 1, 6 (May 1953): 92; Capt. N.G. Fraser, Monthly Psychiatric Report July 1953, August 2, 1953, LAC: RG 24-C-3, vol. 18397; Minutes of Conference at BCOF HQ, August 15, 1950, AWM: file 417/20/32, pt. I: Medical Policy; and Bill Trevett, interview by author, Wiltshire, UK, November 2010.

64 W.S. Stanbury, Red Cross in the Far East, July 1952, Canadian War Museum (CWM): 58C 3 22.1; and Oates, "Memories of Kure Japan."

65 29 BGH Summary of Events and Info, October 1951, TNA: WO 281/1278; Historical Notes: Medical Services, BCFK, TNA: WO 308/21; HQ BCFK to Under Secretary of State, Annual Report on Medical Coordination Overseas, December 3, 1952, TNA: DEFE 3/317; Brig. J.E. Snow, 29 BGH – Monthly Liaison Letter, November 1951, TNA: WO 281/1278; and Main Admin HQ BCFK, Est. BCGH, November 12, 1951, TNA: WO 281/1278.

66 O'Neill, *Combat Operations*, 166.
67 Anderton, "The Birth of the British Commonwealth Division," 47; Col. J.E. Andrew and Brig. Ken A. Hunter, "The Royal Canadian Army Medical Corps in the Korean War," *Canadian Medical Association Journal* 72 (February 1, 1955): 180; and Historical Notes: Medical Services, BCFK, TNA: WO 308/21.
68 Farrar-Hockley, *Combat Operations*, 375.
69 I.M. Hurrell, Internal Memorandum, August 26, 1952, TNA: FO 371/99613.
70 Gen. Mike West to Sir John Crocker, October 29, 1952, NAA: CRS A2107.K1.05 (supplement).
71 ISMC, September 4, 1946, Minutes of Meeting, LAC: RG 24, acc. 1983-1984/167, box 7717, 20-1-1, pt. 1, as quoted in Bill Rawling, *The Myriad Challenges of Peace: Canadian Forces Medical Practitioners since the Second World War* (Ottawa: Canadian Government Publishing, 2004), 34; Col. G.L. Morgan Smith, "The Royal Canadian Army Medical Corps of Today," *Canadian Services Medical Journal* 10, 1 (July/August 1954): 20; and Working Party on Revised Est. of MOs: Memo by AMD1, RAMC: Peace Establishment Officers, 1953, TNA: WO 32/10383.
72 Army Medical Advisory Board, Meetings July 1, 1949 – September 1954, December 8, 1950, 4, TNA: WO 32/13465.
73 "Discussion on Military Medical Problems in Korea," *Proceedings of the Royal Society of Medicine* 46 (10 June 1953): 1038.
74 Ibid.
75 Lt. Col. A. MacLennan (26 Field Ambulance) 1 Commonwealth Division, Questionnaire on Korean Campaign, 1950–52, Wellcome Library and Archives (WLA): Muniments Collection, 761/4, box 158.
76 Arthur Helliwell, "Untitled," *The People* (1952), as quoted in Carew, *Commonwealth at War*, 259.
77 BBCZMU War Diary 1952, TNA: WO 281/898; and Maj. R.A. Smillie, RCAMC, Situation Report, September 1952, TNA: WO 281/898.
78 The following chart shows the average daily holdings and number of evacuations from Korea from June to October 1952. It demonstrates how evacuations dropped once the British Commonwealth Communications Zone Medical Unit was formed.

	June	July	August	September	October
Average holdings in Korea	172	205	237.6	266.2	278.3
Evacuations from Korea	479	473	424	274	285

Source: ADMS Monthly Liaison Letter Serial No. 17, October 1952, TNA: WO 281/887.

79 O'Neill, *Combat Operations*, 105; Grey, *Commonwealth Armies*, 121, 131.
80 Grey, ibid., 58–59.
81 Ibid.
82 Ibid.
83 Ibid., 65.
84 Ibid., 126–27.
85 Canadian Joint Staff, Washington DC, to C.P. Stacey, DHH, DND: 112.3H1.009 (D113).
86 Grey, *Commonwealth Armies*, 151.
87 Ibid., 105.
88 Col. J.S. McCannel, Study on Commonwealth Medical Services in Korea, June 12, 1954, DHH, DND: 681.013 (D48).

89 Historical Notes: Medical Services, BCFK, TNA: WO 308/21; Maj. J.H. Cater, Minutes of ADMS Conference, February 2, 1953, TNA: WO 281/888; and MacLennan, (26 Field Ambulance) 1 Commonwealth Division, Questionnaire on Korean Campaign, 1950–52, WLA: Muniments Collection, 761/4, box 158.
90 Andrew and Hunter, "The Royal Canadian Army Medical Corps in the Korean War," 180.
91 Ibid.
92 Report of Visit of ADMS to Korea, April 17–21, 1951, TNA: WO 32/21831; Col. Geoffrey Anderton, 1 Commonwealth Division, Questionnaire on Korean Campaign, 1950–52, WLA: Muniments Collection, 761/4, box 158.
93 French, *Army, Empire and the Cold War*, 141.
94 25 FDS War Diaries, 1951–53, LAC: RG 24-C-3, vols. 18395–97.
95 Barclay, *First Commonwealth Division*, 44.
96 25 FDS War Diaries, 1951–53, LAC: RG 24-C-3, vols. 18395–97.
97 Lt. Col. John C. Blaxland, "The Armies of Canada and Australia: Closer Collaboration?" *Canadian Military Journal* 3, 3 (Autumn 2002): 46.
98 Grey, *Commonwealth Armies*, 190; and Devine, "La Belle Alliance," 51.
99 Roland Wilson, *Official Year Book of the Commonwealth of Australia No. 37: 1946 and 1947* (Canberra: Commonwealth Bureau of Census and Statistics, 1948), 1148–49; Christopher Clark-Coulthard, *Duntroon: The Royal Military College of Australia, 1911–1986* (Sydney: Allen and Unwin, 1986); and Jeffrey Grey, *Australian Brass: The Career of Lieutenant General Sir Horace Robertson* (Cambridge: Cambridge University Press, 1992), 3.
100 Grey, ibid., 3.
101 Capt. W.G. Clever, "A Brief History: British Canadian Military Medical Services," *Canadian Army Journal* 8, 4 (October 1954): 148; and Hub Gray, *Beyond the Danger Close: The Korean Experience Revealed: 2nd Battalion Princess Patricia's Canadian Light Infantry* (Calgary: Bunker to Bunker Books, 2003), 121.
102 Clever, ibid., 150.
103 Nicholson, *Canada's Nursing Sisters*, 254–55; and David S. Whittingham, RCAMC Papers vol. 1, 1951–53, CWM: 58C 3 22.1.
104 Grey, *Commonwealth Armies*, 105.
105 Ibid.
106 Ibid.
107 Farrar-Hockley, *An Honourable Discharge*, 366.
108 Field Marshal Sir William Slim, as quoted in Farrar-Hockley, ibid., 366.
109 Farrar-Hockley, *A Distant Obligation*, 115.
110 David J. Bercuson, *Blood on the Hills: The Canadian Army in the Korean War* (Toronto: University of Toronto Press, 1999), 35–39; Brent Byron-Watson, *Far Eastern Tour: Canadian Infantry in Korea, 1950–1953* (Montreal and Kingston: McGill-Queen's University Press, 2002), 7.
111 Australian War Memorial, "People Profiles: General Francis George (Frank) Hassett, AC, KBE, CB, DSO," http://www.awm.gov.au/people/8445.asp; O'Neill, *Combat Operations*, 172; and McGibbon, *Politics and Diplomacy*, 48.
112 "High US Honor for Australian," *Barrier Miner*, March 28, 1951; Liddell Hart Centre for Military Archives, "Summary Guide: GB99 KCLMA Anderton," August 8, 2005, http://www.kingscollections.org/catalogues/lhcma/collection/a/an30-001?searchterms=Anderton and "Canadian for Australian Army Course," *Cairns Post*, December 19, 1950.
113 "News of the Medical Services: Canadian Armed Forces," *Canadian Medical Association Journal* 62, 3 (March 1950): 297; and Harold Russell, "24th Canadian Field Ambulance,

Royal Canadian Army Medical Corps," *Canadian Military History* 8, 1 (Winter 1999): 69–70.
114 J.H. Gorman, J.S. Logan, and D.A.D. Montgomery, "Historical Review: The Evacuation of Burma: Fifty Years Ago," *Ulster Medical Journal* 61, 2 (October 1992): 169.
115 For full chronology of events, see Appendix A.

Chapter 3: For the Common Good

1 Gen. Bruce C. Clarke, interview by Jerry Hess, January 14, 1970, Harry S. Truman Library and Museum, http://www.trumanlibrary.org/oralhist/clarkeb.htm.
2 David French, *Army, Empire and the Cold War: The British Army and Military Policy, 1945–1971* (Oxford: Oxford University Press, 2012), 141; Max Hastings, *The Korean War* (London: Macmillan, 2000), 286–87; Gen. Sir Anthony Farrar-Hockley, *The British Part in the Korean War*, vol. 1, *A Distant Obligation* (London: HMSO, 1990), 136–38; Brig. Cyril N. Barclay, *The First Commonwealth Division: The Story of British Commonwealth Land Forces in Korea, 1950–1953* (Aldershot: Gale and Polden, 1954), 110; Ian McGibbon, *New Zealand and the Korean War*, vol. 1, *Politics and Diplomacy* (Auckland: Oxford University Press, 1992), 41–47; and Jeffrey Grey, *The Commonwealth Armies and the Korean War: An Alliance Study* (Manchester: Manchester University Press, 1988), 77.
3 McGibbon, *Politics and Diplomacy*, 301.
4 Patrick Mileham, Richard Lane, David Rowland, and Philip Wilkinson, "Panel – Morale in the Armed Forces," *Royal United Service Institute Journal* 146, 2 (2001): 46.
5 Maj. Gen. H.J. Coates, "Morale on the Battlefield," *Australian Defence Force Journal* (*ADFJ*) 45 (March/April 1984): 6.
6 Edgar Jones, *Morale, Psychological Wellbeing of UK Armed Forces and Entertainment: A Report for the British Forces Foundation* (London: KCL Institute of Psychiatry, January 2012), 12–13.
7 Ernest Andrade Jr., "Review of *Morale: A Study of Men and Courage: The Second Scottish Rifles at the Battle of Neuve Chapelle, 1915* by John Baynes," *Military Affairs* 32, 2 (October 1968): 91.
8 Sergio Catignani, "Motivating Soldiers: The Example of the Israeli Defence Forces," *Parameters* 34, 3 (Autumn 2004): 113–14; L.H. Ingraham and F.J. Manning, "Psychiatric Battle Casualties: The Missing Column in a War without Replacements," *Military Review* 60, 8 (1980): 19–29; Col. Reuven Gal, "Unit Morale: From Theoretical Puzzle to an Empirical Illustration – An Israeli Example," *Journal of Applied Social Psychology* 16, 6 (1986): 555; *Developing Leaders: A Sandhurst Guide* (Camberley: Ministry of Defence, 2012), 1–91; Keith Grint, *The Arts of Leadership* (Oxford: Oxford University Press, 2001), 1–34; and Victoria Nolan, *Military Leadership and Counterinsurgency: The British Army and Small War Strategy since World War II* (London: Tauris, 2012).
9 Maj. Martin Lewis, "The Promotion and Maintenance of Mental Health in the Military Community: Part II," *Journal of the Royal Army Medical Corps* (*JRAMC*) 96, 2 (February 1951): 102–3, 110.
10 Lt. Frank B. Norbury, "Psychiatric Admissions in a Combat Division in 1952," *Medical Bulletin of US Army Far East* 1, 8 (July 1953): 132.
11 Catignani, "Motivating Soldiers," 114.
12 Robert J. O'Neill, *Australia in the Korean War 1950–1953*, vol. 2, *Combat Operations* (Canberra: Australian War Memorial and the Australian Government Publication Service, 1985), 240.
13 Ibid.
14 Grey, *Commonwealth Armies*, 106.
15 O'Neill, *Combat Operations*, 240.

16 Lt. Col. Herbert Fairlie Wood, *Strange Battleground: The Operations in Korea and Their Effects on the Defence Policy of Canada* (Ottawa: Queen's Printer and Controller of Stationery, 1966), 59–69; and O'Neill, *Combat Operations,* 105–7.
17 Grey, *Commonwealth Armies,* 135–41.
18 Maj. Gen. A.J.H. Cassels, 1 Commonwealth Division Periodic Report, May 1 – October 15, 1951, National Archives of Australia (NAA): CRS A2107, item K11.09.
19 O'Neill, *Combat Operations,* 241.
20 Ibid., 242.
21 Ibid.
22 Ibid.
23 Grey, *Commonwealth Armies,* 142.
24 Ibid.
25 Ibid.
26 Lt. M.F. Reynolds, Korea: Battle Experience Questionnaire, The National Archives at Kew (TNA): WO 231/90.
27 G. Paterson, interview, Imperial War Museum Sound Archive (IWMSA): acc. no. 19094, reels 1, 4.
28 French, *Army, Empire and the Cold War,* 142.
29 Col. Davey was a nickname for Lt. Col. David Rose. R.J. Carriage, interview, IWMSA: acc. no. 18267/3, as quoted in French, *Army, Empire and the Cold War,* 142; and Remembering: Scotland at War, "It Was Easier to Put Me in the Black Watch 'National Service,'" http://www.rememberingscotlandatwar.org.uk/Accessible/Exhibition/87/It-was-easier-to -put-me-in-the-Black-Watch-National-Service.
30 Australian War Memorial, "Capt. Reg Saunders," http://www.awm.gov.au/exhibitions/ korea/faces/saunders/.
31 Welfare in the Canadian Army, November 13, 1952, Library and Archives Canada (LAC): RG 24, acc. 1983-84/167, vol. 3, box 4903, file 3125-33/29; Albert E. Cowdrey, *The Medics' War* (Washington, DC: Center of Military History, 1987), 146; Hastings, *Korean War,* 369; Barclay, *First Commonwealth Division,* 3; and Brian Catchpole, "The Commonwealth in Korea," *History Today* 48, 11 (November 1998), http://www.historytoday.com/ brian-catchpole/commonwealth-korea.
32 Infantry Liaison Letter, 2 RAR, July 1953, Australian War Memorial (AWM) 85, item no. 3/5; 1 Commonwealth Division Periodic Report, April 1, 1953 – August 1, 1953, TNA: WO 308/65; 1 Commonwealth Division Periodic Report, July 1, 1952 – October 31, 1952, TNA: WO 308/64; Welfare in Canadian Army, November 13, 1952, LAC: RG 24, acc. 1983-1984/167, vol. 3, box 4903, file 3125-33/29; Tom Hickman, *The Call-Up: A History of National Service* (London, UK: Headline, 2005), 83; and Catchpole, "The Commonwealth in Korea."
33 US Army Survey, as quoted in Stanley Sandler, *The Korean War: No Victors, No Vanquished* (Lexington, KY: University of Kentucky Press, 1999), 131–32.
34 Alex Easton, interview by Remembering: Scotland at War, 2009.
35 Lt. Gen. Matthew B. Ridgway, 3 RAR War Diary, January 21, 1951, AWM85, item no. 2/11.
36 Gen. James Van Fleet, as quoted in Hastings, *The Korean War,* 208.
37 *The Steel Helmet,* as quoted in Peter Wollen, *Signs and Meaning in the Cinema,* 5th ed. (London: Macmillan, 2013).
38 Hugh Deane, *The Korean War, 1945–1953* (San Francisco: China Books and Periodicals, 1999), 29–30.
39 President Harry S. Truman, as quoted in Deane, ibid., 29.

40 O'Neill, *Combat Operations*, 239.
41 Paul M. Edwards, *The Korean War,* American Soldiers' Lives: Daily Life through History (Westport, CT: Greenwood, 2006), 92–94; Eric Taylor, *Wartime Nurse: One Hundred Years from the Crimea to Korea, 1854–1954* (London: Robert Hale, 2001), 204; and Bill Trevett, interview by author, Wiltshire, UK, November 2010.
42 As quoted in Taylor, ibid., 204.
43 Col. Bernd Horn, "Fear," in *The Military Leadership Handbook,* ed. Col. Bernd Horn and Robert W. Walker (Toronto: Dundurn Press; Canadian Defence Academy Press, 2008), 291.
44 Mark Johnson, *At the Front Line: Experiences of Australian Soldiers in World War II* (Cambridge: Cambridge University Press, 1996), 54; Office of Surgeon General, USA, Memo 330.11 for CG AGF: Prevention of Manpower Loss from Psychiatric Disorders, September 16, 1944, National Archives and Records Administration (NARA): Army Ground Forces Statistical Section Files, 330.11 (S); and Robert R. Palmer, *The Procurement of Enlisted Personnel: The Problem of Quality* (Washington, DC: US Government Printing Office, 1948), 228.
45 Maj. Raymond Sobel, "Anxiety-Depressive Reactions after Prolonged Combat Experience – the 'Old Sergeant Syndrome,'" *Bulletin of the US Army Medical Department* Nov 9 (Supplement) (1949): 137.
46 Ibid.
47 William D. Henderson, *Cohesion: The Human Element in Combat* (Washington, DC: National Defense University Press, 1985), 4, as quoted in Catignani, "Motivating Soldiers," 110.
48 Gal, "Unit Morale," 559.
49 Ibid., 559; and Ingraham and Manning, "Psychiatric Battle Casualties," 19–29.
50 Morris Janowitz, *The Professional Soldier: A Social and Political Portrait* (Glencoe, IL: Free Press, 1960), 21; Frederick J. Manning and Larry H. Ingraham, "An Investigation into the Value of Unit Cohesion in Peacetime," in *Contemporary Studies in Combat Psychiatry,* Contributions in Military Studies No. 62, ed. Gregory Belenky (Westport, CT: Greenwood, 1987), 49; Field Marshal Montgomery, *Morale in Battle* (1946), as quoted in Coates, "Morale on the Battlefield," 9.
51 Hew Strachan, ed., *The British Army, Manpower and Society into the Twenty-First Century* (London: Frank Cass, 2000), xvii–xviii.
52 Capt. Rutherford, 3 RAR War Diary Medical Report, May 1953, AWM85, item no. 639175; and O'Neill, *Combat Operations*, 131, 219, 267.
53 O'Neill, ibid., 219, 267.
54 The US Army's individual rotation policy has been sharply criticized. Military sociologists Paul L. Savage and Richard A. Gabriel have argued that individual rotation had a negative impact on the well-being of troops, particularly in Vietnam. There are no definitive statistics to confirm or disprove this controversial thesis. Paul L. Savage and Richard A. Gabriel, "Cohesion and Disintegration in the American Army: An Alternative Perspective," *Armed Forces and Society* 2 (1976): 341; Anthony Kellett, "Combat Motivation," in *Contemporary Studies in Combat Psychiatry,* ed. Belenky, 208; James Griffith, "Measurement of Group Cohesion in US Army Units," *Basic and Applied Social Psychology* 9, 2 (1988): 152; and Col. Albert Julius Glass, "History and Organization of a Theater Psychiatric Service before and after 30 June 1951," in *Recent Advances in Medicine and Surgery: Based on Professional Medical Experiences in Japan and Korea 1950–1953,* vol. 2, Medical Science Publication No. 4, United States Army Medical Department (Washington, DC: Walter Reed Army Medical Service Graduate School, 1954).

55   Hugh McManners, *The Scars of War* (London: HarperCollins, 1994), 31.
56   Director General of Military Training, Statement issued in advance of Chief of Imperial General Staff Conference, October 17, 1951, TNA: WO 33/2710.
57   Gen. Sir Anthony Farrar-Hockley, *The British Part in Korean War*, vol. 2, *An Honourable Discharge* (London: HMSO, 1995), 63.
58   Ibid.
59   Ibid.
60   Brent Byron-Watson, *Far Eastern Tour: Canadian Infantry in Korea, 1950-1953* (Montreal and Kingston: McGill-Queen's University Press, 2002), 36.
61   Ibid., 37.
62   "Korea Scandal: Report That Will Shock You!" *Sunday Dispatch*, January 6, 1952.
63   Farrar-Hockley, *An Honourable Discharge*, 355.
64   British winter gear typically consisted of "a string vest, long johns, under-trousers, trousers, parka with a wired hood, and thick rubber-soled boots." Ashley Cunningham-Boothe and Peter Farrar, eds., *British Forces in the Korean War* (West Yorkshire: British Korean Veterans Association, 1989), 13; Maj. P.M. Bretland, MB, ChB, "The Principles of Prevention of Cold Injuries: Notes on the Problem as Encountered, and the Methods Used, in Korea," *Journal of the Royal Army Medical Corps* 100, 2 (April 1954): 92.
65   Cunningham-Boothe and Farrar, ibid., 12.
66   Brig. H.L. Cameron to Mr. T.D. Anderson, General Secretary of Canadian Legion, October 1, 1952, LAC: RG 24, acc. 1983-1984/167, box 4912, file 3127-33/29, pt. 2; Les Peate, "Korean War: Food for Thought," *Esprit de Corps*, March 1997, https://www.highbeam.com/doc/1G1-30448491.html.
67   Ibid.
68   Hickman, *The Call-Up*, 80; Barclay, *First Commonwealth Division*, 184.
69   Hickman, ibid., 80.
70   1 Commonwealth Division Periodic Report, July 1, 1952 – October 31, 1952, TNA: WO 308/64; 1 Commonwealth Division Periodic Report No. 3, October 1, 1952 –March 31, 1953, TNA: WO 308/60; HQ British Commonwealth Forces Korea Periodic Report No. 5, October 1, 1953 – March 31, 1954, TNA: WO 308/1; 1 Commonwealth Division Periodic Report No. 9, October 1, 1955 – June 30, 1956, TNA: WO 308/62; Korean Campaigns: Welfare and Entertainment, TNA: WO 308/6; Cunningham-Boothe and Farrar, *British Forces in the Korean War*, 13.
71   Welfare in the Canadian Army, November 13, 1952, LAC: RG 24, acc. 1983-1984/167, vol. 3, box 4903, file 3125-33/29; Adjutant General, HQ British Commonwealth Force Korea, Six Monthly Report, April 1 – September 30, 1954, TNA: WO 308/7; Col. John Wallis, Welfare – Donations by Benevolent Organisations – Shipment at Public Expense, December 5, 1952, LAC: RG 24, acc. 1983-1984/167, vol. 3, box 4903, file 3125-33/29; Tuckett Ltd. to Col. John Wallis, February 27, 1952, LAC: RG 24, acc. 1983-1984/167, box 4912, file 3127-33/29, pt. 2; Mr. C.K. Hogan to Col. John Wallis, October 21, 1952, LAC: RG 24, acc. 1983-1984/167, box 4912, file 3127-33/29, pt. 2; Mr. G.L. Austin to Col. John Wallis, December 17, 1952, LAC: RG 24, acc. 1983-1984/167, box 4912, file 3127-33/29, pt. 2; Col. John Wallis to Mr. E.J. Young, November 23, 1953, LAC: RG 24, acc. 1983-1984/167, box 4711, file 3127-1, pt. 1; Mr. G.L. Austin to Col. John Wallis, January 8, 1953, LAC: RG 24, acc. 1983-1984/167, box 4912, file 3127–33/29, pt. 2.
72   The Commonwealth Division also subscribed to a number of newspapers. *Japan News* and *Stars and Stripes* had the widest distribution. The former was a regional English-language publication, while the US Army produced the latter. During the war, they reached a peak circulation of 26,000 and 75,000, respectively. Produced by officers from

the Royal Army Educational Corps, the division's own broadsheet was called *Crown News*. It featured regional news from each of the Commonwealth countries and boasted a French-language section. 1 Commonwealth Division Periodic Report, July 1, 1952 – October 31, 1952, TNA: WO 308/64; British Commonwealth Force Korea Periodic Report, April 1, 1953 – August 1, 1953, TNA: WO 308/65.

73 Jeffrey A. Keshen, *Saints, Sinners, and Soldiers: Canada's Second World War* (Vancouver: UBC Press, 2004), 124.

74 Lindsey Koren, "Smithsonian Traveling Exhibition Offers Fascinating Look at Military Mail and Communication," Mail Call, Smithsonian Institution Traveling Exhibition Service, 2011, http://www.sites.si.edu/exhibitions/exhibits/mailCall/#press.

75 Historical Notes: A Branch Including Chaplains, Provost & Education, TNA: WO 308/9; British Commonwealth Force Korea Periodic Report No. 8, April 1, 1955 – September 30, 1955, TNA: WO 308/61; Brig. J.M. Rockingham, Report on Welfare – 25 Cdn Infantry Brigade, December 24, 1951, LAC: RG 24, acc. 1983-1984/167, vol. 3, box 4903, file 3125-33/29; Local Army Welfare Officer, "Six Years of Army Welfare," *Royal United Services Institute Journal* 91, 561 (1946): 52–55; Maj. Gen. W.H.S. Macklin, Welfare – 25 Cdn Infantry Brigade, July 12, 1951, LAC: RG 24, acc. 1983-1984/167, vol. 3, box 4903, file 3125-33/29; and Maj. Gen. W.H.S. Macklin to Rockingham, November 21, 1951, LAC: RG 24, acc. 1983-1984/167, vol. 3, box 4903, file 3125-33/29.

76 Welfare in the Canadian Army, November 13, 1952, LAC: RG 24, acc. 1983-1984/167, vol. 3, box 4903, file 3125-33/29; Rockingham, Report on Welfare – 25 Cdn Infantry Brigade, December 24, 1951, LAC: RG 24, acc. 1983-1984/167, vol. 3, box 4903, file 3125-33/29; and Local Army Welfare Officer, "Six Years of Army Welfare," 52–55.

77 Michael F. Snape, *God and the British Soldier: Religion and the British Army in the First and Second World Wars* (London: Routledge, 2005), 222.

78 Basic Facts about the Navy, Army and Air Force Institutes, 1958, TNA: DEFE 7/21; "Commonwealth Forces' Record in Korea: A Successful Experiment," *Times*, July 21, 1953; Capt. Donald Anderson, "Navy, Army, and Air Force Institutes in War and Peace," *Royal United Services Institute Journal* 85, 537 (1940): 64–65; Meyer Scolnick and Joseph L. Packer, "Evolution of the Army and Air Force Exchange Service," *US Air Force Judge Advocate General Law Review* 8, 5 (1966): 19–36; and 1 Commonwealth Division Periodic Report, April 1, 1953 – August 1, 1953, TNA: WO 308/65.

79 Seoul was roughly thirty-five miles behind the division's front lines. Tokchon served as the division's headquarters and was in the area of Uijeongbu, around fifteen miles from the front. Teal Bridge was six and a half miles southwest of the juncture of the Imjin and Han Rivers. It was also close to the front. William R. Farquhar Jr. and Henry A. Jeffers Jr., *Building the Imjin: Construction of Libby and Teal Bridges during the Korean War (October 1952 – July 1953)*, Studies in Military Engineering No. 5 (Fort Belvoir, VA: US Army Corps of Engineers, 1989), 7; and Lt. Col. A. MacLennan (26 Field Ambulance) 1 Commonwealth Division, Questionnaire on Korean Campaign Answers, 1950–52, Wellcome Library and Archives (WLA): Muniments Collection, 761/4, box 158.

80 Talk with Capt. Fenny on Welfare in the Far East, May 21, 1952, LAC: RG 24, acc. 1983-1984/167, vol. 3, box 4903, file 3125-33/29; and Welfare in Canadian Army, November 13, 1952, LAC: RG 24, acc. 1983-1984/167, vol. 3, box 4903, file 3125-33/29.

81 1 Commonwealth Division Periodic Report No. 7, August 2, 1953 – May 1, 1954, TNA: WO 308/31.

82 Lt. Col. Howard N. Cole, *NAAFI in Uniform* (Lewes, East Sussex: Navy, Army and Air Force Institute, 1982), 178.

83 "Commonwealth Forces' Record in Korea."

84   Rockingham, Report on Welfare – 25 Cdn Infantry Brigade, December 24, 1951, LAC: RG 24, acc. 1983-1984/167, vol. 3, box 4903, file 3125-33/29; "Commonwealth Forces' Record in Korea"; 1 Commonwealth Division Periodic Report, April 1, 1953 – August 1, 1953, TNA: WO 308/65; and 1 Commonwealth Division Periodic Report, November 1, 1952 – April 1, 1953, TNA: WO 308/30.

85   Robin McKechney, as quoted in Cole, *NAAFI in Uniform*, 176–77.

86   HQ British Commonwealth Forces Korea Periodic Report No. 5, October 1, 1953 – March 31, 1954, TNA: WO 308/1; 1 Commonwealth Division Periodic Report, July 1, 1952 – October 31, 1952, TNA: WO 308/64; and Cole, ibid., 178–80.

87   Cole, ibid., 180.

88   Ibid., 175.

89   HQ British Commonwealth Forces Korea Periodic Report No. 5, October 1, 1953 – March 31, 1954, TNA: WO 308/1.

90   Anonymous soldier, as quoted in Byron-Watson, *Far Eastern Tour*, 135.

91   David J. Bercuson, *Blood on the Hills: The Canadian Army in the Korean War* (Toronto: University of Toronto Press, 1999), 174–75.

92   The Canadian Red Cross also ran 25 Canadian Infantry Brigade Recreation Centre or Maple Leaf Park in Korea. It included "a gymnasium, hobby centre, library, theatre, lounge, dry and wet canteens, writing rooms and a gift shop." 1 Commonwealth Division Periodic Report No. 7, August 2, 1953 – May 1, 1954, TNA: WO 308/31; Reduction of Forces in Far East, November 24, 1954, LAC: RG 24, acc. 1983-1984/167, vol. 3, box 4904, file 3125-33/29/15; Welfare in the Canadian Army, November 13, 1952, LAC: RG 24, acc. 1983-1984/167, vol. 3, box 4903, file 3125-33/29; Rundown of Canadian Troops – Far East – Welfare Amenities, April 14, 1955, LAC: RG 24, acc. 1983-1984/167, vol. 3, box 4904, file 3125-33/29/15; Welfare in the Canadian Army, November 13, 1952, LAC: RG 24, acc. 1983-1984/167, vol. 3, box 4903, file 3125-33/29.

93   Betty Wamsley, Maple Leaf Club Opens in Tokyo, n.d., LAC: RG 24, acc. 1983-1984/167, vol. 3, box 4903, file 3125-33/29.

94   Welfare in the Canadian Army, November 13, 1952, LAC: RG 24, acc. 1983-1984/167, vol. 3, box 4903, file 3125-33/29; Cunningham-Boothe and Farrar, *British Forces in the Korean War*, 51–52; and Frances Martin Day, Phyllis Spence, and Barbara Ladouceur eds., *Memoirs of the Canadian Red Cross Corps* (Vancouver: Ronsdale Press, 1998), 343–52.

95   Hickman, *The Call-Up*, 78–79.

96   Rex Sheppard, interview by Legasee: The Veteran Archive, 2011, http://www.legasee.org.uk/the-archive/rex-shepherd/.

97   Bill Trevett, interview by author, Wiltshire, UK, November 2010.

98   Jones, *Morale, Psychological Wellbeing*, 43.

99   HQ British Commonwealth Forces Korea Periodic Report No. 6, April 1954 –September 30, 1954, TNA: WO 308/2; 1 Commonwealth Division Periodic Report No. 9, October 1, 1955 – June 30, 1956, TNA: WO 308/62; and Hickman, *The Call-Up*, 142.

100 1 Commonwealth Division Periodic Report No. 9, October 1, 1955 – June 30, 1956, TNA: WO 308/62.

101 Ibid.

102 Welfare in the Canadian Army, November 13, 1952, LAC: RG 24, acc. 1983-84/167, vol. 3, box 4903, file 3125-33/29.

103 Historical Notes: A Branch Including Chaplains, Provost & Education, TNA: WO 308/9; and 1 Commonwealth Division Periodic Report, July 1, 1952 – October 31, 1952, TNA: WO 308/64.

104 1 Commonwealth Division Periodic Report, July 1, 1952 – October 31, 1952, TNA: WO 308/64; 1 Commonwealth Division Periodic Report, November 1, 1952 – April 1, 1953,

TNA: WO 308/30; and 1 Commonwealth Division Periodic Report, April 1, 1953 – August 1, 1953, TNA: WO 308/65.

105 Jones, *Morale, Psychological Wellbeing,* 42.
106 Maj. Gen. W.H.S. Macklin to Brooke Claxton, August 12, 1953, LAC: RG 24, acc. 1983-1984/167, box 4914, file 3128-33/29, pt. 4; Adjutant General, Report to Treasury, September 3, 1953, LAC: RG 24, acc. 1983-84/167, box 4914, file 3128-33/29, pt. 4; 1 Commonwealth Division Periodic Report, July 1, 1952 – October 31, 1952, TNA: WO 308/64; Claude F. Luke, "The Work of the Navy, Army and Air Force Institutes Entertainment Branch," *Royal United Services Institute Journal* 86, 541 (1941): 88–94.
107 Commonwealth Division Periodic Report, July 1, 1952 – October 31, 1952, TNA: WO 308/64; 1 Commonwealth Division Periodic Report No. 3, October 1, 1952 – March 31, 1953, TNA: WO 308/60; and Welfare in the Canadian Army, November 13, 1952, LAC: RG 24, acc. 1983-1984/167, vol. 3, box 4903, file 3125-33/29.
108 Carole Carr, as quoted in Hickman, *The Call-Up,* 83.
109 Historical Notes: A Branch Including Chaplains, Provost & Education, TNA: WO 308/9.
110 1 Commonwealth Division Periodic Report No. 3, October 1, 1952 – March 31, 1953, TNA: WO 308/60; 1 Commonwealth Division Report No. 5, October 1, 1953 – March 31, 1954, TNA: WO 308/1; and Historical Notes British Commonwealth Forces Korea: Britcom Forward Maintenance Area/Sub Area North, TNA: WO 308/17.
111 Deputy Assistant Chaplain General W.S. James to Deputy Assistant Adjutant General, Historical Review – Royal Army Chaplain's Department, Korean Theatre, December 1953, TNA: WO 308/9.
112 Adjutant General, HQ British Commonwealth Forces Korea, Six Monthly Report April 1 – September 30, 1954, TNA: WO 308/7.
113 Deputy Assistant Chaplain General W.S. James to Deputy Assistant Adjutant General, Historical Review – Royal Army Chaplain's Department, Korean Theatre, December 1953, TNA: WO 308/9.
114 Ibid.
115 Florence Bell, as quoted in Day, Spence, and Ladoceur, *Memoirs of the Canadian Red Cross Corps,* 346; Rockingham, Report on Welfare – 25 Cdn Infantry Brigade, December 24, 1951, LAC: RG 24, acc. 1983-1984/167, vol. 3, box 4903, file 3125-33/29; and Adjutant General, Headquarters British Commonwealth Forces Korea, Six Monthly Report April 1 – September 30, 1954, TNA: WO 308/7.
116 Adjutant General, HQ British Commonwealth Forces Korea, Six Monthly Report: April 1 – September 30, 1954, TNA: WO 308/7; Historical Notes: the Role of the RAEC in the Korean War 1950–53, TNA: WO 308/9; and British Commonwealth Forces Korea No. 9, October 1, 1955 – June 30, 1956, TNA: WO 308/62.

Chapter 4: Weathering the Storm

1 Interview with author, 2011.
2 Ibid.
3 Ibid.
4 Ibid.
5 Jeffrey Grey, *The Commonwealth Armies and the Korean War: An Alliance Study* (Manchester: Manchester University Press, 1988), 27.
6 Bill Rawling, *The Myriad Challenges of Peace: Canadian Forces Medical Practitioners since the Second World War* (Ottawa: Canadian Government Publishing, 2004), 48–49.
7 Albert E. Cowdrey, *The Medics' War: The US Army in Korea* (Washington, DC: Center of Military History, 1987), 92.

8   Richard Trembath, *A Different Sort of War: Australians in Korea 1950–53* (Melbourne: Australian Scholarly Publishing, 2005), 11–14.

9   This chapter does not discuss the experience of Commonwealth prisoners of war held by the North Koreans and the Chinese. For further details, see Appendix B.

10   Col. Geoffrey Anderton, Assistant Director of Medical Services (ADMS), 1 Commonwealth Division, Questionnaire on Korean Campaign, 1950–52, Wellcome Library and Archives (WLA): Muniments Collection, 761/4, box 158; and Brig. Cyril N. Barclay, *The First Commonwealth Division: The Story of British Commonwealth Land Forces in Korea, 1950–1953* (Aldershot: Gale and Polden, 1954), 44.

11   Edgar Jones and Ian Palmer, "Army Psychiatry in the Korean War: The Experience of 1 Commonwealth Division," *Military Medicine* 165, 4 (2000): 256; Edgar Jones and Simon Wessely, *Shell Shock to PTSD: Military Psychiatry from 1900 to the Gulf War* (London: Taylor and Francis, 2005), 120; and Capt. J.J. Flood, "Psychiatric Casualties in UK Elements of Korean Force: Dec 1950 – Nov 1951," *Journal of the Royal Army Medical Corps* (*JRAMC*) 100, 1 (January 1954): 41.

12   Col. Geoffrey Anderton, "The Birth of the British Commonwealth Division Korea," *JRAMC* 99, 2 (January 1953), 47; Barclay, *First Commonwealth Division*, 87; Historical Notes: Medical Services, British Commonwealth Forces Korea (BCFK), The National Archives at Kew (TNA): WO 308/21; Col. (Ret.) Albert J. Glass and Franklin D. Jones, *Psychiatry in the United States Army: Lessons for Community Psychiatry*, ed. Franklin D. Jones, Linette R. Sparacino, and Joseph M. Rothberg (Bethesda, MD: Uniformed Services University of Health Sciences, 2005).

13   Jones and Wessely, *Shell Shock to PTSD*, 122.

14   Ibid.

15   Col. Albert J. Glass, "History and Organization of a Theatre Psychiatric Service before and after 30 June 1951," in *Recent Advances in Medicine and Surgery*.

16   Ibid.

17   Psychiatric Classifications and Criteria, 1958–67, Library and Archives Canada (LAC): RG 24, acc. 1983-1984/167 GAD, box 7985, file C-2-6720-1; and Col. Anderton, Role of 25 Canadian Field Dressing Station (25 FDS), August 9, 1951, LAC: RG 24-C-3, vol. 18395; Maj. R.G. Davies, Monthly Psychiatric Report, August 7, 1953, LAC: RG 24-C-3, vol. 18397.

18   Jones and Wessely, *Shell Shock to PTSD*, 120.

19   War Office, Report on Health of Army 1951–52, TNA: WO 279/610; ADMS War Diary, 1951–52, TNA: WO 281/886-7; 25 FDS War Diary, October-December 1952, LAC: RG 24-C-3, vol. 18396; 25 FDS – Monthly Progress Report, May 1953, LAC: RG 24-C-3, vol. 18397; ADMS Conference, January 12, 1953, TNA: WO 281/888; Maj. F.C.R. Chalke, Monthly Psychiatric Report – May 1952, June 13, 1952, TNA: WO 281/887; Maj. J.S. Hitsman, Appreciation of Movement of 25 FDS, May 1952, LAC: RG 24-C-3, vol. 18395; Brig. J.E. Snow, 29 BGH Monthly Liaison Letter March 1952, Mar 11, 1952, TNA: WO 281/892; "Canadian Armed Forces: News of the Medical Services," *Canadian Medical Association Journal* 63 (September 1950): 304; and Brig. C.S. Thompson to Dr. G.H. Hutton, September 23, 1946, LAC: RG 24, vol. 19, 466, in Terry Copp and Bill McAndrew, *Battle Exhaustion: Soldiers and Psychiatrists in the Canadian Army, 1939–1945* (Montreal and Kingston: McGill-Queen's University Press, 1990), 157.

20   Minutes of ADMS Conference, January 4, 1954, TNA: WO 281/889; Capt. N.G. Fraser to Mrs. C.C. Fraser and Mr. Rupert Fraser, May 3, 1953, Personal Letters of N.G. Fraser, Glasgow, UK; Dr. Leslie Bartlet, email message to author, September 22, 2011; and Leslie Bartlet, "A National Service Psychiatrist's Story," *Journal of the Royal Army Medical Corps* 156, 4 (December 2010): 273–75.

21 "KO" is not an acronym but "a military alpha designation of the unit." Raymond M. Scurf-ield, *A Vietnam Trilogy, Veterans and Post Traumatic Stress: 1968, 1989, 2000* (New York: Algora, 2004), 17.

22 James A. Martin, Linette R. Sparacino, and Gregory Belenky, *The Gulf War and Mental Health: A Comprehensive Guide* (Westport, CT: Greenwood, 1996), 10.

23 Glass, "History and Organization."

24 Ashworth, Sparacino, and Belenky, *Gulf War and Mental Health*, 10.

25 Copp and McAndrew, *Battle Exhaustion*, 157.

26 Col. J.E. Andrew and Brig. Ken A. Hunter, "The Royal Canadian Army Medical Corps in the Korean War," *Canadian Services Medical Journal* (July/August 1954): 5-15; Adjutant General (AG) War Diary, LAC: RG 24, vol. 18, 221; and Account of Recruitment – No. 6 Personnel Depot, Toronto, Directorate of History and Heritage (DHH), Department of National Defence (DND): 112.3H1.001 (D9).

27 David J. Bercuson, *Blood on the Hills: The Canadian Army in the Korean War* (Toronto: University of Toronto Press, 1999), 39-59; and Brent Byron-Watson, *Far Eastern Tour: Canadian Infantry in Korea, 1950-1953* (Montreal and Kingston: McGill-Queen's University Press, 2002), 18-25.

28 Bercuson, ibid., 54; "Notes on Fighting in Korea – 25 Aug. 1950," September 18, 1950, DHH, DND 112.3M2 (D347).

29 Bercuson, ibid., 58-60.

30 DHH, DND, *Historical Report No. 72: Canadian Participation in the Korean War Part II* (Ottawa: Government of Canada, 1955); Maj. Chalke, Monthly Psychiatric Report May 1952, June 13, 1952, TNA: WO 281/887; and Col. G.L. Morgan Smith, ADMS Monthly Liaison Letter Serial 13, June 1952, TNA: WO 281/887.

31 James V. Arbuckle, *Military Forces in 21st Century Peace Operations: No Job for a Soldier?* (New York: Routledge, 2006), 61.

32 Robert J. O'Neill, *Australia in the Korean War 1950-1953*, vol. 2, *Combat Operations* (Canberra: Australian War Memorial and the Australian Government Publication Service , 1985), 131, 219, 267.

33 Ibid., 219, 267.

34 Ibid.

35 Ibid., 267.

36 Ibid.

37 Capt. Rutherford, 3rd Battalion Royal Australian Regiment (3 RAR) War Diary, May 1953, Australian War Memorial (AWM): AWM85, item 639175.

38 Glass, "History and Organization."

39 Ibid.

40 Tom Hickman, *The Call-Up: A History of National Service* (London, UK: Headline, 2005), 100; Jason T. Fensome, "The Administrative History of National Service in Britain, 1950-1963" (PhD dissertation, Cambridge University, 2001), 15, 57-58.

41 Maj. Chalke, Monthly Psychiatric Report, January 1953, TNA: WO 281/888; Col. G.L. Morgan Smith, ADMS Monthly Liaison Letter Serial No. 20, January 1953, TNA: WO 281/888.

42 Grey, *Commonwealth Armies*, 39.

43 Ibid.

44 Lt. Col. Harry Pozner, "Some Aspects of Post-War Army Psychiatry," *JRAMC* 94, 1 (January 1950): 44-45.

45 Ibid.

46 Lt. Col. Elspeth C. Ritchie, "Psychiatry in the Korean War: Perils, PIES and Prisoners of War," *Military Medicine* 167, 11 (2002): 898; Hans Pols and Stephanie Oak, "War &

Military Mental Health: The US Psychiatric Response in the 20th Century," *American Journal of Public Health* 97, 12 (December 2007): 2136; Historical Notes: Medical Services, BCFK, TNA: WO 308/21; and Cowdrey, *Medics' War*, 91–92, 128.

47 Flood, "Psychiatric Casualties in UK Elements," 42–47.

48 From June 1950 to November 1951, US battle casualties peaked at 460 per 1,000. Frank A. Reister, *Battle Casualties and Medical Statistics: United States Army Experience in the Korean War* (Washington, DC: Surgeon General, Department of the Army, 1973), US Army Medical Department, Office of Medical History, http://history.amedd.army.mil/booksdocs/korea/reister/reister.html; and Jones and Wessely, *Shell Shock to PTSD*, 121.

49 Eric T. Dean Jr., *Shook over Hell, Post-Traumatic Stress, Vietnam and the Civil War* (Cambridge, MA: Harvard University Press, 1997), 40; and Jones and Wessely, ibid., 121.

50 25 FDS War Diary, 1951–53, LAC: RG 24-C-3, vols. 18395–97.

51 Glass, "History and Organization"; Cowdrey, *The Medics' War*, 248; and Lt. Frank B. Norbury, "Psychiatric Admissions in a Combat Division in 1952," *Medical Bulletin of US Army Far East* 1, 8 (July 1953): 131.

52 25 FDS War Diary, 1951–53, LAC: RG 24-C-3, vols. 18395–97.

53 Psychiatric Classifications and Criteria, 1958–67, LAC: RG 24, 1983-84/167 GAD, box 7985, file C-2-6720-1.

54 David K. Henderson and Robert D. Gillespie, *A Textbook of Psychiatry for Students and Practitioners*, 7th ed. (Oxford: Oxford University Press, 1950), 146.

55 Ibid.

56 25 FDS War Diary, 1951–53, LAC: RG 24-C-3, vols. 18395–97.

57 Psychiatric Classifications and Criteria, 1958–67, LAC: RG 24, 1983-84/167 GAD, box 7985, file C-2-6720-1.

58 Acting Director of Medical Services Stanley Shier to Medical Officers, September 9, 1947, LAC: RG 24, 1983-84/167 GAD, box 7985, file C-2-6720-1.

59 Ibid.

60 Franklin D. Jones, "Military Psychiatry since World War II," in *American Psychiatry after World War II (1944–1994)*, ed. Roy W. Menninger and John C. Nemiah (Washington, DC: American Psychiatric Press, 2000), 13.

61 Capt. N.G. Fraser, Monthly Psychiatric Report, July 1953, LAC: RG 24-C-3, vol. 18397.

62 Dr. Leslie Bartlet, email message to author, September 22, 2011.

63 Hyam Bolocan, "Functions of a Psychiatric Consultant to a Division, and to an Army," in *Recent Advances in Medicine and Surgery*.

64 RCAMC Study Papers: Medical General Series – Psychiatric Casualties in Battle, Canadian War Museum (CWM): Textual Records 58C 3 22.1.

65 In May 1952, a patient was admitted to 25 Field Dressing Station for the treatment of "post-traumatic syndrome." This represents one of the first times that the term was used in reference to battle exhaustion. 25 FDS War Diary, May 1952, June 1952, LAC: RG 24-C-3, vol. 18397; and Bill Rawling, *Death Their Enemy: Canadian Medical Practitioners and War* (Quebec: AGMV, 2001), 251.

66 Ibid.

67 Jones and Wessely, *Shell Shock to PTSD*, 123.

68 Paul Sneath, Papers Related to Defence Medical and Dental Services Advisory Board Part III, LAC: MG 31, 17, no. 87.

69 Ben Shephard, *A War of Nerves: Soldiers and Psychiatrists in the Twentieth Century* (Cambridge, MA: Harvard University Press, 2001), 327; and Christopher G. Blood and Eleanor D. Gauker, "The Relationship between Battle Intensity and Disease Rates among Marine Corps Infantry Units," *Military Medicine* 158, 4 (2000): 340–41.

70 Jones and Wessely, *Shell Shock to PTSD*, 123.

71 "Commonwealth Forces' Record in Korea: A Successful Experiment," *Times of London*, July 21, 1953.

72 Commonwealth Division Periodic Report, October 16, 1951 – February 15, 1952, TNA: WO 308/28; and 25 FDS War Diary, 1952, LAC: RG 24-C-3, vol. 18396.

73 Capt. Robert J. Lavin, MC, 7th Division Neuropsychiatric Report: US Army 7th Infantry Division, 1952, National Archives and Records Administration (NARA): RG 112, Records of US Army Surgeon General, 7th Infantry Division, Annual Reports, 1950–53, box 221; and Capt. Simon L. Feigin, "Neuropsychiatric Casualties as a Result of Combat Involving Hill 266 ('Old Baldy')," *Medical Bulletin of US Army Far East* 1, 8 (July 1953): 134.

74 Jones and Wessely, *Shell Shock to PTSD*, 125; and Edgar Jones and Simon Wessely, "Hearts, Guts and Minds: Somatisation in the Military from 1900," *Journal of Psychosomatic Research* 56 (2004): 425–29.

75 Ibid., 126.

76 Lt. Col. N.H. McNally, Canadian Section BCGH, June 1952, LAC: RG 24-C-1-c, vol. 35954, file 2001/812/BC.

77 Ibid.

78 Dr. Leslie Bartlet, email message to author, September 22, 2011.

79 Col. G.L. Morgan Smith, Medical Admin Instructions, Serial No. 12, August 3, 1952, TNA: WO 281/1952; and Col. A.N.T. Meneces, BCGH: Monthly Liaison Letter – June 1952, June 27, 1952, TNA: WO 281/892.

80 Psychiatric Classifications and Criteria, 1958–67, LAC: RG 24, 1983-84/167 GAD, box 7985, file C-2-6720-1.

81 The study was conducted at "the US Naval Hospital, Bethesda, Maryland, and the Walter Reed General Hospital, Washington, DC." The majority of patients "had sustained compound fractures and other serious injuries that required prolonged treatment and sometimes repeated operations." The sample size was relatively small and involved only seventy-five men. Douglas Noble, Marion E. Roudebush, and Douglas Price, "Studies of Korean War Casualties, Part I: Psychiatric Manifestations in Wounded Men," *American Journal of Psychiatry* 108, 7 (January 1, 1952): 495–96; and Report of DGMS: Representative on Attendance at American Psychiatric Association, May 7–10, 1951, LAC: RG 24, 1983-84/167 GAD, box 7985, file C-2-6720-1.

82 Adrian Roberts, *Synopsis of Causation: Cold Injury* (London: Ministry of Defence, September 2008), 3–4; "Cold in Korea," *Lancet* 260, 6727 (August 2, 1952): 233; and Simon C. Gandevia, "An Australian Army Doctor – Bryan Gandevia," in *War Wounds: Medicine and the Trauma of Conflict*, ed. Ashley Ekins and Elizabeth Stewart (Wollombi: Exisle, 2011), 111–12.

83 "Cold Weather Clothing for Korea," *British Medical Journal (BMJ)* 2, 4745 (December 15, 1951): 1457.

84 Jones and Wessely, *Shell Shock to PTSD*, 126.

85 Ibid.; H.E. Hanson and R.F. Goldman, "Cold Injury in Man: A Review of Its Etiology and Discussion of Its Prediction," *Military Medicine* 134, 11 (October 1969): 1307–16.

86 Maj. J.M. Adam and W.S.S. Ladell, Dept. of Scientific Adviser to Army Council: Report of Field Studies on Troops of Commonwealth Division in Korea, Winter 1951–52, June 28, 1954, TNA: WO 348/117.

87 Ibid.

88 Samuel C. Bullock, Luther L. Mays, and Albert N. Berenberg, "A Study of the Personality Traits of Frostbite Casualties," in *Cold Injury – Korea 1951–1952*, by United States Army Medical Research Laboratory (Fort Knox, KY: United States Army Medical Research Laboratory, 1953), 664–735; James B. Sampson, "Anxiety as a Factor in the Incidence of Combat Cold Injury: A Review," *Military Medicine* 149 (February 1984): 89; and Lt. Col. Kenneth Orr, "Developments in Prevention and Treatment of Cold Injury," in *Recent Advances in Medicine and Surgery.*

89 Jones and Wessely, *Shell Shock to PTSD*, 127.

90 Maj. P.M. Bretland, "The Principles of Prevention of Cold Injuries: Notes on the Problem as Encountered, and the Methods Used, in Korea," *JRAMC* 100, 2 (April 1954): 96; Col. J.S. McCannel, Study on Commonwealth Medical Services in Korea, June 12, 1954, DHH, DND: 681.013 (D48); and "Discussion on Military Medical Problems in Korea," *Proceedings of Royal Society of Medicine* 46 (June 10, 1953): 1044.

91 Col. G.L. Morgan Smith, Monthly Liaison Letter, December 1952, TNA: WO 281/887.

92 Col. Albert J. Glass, "Psychiatry in the Korean Campaign: A Historical Review," *US Armed Forces Medical Journal* 4 (1953): 1387–1401; Maj. Gen. A.J.H. Cassels to CIGS Field Marshal Sir William Slim, March 19, 1952, TNA: WO 216/515; and "Discussion on Military Medical Problems in Korea," 1044.

93 DGAMS Sir Neil Cantlie to Sir John Crocker, February 1952, TNA: WO 216/515.

94 Maj. Gen. A.J.H. Cassels to CIGS Field Marshal Sir William Slim, March 19, 1952, TNA: WO 216/515.

95 Ibid.

96 Ibid.

97 C-in-C Far Eastern Land Forces Gen. Sir Charles F Keightley to CIGS Field Marshal Sir William J Slim, Note on Self Inflicted Wounds, April 22, 1952, TNA: WO 216/515.

98 Ibid.

99 Ibid.

100 Ibid.

101 Ibid.

102 There are no Commonwealth records that reveal whether or not anyone was successfully prosecuted for a self-inflicted injury during the Korean War. Registrar Judge Advocate General, Courts-Martial in Korea for Cowardice, Desertion and Mutiny – Parliamentary Questions, January 1954, TNA: WO 93/59.

103 25 FDS War Diary, 1951–53, LAC: RG 24-C-3, vols. 18395–97.

104 Psychiatric Classifications and Criteria, 1958–67, LAC: RG 24, 1983-84/167 GAD, box 7985, file C-2-6720-1.

105 Ibid.

106 25 FDS War Diary, 1953, LAC: RG 24-C-3, vol. 18397.

107 Capt. N.G. Fraser, 25 FDS Monthly Psychiatric Report August 1953, September 2, 1953, LAC: RG 24-C-3, vol. 18397.

108 Ibid.

109 Ibid.

110 Ibid.

111 Ibid.

112 AG BCFK, Six Monthly Report: April 1 – September 30, 1954, TNA: WO 308/7; HQ BCFK Periodic Report No. 5, October 1, 1953 – March 31, 1954, TNA: WO 308/1; Korean Campaigns: Welfare and Entertainment, TNA: WO 308/6; and War Office, Report on Health of Army 1955, July 3, 1959, TNA: WO 279/617.

113 Hyam Bolocan, "Functions of a Psychiatric Consultant to a Division, and to an Army," in *Recent Advances in Medicine and Surgery*.

114 Norman M. Camp, "Ethical Challenges for the Psychiatrist during the Vietnam Conflict," in *Military Psychiatry: Preparing in Peace for War*, ed. Franklin D. Jones et al. (Washington, DC: US Government Printing Office, 1994), 134.

115 Flood, "Psychiatric Casualties in UK Elements," 41; Hans Binneveld, *From Shell Shock to Combat Stress: A Comparative History of Military Psychology* (Amsterdam: Amsterdam University Press, 1998), 137; Col. Donald B. Peterson and Brig. Gen. Rawley E. Chambers, "Restatement of Combat Psychiatry," *American Journal of Psychiatry* 109, 4

(October 1952), 249–54; and Col. Albert J. Glass, "Psychotherapy in the Combat Zone," *American Journal of Psychiatry* 110, 10 (1954): 725–31.

116 RCAMC Study Papers Vol. I, Tactics Series – Précis 3, 1952, CWM: Textual Records 58C 3 22.1; Montgomery, Questionnaire on Korean Campaign, 1952, WLA: Muniments Collection, 761/4, box 158; Army Medical Advisory Board, Meetings July 1, 1949 – September 1954, December 8, 1950, 4, TNA: WO 32/13465; and Col. G. Anderton, ADMS 1 Commonwealth Division, Questionnaire on Korean Campaign, 1950–52, WLA: Muniments Collection, 761/4, box 158.

117 Glass, "History and Organization."

118 Ibid.

119 Ibid.

120 25 FDS War Diary, 1951–53, LAC: RG 24-C-3, vols. 18395–97; Flood, "Psychiatric Casualties in UK Elements," 43; and Richard A. Newman, "Combat Fatigue: A Review of the Korean Conflict," *Military Medicine* (October 1964): 926.

121 I. Philips Frohman, "The Barbiturates," *American Journal of Nursing* 54, 4 (April 1954): 432.

122 Shephard, *War of Nerves*, 209–10; and William Sargant, "Physical Treatment of Acute War Neuroses," *British Medical Journal* 2 (1942): 574–76.

123 William Sargant, *The Unquiet Mind: The Autobiography of a Physician in Psychological Medicine* (London: Heinemann, 1967), 114, as quoted in Terry Copp and Mark Osborne Humphries, *Combat Stress in the 20th Century: The Commonwealth Perspective* (Kingston, ON: Canadian Defence Academy Press, 2010), 128; Shephard, *War of Nerves*, 207–8; and "Psychiatry: Condensed from an Article Written by Brig. A. Torrie, MB, and Maj. R.H. Ahrenfeldt," *JRAMC* 90, 6 (June 1948): 332.

124 25 FDS War Diary, 1951–53, LAC: RG 24-C-3, vols. 18395–97; Capt. Richard L. Conde, US Army 7th Infantry Division, Annual Report of Neuropsychiatric Services, January 1, 1951 – December 31, 1951, NARA: RG 112, Records of the US Army Surgeon General, 7th Infantry Division, Annual Reports, 1950–53, box 221; Flood, "Psychiatric Casualties in UK Elements," 43; and Norbury, "Psychiatric Admissions," 131.

125 25 FDS War Diary, 1951, LAC: RG 24-C-3, vol. 18395; ADMS War Diary, February 1952, TNA: WO 281/887; and Capt. N.G. Fraser to Mrs. C.C. Fraser and Mr. Rupert Fraser, March 22, 1953, Personal Letters of N.G. Fraser, Glasgow, UK.

126 ADMS War Diary, 1951–53, TNA: WO 281/886-888; Capt. N.G. Fraser to Mrs. C.C. Fraser and Mr. Rupert Fraser, March 1953, Personal Letters of N.G. Fraser, Glasgow, UK; Col. Byron L. Steger, "Medical Societies in Korea," *Medical Bulletin of the US Army Far East* 1, 6 (May 1953): 92; Lt. N.G. Fraser to Mrs. C.C. Fraser and Mr. Rupert Fraser, 4, 22 Jan. 1953, Personal Letters of N.G. Fraser, Glasgow, UK; and Capt. N.G. Fraser, Monthly Psychiatric Report July 1953, August 2, 1953, LAC: RG 24-C-3, vol. 18397.

127 Capt. N.G. Fraser to Mrs. C.C. Fraser and Mr. Rupert Fraser, July 10, 1953, Personal Letters of N.G. Fraser, Glasgow, UK.

128 25 FDS War Diary, 1951–53, LAC: RG 24-C-3, vols. 18395–97; Dr. Leslie Bartlet, email message to author, September 22, 2011; and Flood, "Psychiatric Casualties in UK Elements."

129 Col. Albert J. Glass, "Psychotherapy in the Combat Zone," 727.

130 Ibid., 728.

131 Capt. H.C.J. L'Etang, "A Criticism of Military Psychiatry in the Second World War: Part III Historical Survey," *JRAMC* 97, 5 (November 1951): 326; Bolocan, "Functions of a Psychiatric Consultant"; Newman, "Combat Fatigue," 926; and Rawling, *Death Their Enemy*, 252.

132   No records were kept of the number of men returned to their original units. Commonwealth RTU figures are indicative only of the number of men who returned to some form of active duty (e.g., combat, support roles). 25 FDS War Diary, 1951-53, LAC: RG 24-C-3, vols. 18395-97; War Office, Report on the Health of the Army 1951-52, TNA: WO 279/610; Ritchie, "Psychiatry in the Korean War," 900; and Norbury, "Psychiatric Admissions," 131.

133   Ritchie, ibid., 900.

134   Flood, "Psychiatric Casualties in UK Elements," 47.

135   Shephard, *War of Nerves*, 325-27; Jones and Wessely, *Shell Shock to PTSD*, 88; and Copp and Humphries, *Combat Stress*, 153.

136   Shephard, *War of Nerves*, 342.

137   ADMS War Diary, 1951-53, TNA: WO 281/886-888; 25 FDS War Diary, 1951-53, LAC: RG 24-C-3, vols. 18395-97; and 29 BGH and BCGH War Diary, 1950-53, TNA: WO 281/892, 281/1274-1278.

138   29 BGH: Situation Report – UK Troops, Fortnight Ending 22 Dec. 1950, TNA: WO 281/1274.

139   Glass, "Psychiatry in the Korean Campaign," 1563-83.

140   Capt. R.G. Godfrey, Monthly Psychiatric Report – September 1952, October 9, 1952, TNA: WO 281/887.

141   Eric Taylor, *Wartime Nurse: One Hundred Years from the Crimea to Korea, 1854-1954* (London: Robert Hale, 2001), 202-3; Lt. Col. Howard N. Cole, *Navy, Army and Air Force Institute in Uniform* (Lewes, East Sussex: Navy, Army and Air Force Institute, 1982), 175; Maj. B.D. Jaffey, Casualty Evacuation in Korea, 37 Canadian Field Ambulance, September 1952, LAC: RG 24, vol. 18, 385; Dr. W.S. Stanbury, Canadian Red Cross in the Far East, July 1952, CWM: 58C 3 22.1; Dr. Leslie Bartlett, email message to author, September 22, 2011; and Rawling, *Death Their Enemy*, 242-43.

142   Bill Trevett, interview with author, Wiltshire, UK, November 2010.

143   Ruth Stone, "Nursing aboard Her Majesty's Hospital Ship Maine," in *British Forces in the Korean War*, ed. Ashley Cunningham-Boothe and Peter Farrar (West Yorkshire: British Korean Veterans Association, 1989), 114; and Taylor, *Wartime Nurse*, 194-96.

144   Stone, ibid., 119.

145   Psychiatric evacuations to BCGH ranged from 2 to 15 percent of all Commonwealth evacuations to the hospital. However, the numbers were usually around the 5-7 percent mark. 25 FDS War Diary, 1951-52, LAC: RG 24-C-3, vols. 18395-96; Weekly Returns of UK Patients Transferred to BCOF Hospital from Korea via US Units, 1951, TNA: WO 281/892, 1275-78; War Office, Report on Health of Army 1951-52, TNA: WO 279/610; Historical Notes: Medical Services, BCFK, TNA: WO 308/21; 29 BGH War Diary, 1951, TNA: WO 281/1275-1278; BCGH War Diary, 1952, TNA: WO 281/892; and BCFK Periodic Report No. 3, October 1, 1952 – March 31, 1953, TNA: WO 308/60.

146   Col. A.N.T. Meneces, BCGH: Monthly Liaison Letter – July 1952, August 15, 1952, TNA: WO 281/892; 29 BGH: Situation Report – UK Troops, Fortnight Ending 22 December 1950, TNA: WO 281/1274; 25 FDS War Diary, 1951, LAC: RG 24-C-3, vol. 18395; and Dr. Kenneth Davison, interview with author, Newcastle upon Tyne, UK, November 17, 2010.

147   Flood, "Psychiatric Casualties in UK Elements," 40-47; Brig. J.E. Snow, 29 BGH – Monthly Liaison Letter March 1951, TNA: WO 281/1276; 25 FDS War Diary, October-December 1952, LAC: RG 24-C-3, vol. 18396; Minutes of ADMS Conference, January 4, 1954, TNA: WO 281/889; ADMS War Diary, May 1953, TNA: WO 281/888; Capt. N.G. Fraser, Letters to Mrs. C.C. Fraser and Mr. Rupert Fraser, March-August 1953, Personal Letters of N.G. Fraser, Glasgow, UK; Dr. Leslie Bartlet, email message to author, September 22, 2011; F.C.R. Chalke, Monthly Psychiatric Report – May 1952, June 13, 1952, TNA: WO 281/887; J.C.B. Whycherley, Roll of Officers for Month Ending 31 January

1952, TNA: WO 281/892; and Maj. J.S. Hitsman, Appreciation of Movement of 25 FDS, May 1952, LAC: RG 24-C-3, vol. 18395.
148 Lt. Col. E.H. Ainslie, Canadian Section BCGH War Diary, February 1953, LAC: RG 24-C-1-c, vol. 35954, file 2001-812/BC.
149 No. 6 Convalescent Training Depot, RAMC War Diary, 1951–52, TNA: WO 281/906-907; and Historical Notes: Medical Services BCFK, 1953, TNA: WO 308/21.
150 Maj. R. Fuller, No. 6 Convalescent Depot, RAMC War Diary, Appendix No. 2, July 19, 1951, TNA: WO 281/906.
151 BCFK Periodic Report No. 8, April 1, 1955 – September 30, 1955, TNA: WO 308/61; 29 BGH War Diary, 1951, TNA: WO 281/1275-1278; and Dr. W.S. Stanbury, Canadian Red Cross in the Far East, July 1952, CWM: 58C 3 22.1.
152 Glass, "History and Organization."
153 Evacuation Policy: Korean Theatre of Operations, May 23, 1951, LAC: RG 24, 1983-1984/048, box 2153, file 5835-I, pt. 1.
154 David Oates, "Memories of Kure Japan: A Personal Experience," Memories of Kure Japan: A Medic in the Korean War, http://www.kurememories.com/page4.htm.
155 Lt. Col. Harold M. Wright, *Salute to the Air Force Medical Branch on the 75th Anniversary of the Royal Canadian Air Force* (Ottawa: Self Published, 1999), 206.
156 Rawling, *Myriad Challenges*, 79.
157 Ibid.
158 Ibid., 122–23, 247–49, 259; Col. for Vice-AG to the Secretary, Medical Services Coordinating Committee, October 30, 1958, TNA: Ministry of Pensions and National Insurance (PIN) 14/44; Committee Examining Ministry of Defence/National Health Service Collaboration, Use of Service Hospitals for Pensioners, September 15, 1978, TNA: PIN 59/483; and World Veterans Federation, *Social Affairs Rehabilitation, Comparative Report: Legislation Affecting Disabled Veterans and Other War Victims* WVF-DOC/830 (Paris: World Veterans Federation, September 1955), 7–10.
159 Queen Alexandra's Royal Army Nursing Corps, "Information and History about Netley Royal Victoria Military Hospital," QARANC, http://www.qaranc.co.uk/netleyhospital.php; N.C. Croft Cohen, Commissioner of Board of Control, Report on Netley, December 10, 1957, TNA: MH 95/34; and E.N. Butler, Commissioner of Board of Control, August 30, 1951, TNA: MH 95/34.
160 Commissioner of Board of Control, December 10, 1956, TNA: MH 95/34.
161 Cyril M.T. Hastings, Commissioner of Board of Control, Report on Netley, May 20, 1959, TNA: MH 95/34; E.N. Butler, Commissioner of Board of Control, August 30, 1951, October 14, 1952, September 23, 1953, TNA: MH 95/34; and Commissioner of Board of Control, February 27, 1950, June 10, 1955, TNA: MH 95/34.
162 Veterans Affairs Canada, "Ste Anne's Hospital – Our History," http://www.veterans.gc.ca/eng/steannes/stannehis5 (accessed 4 October 2012) Canada, House of Commons Standing Committee on National Defence, March 13, 2008 (Ms. Rachel Corneille Gravel).
163 Ibid.
164 It is more than likely that Australian veterans would have been treated at one of the Repatriation General Hospitals located in major cities like Sydney, Brisbane, and Melbourne. G.J. Downs, "Australia," *Journal of International and Comparative Social Welfare* 10, 1 (1994): 15, 23.
165 Psychiatric Classifications and Criteria, 1958–67, LAC: RG 24, 1983-84/167 GAD, box 7985, file C-2-6720-1; Rawling, *Death Their Enemy*, 252; and L'Etang, "A Criticism of Military Psychiatry," 326.
166 Dr. John Beswick, as quoted in John Melady, *Canada's Forgotten War* (Toronto: Macmillan of Canada, 1983), 152.

167   Col. G.L. Morgan Smith, ADMS Monthly Liaison Letter Serial 15, August 1952, TNA: WO 281/887.
168   Ibid.

Chapter 5: Forever Changed

1   25 Canadian Field Dressing Station (25 FDS) War Diaries, 1951–53, Library and Archives Canada (LAC): RG 24-C-3, vols. 18395–97; War Office, Report on Health of the Army 1951–52, The National Archives at Kew (TNA): WO 279/610.
2   War Office, Report on Health of the Army 1953, July 31, 1956, TNA: WO 279/614.
3   World Veterans Federation (WVF), *Social Affairs Rehabilitation, Comparative Report: Legislation Affecting Disabled Veterans and Other War Veterans*, WVF-DOC/830 (Paris: WVF, September 1955), 4–49.
4   Stephen Garton, *The Cost of War: Australians Return* (Melbourne: Oxford University Press, 1996), 80.
5   Pension and Rehabilitation Schemes of Dominions 1950s, TNA: PIN 15/3069; Report on War Pensioners for 1964, July 1965, TNA: PIN 18/500; WVF, *Social Affairs Rehabilitation*, 15–33.
6   Commonwealth of Australia, *House of Representatives*, September 26, 1956 (Mr. Bryant Gordon); Commonwealth of Australia, *Senate*, September 16, 1959 (Sir Walter Cooper).
7   Pension and Rehabilitation Schemes of Dominions 1950s, TNA: PIN 15/3069.
8   Ibid.
9   Allowance for Lowered Standard of Occupation: Memo for War Pensions Committees, 1964, TNA: PIN 59/84.
10 Notes on War Pension Schemes of UK, Canada, Australia, NZ, and South Africa, September 1945, TNA: PIN 15/3069; Report on War Pensioners for 1964, July 1965, TNA: PIN 18/500; and Department of Veterans' Affairs, *Pensioner Summary*, (Canberra: Government of Australia, December 2011).
11 Garton, *The Cost of War*, 167–69.
12 There were some exceptions. If the veteran had a minor disability, he received compensation in one payment. However, countries varied in what they considered a "minor" disability. In the United Kingdom, veterans with 20 percent disability or less qualified, whereas Canadian veterans were eligible only if they were less than 5 percent disabled. WVF, *Social Affairs Rehabilitation*, 32–33.
13 Alice Aiken and Amy Buitenhuis, *Supporting Canadian Veterans with Disabilities* (Kingston, ON: Defence Management Studies Program, Queen's University, 2011), 4; Les Peate, Korea Veterans Association of Canada, email to author, June 16, 2012; and WVF, *Social Affairs Rehabilitation*, 32.
14 Notes on War Pension Schemes of UK, Canada, Australia, NZ, and South Africa, September 1945, TNA: PIN 15/3069; G.J. Downs, "Australia," *Journal of International and Comparative Social Welfare* 10, 1 (1994): 7, 10; and WVF, ibid., 22–23.
15 Commonwealth of Australia, *House of Representatives*, April 22, 1959 (Sir Wilfrid Kent Hughes); WVF, ibid., 38–41.
16 WVF, ibid., 40.
17 Ibid.; Canadian Forces Advisory Council, *The Origins and Evolution of Veterans Benefits in Canada* (Ottawa: Veterans Affairs Canada, 2004).
18 WVF, *Social Affairs Rehabilitation*, 40–41.
19 Garton, *The Cost of War*, 98.
20 Downs, "Australia," 20; and WVF, *Social Affairs Rehabilitation*, 47–49.
21 Aiken and Buitenhuis, *Supporting Canadian Veterans*, 6; and Garton, *The Cost of War*, 80–81.

22 "The Wounded Man Speaks," 1919, as quoted in Garton, *The Cost of War*, 107.
23 Aiken and Buitenhuis, *Supporting Canadian Veterans*, 6.
24 Anon. to Miss Carr, May 1957, TNA: PIN 15/4084; Garton, *The Cost of War*, 84; and WVF, *Social Affairs Rehabilitation*, 4–6.
25 Pension and Rehabilitation Schemes of Dominions 1950s, TNA: PIN 15/3069; Commonwealth of Australia, *Senate*, September 16, 1959 (Sir Walter Cooper).
26 Government of New Zealand, War Pensions Act, 1954; Commonwealth of Australia, ibid.; and Stephen Uttley, "New Zealand," *Journal of International and Comparative Social Welfare* 10, 1 (1994): 46.
27 Uttley, ibid., 46.
28 Report on War Pensioners for 1954, June 1955, TNA: PIN 19/275; Report on War Pensioners for 1964, July 1965, TNA: PIN 18/500; and Commonwealth of Australia, *Senate*, September 16, 1959 (Sir Walter Cooper).
29 A.E.W. Ward to Dennys, Royal Warrant – Onus of Proof, July 3, 1956, TNA: PIN 59/2; Commonwealth of Australia, *House of Representatives*, October 13, 1955 (Mr. Kim Beazley); Law Commission, *A New Support Scheme for Veterans: A Report on the Review of the War Pensions Act 1954* (Wellington, NZ: Law Commission, May 2010), 78; and Commonwealth of Australia, *Senate*, September 16, 1959 (Sir Walter Cooper).
30 A.E.W. Ward to Dennys, Royal Warrant – Onus of Proof, July 3, 1956, TNA: PIN 59/2; and WVF, *Social Affairs Rehabilitation*.
31 Report on War Pensioners for 1955, 1956, TNA: PIN 19/277; Commonwealth of Australia, *House of Representatives*, October 13, 1955 (Mr. Malcolm McColm); Stephen Uttley, "New Zealand," 47; and Canadian Forces Advisory Council, *The Origins and Evolution of Veterans Benefits in Canada*.
32 Gen. Sir Anthony Farrar-Hockley, *The British Part in the Korean War*, vol. 1, *A Distant Obligation* (London: HMSO, 1990), ix; Col. Charles P. Stacey, "The Development of the Canadian Army," *Canadian Army Journal* 6, 4 (July 1952): 19; and William C. Johnston, *A War of Patrols: Canadian Army Operations in Korea* (Vancouver: UBC Press, 2003), 373.
33 Report on War Pensioners for 1955, 1956, TNA: PIN 19/277; and Canadian Forces Advisory Council, *The Origins and Evolution of Veterans Benefits in Canada*.
34 UK, House of Commons, *Debates*, March 14, 1960, Hansard, series 5, vol. 619, cc. 923–24.
35 Pension and Rehabilitation Schemes of Dominions 1950s, TNA: PIN 15/3069; Uttley, "New Zealand," 46; and WVF, *Social Affairs Rehabilitation*, 15–20.
36 Thomas to Mr. Trew, December 20, 1957, TNA: PIN 2894.
37 Garton, *The Cost of War*, 109–10.
38 Ibid.
39 Ibid.
40 Travis E. Dancey, "The Interaction of the Welfare State and the Disabled," *Canadian Medical Association Journal* 103 (1970): 274–77; and Travis E. Dancey, "Treatment in the Absence of Pensioning for Psychoneurotic Veterans," *American Psychiatric Journal* 107 (1950): 347.
41 Dancey, "Treatment in the Absence of Pensioning," 347.
42 Notes on War Pension Schemes of UK, Canada, Australia, NZ, and South Africa, September 1945, TNA: PIN 15/3069; and Pension and Rehabilitation Schemes of Dominions 1950s, TNA: PIN 15/3069.
43 Ibid.
44 Garton, *The Cost of War*, 88.
45 Ibid.

46 Ibid.

47 Ivan P. Ryan, Korea Veterans Association of Australia, email to author, May 24, 2012.

48 Report on War Pensioners for 1964, July 1965, TNA: PIN 18/500; and Committee Examining MoD/NHS Collaboration, Use of Service Hospitals for War Pensioners, September 15, 1978, TNA: PIN 59/483.

49 Bill Rawling, *The Myriad Challenges of Peace: Canadian Forces Medical Practitioners since the Second World War* (Ottawa: Canadian Government Publishing, 2004), 122–23, 247–49, 259; Col. for Vice-Adj. Gen. to the Secretary, Medical Services Coordinating Committee, October 30, 1958, TNA: PIN 14/44; Committee Examining MoD/NHS Collaboration, Use of Service Hospitals for War Pensioners, September 15, 1978, TNA: PIN 59/483; and WVF, *Social Affairs Rehabilitation*, 7–10.

50 Atkinson, Memo – Decentralisation of Action – Other Rank Pensioners Receiving Psychiatric Treatment, TNA: PIN 59/216; F.J. Marcham, Norcross Awards: Report on the Service Patient Scheme for Mental Cases, April 1959, TNA: PIN 15/4084; Commonwealth of Australia, *Senate*, June 22, 1950 (Sir Walter Cooper); Garton, *The Cost of War*, 167–69; Dancey, "The Interaction of the Welfare State and the Disabled," 275–77; and WVF, *Social Affairs Rehabilitation*, 7–10.

51 "Teaching Mental Health: Discussion by the Royal Medico-Psychological Association," *Lancet* 265, 6861 (February 26, 1955): 449; Duncan Macmillan, "Recent Developments in Community Mental Health," *Lancet* 281, 7281 (March 16, 1963): 567–68; Liam Clarke, "The Opening of Doors in British Mental Hospitals in the 1950s," *History of Psychiatry* 4 (1993): 527–51; and Lord Stonham, House of Lords Official Report, July 16, 1959, TNA: PIN 19/202.

52 Anon. to Mr. Birtles, October 17, 1957, TNA: PIN 15/4084; Anon. to the Secretary, Mental Hospital Management Committee, January 9, 1951, TNA: PIN 59/216; Commonwealth of Australia, *Senate*, June 22, 1950 (Sir Walter Cooper); Garton, *The Cost of War*, 167–69; Dancey, "The Interaction of the Welfare State and the Disabled," 275–77; and Dancey, "Treatment in the Absence of Pensioning," 348–49.

53 Anon. to Mr. Birtles, October 17, 1957, TNA: PIN 15/4084; Report on War Pensioners for 1955, 1956, TNA: PIN 19/277; Anon. to Secretary, Mental Hospital Management Committee, January 9, 1951, TNA: PIN 59/216; and F.J. Marcham, Norcross Awards: Report on Service Patient Scheme for Mental Cases, April 1959, TNA: PIN 15/4084.

54 Draft of Notes: Facilities for Rehabilitation Available through the Ministry of Labour and National Service, 1959, TNA: PIN 15/2730; Garton, *The Cost of War*, 80; and WVF, *Social Affairs Rehabilitation*, 44–45.

55 Anon. to E.L. Trew, June 19, 1959, TNA: PIN 15/4084; Remploy, "Who We Are," http://www.remploy.co.uk/about-us/whoweare.ashx (accessed 10 November 2011); and WVF, *Social Affairs Rehabilitation*, 45.

56 The British Ex-Services Mental Welfare Society is now known as Combat Stress.

57 Norcross to Mr. Beavan, November 17, 1955, TNA: PIN 15/3144.

58 Combat Stress, "About Us: The History of Combat Stress," http://www.combatstress.org.uk/about-us/history-of-combat-stress/; Norcross to Mr. Beavan, ibid.; and R. Atkinson to Mr. Taylor, June 2, 1964, TNA: PIN 15/3144.

59 Joy Damousi, *Living with the Aftermath: Trauma, Nostalgia and Grief in Post-War Australia* (Cambridge: Cambridge University Press, 2001), 135–40; Ivan P. Ryan, Korea Veterans Association of Australia, email to author, May 24, 2012; and Les Peate, Korea Veterans Association of Canada, email to author, June 16, 2012.

60 Ted Barris, *Deadlock in Korea: Canadians at War 1950–1953* (Toronto: Macmillan of Canada, 1999), 286–306.

61 Arthur Marion, as quoted in Barris, ibid., 288.
62 Ibid.
63 Ibid.
64 Ibid.
65 Damousi, *Living with the Aftermath,* 140.
66 Ibid.
67 Dept. of Health and Social Security – Central Advisory Committee on War Pensions, Minutes of the 97th Meeting, November 18, 1981, TNA: PIN 88/90; Downs, "Australia," 12; Les Peate, Korea Veterans Association of Canada, email to author, June 16, 2012; and Garton, *The Cost of War,* 89, 92, 170–72.
68 Don Flieger, as quoted in Barris, *Deadlock in Korea,* 288.
69 Ibid.
70 Ivan P. Ryan, Korea Veterans Association of Australia, email to author, May 24, 2012.
71 Improvements in War Pensions since September 1945, 1960s, TNA: PIN 59/13; Report on War Pensioners for 1954, June 1955, TNA: PIN 19/275; Report on War Pensioners for 1955, 1956, TNA: PIN 19/277; Report on War Pensioners for 1964, July 1965, TNA: PIN 18/500; WVF Conference, 1967, TNA: PIN 47/100; Downs, "Australia," 10–11; Ivan P. Ryan, Korea Veterans Association of Australia, email to author, May 24, 2012; Law Commission, *A New Support Scheme,* iv, 15, 63, 118, 144, 146; Canada, Parliament, House of Commons Standing Committee on National Defence, *Minutes of Proceedings,* 2nd session, 39th Parliament, Meeting No. 22, April 29, 2008 (Mr. Darragh Mogan); Commonwealth of Australia, *Senate,* September 28, 1955 (William Ashley); Commonwealth of Australia, *Senate,* September 24, 1958 (Justin O'Byrne); and Uttley, "New Zealand," 44, 48–50, 53.
72 Sylvia Wrobel, "Science, Serotonin, and Sadness: The Biology of Antidepressants," *Journal of the Federation of American Societies for Experimental Biology* 21, 13 (November 2007): 3404–17.
73 Thomas A. Ban, "Fifty Years Chlorpromazine: A Historical Perspective," *Neuropsychiatric Diseases and Treatment* 3, 4 (August 2007): 495–500; J.L. Crammer, "Comment: Britain in the Fifties: Leucotomy and Open Doors," *History of Psychiatry* 5, 19 (1994): 394; and Edward Shorter, *A History of Psychiatry: From the Era of the Asylum to the Age of Prozac* (Toronto, Canada: John Wiley and Sons, 1997), 33–68.
74 Edgar Jones, discussion with author, 2012.
75 Canadian Mental Health Association, "History of CMHA," http://ontario.cmha.ca/about-us/history-of-cmha/#.WC99MubQeUk; and Clarke, "The Opening of Doors," 527–51.
76 F.J. Marcham, Norcross Awards: Report on the Service Patient Scheme for Mental Cases, April 1959, TNA: PIN 15/4084; and MPNI, War Pensioners' Welfare Service: Welfare Officers' Guide, 1971, TNA: PIN 14/44.
77 C. Alamo, P. Clervoy, E. Cuenca, F. López Muñoz, and G. Rubio, "History of the Discovery and Clinical Introduction of Chlorpromazine," *Annals of Clinical Psychiatry* 17, 3 (2005): 113–35; and Ban, "Fifty Years Chlorpromazine," 495–500.
78 Gina Bari Kolata, "New Drugs and the Brain," *Science,* New Series 205, 4408 (August 24, 1979): 774.
79 Ban, "Fifty Years Chlorpromazine," 495–500; Heinz E. Lehmann, "Introduction of Chlorpromazine Treatment of Mental Illness in North America," Canadians for Health Research, http://www.chrcrm.org/en/salute-excellence/introduction-chlorpromazine-treatment-mental-illness-north-america.
80 Joanna Moncrieff, "An Investigation into the Precedents of Modern Drug Treatment in Psychiatry," *History of Psychiatry* 10 (1999): 475–90.

81 Ban, "Fifty Years Chlorpromazine," 495–500; and Lehmann, "Introduction of Chlorpromazine Treatment."

82 Andrew Scull, "Psychiatrists and Historical 'Facts' Part One: The Historiography of Somatic Treatments," *History of Psychiatry* 6 (1995): 235–36.

83 Robert Golden, Jeffrey A. Lieberman, Joseph McEvoy, and Scott Stroup, "Drugs of the Psychopharmacological Revolution in Clinical Psychiatry," *Psychiatric Services* 51, 10 (October 1, 2000): 1254–58; Moncrieff, "An Investigation," 475–90; Shorter, *A History of Psychiatry*, 255–72; and Wrobel, "Science, Serotonin and Sadness," 3404–17.

84 Ban, "Fifty Years Chlorpromazine," 495–500.

85 Ibid., 498.

86 Ivan P. Ryan, Korea Veterans Association of Australia, email to author, May 24, 2012; Les Peate, Korea Veterans Association of Canada, email to author, June 16, 2012; and Uttley, "New Zealand," 46–47, 51.

87 Paragraphs on War Pensions Proposed by Mental Welfare Commission for Scotland for Inclusion in Forthcoming Report, April 1971, TNA: PIN 18/616.

88 Ibid.

89 Note of Meeting to Consider the Position of War Pensioners in Hospital, July 13, 1971, TNA: PIN 18/616; L. Errington to Miss Riddelsdell, War Pensioners in Hospital, July 28, 1971, TNA: PIN 35/416; and R.G. Cope to Mr. Pagdin, July 8, 1971, TNA: PIN 18/616.

90 R. Windsor to Overend and Errington, War Pensions and Industrial Injuries, July 2, 1971, TNA: PIN 18/616.

91 Paragraphs on War Pensions Proposed by Mental Welfare Commission for Scotland for Inclusion in Forthcoming Report, April 1971, TNA: PIN 18/616; and Note of a Meeting to Consider the Position of War Pensioners in Hospital, July 13, 1971, TNA: PIN 18/616.

92 Ben Shephard, *A War of Nerves: Soldiers and Psychiatrists in the Twentieth Century* (Cambridge: Harvard University Press, 2001), 355.

93 Edgar Jones and Simon Wessely, *Shell Shock to PTSD: Military Psychiatry from 1900 to the Gulf War* (London: Taylor and Francis, 2005), 128.

94 Ibid.

95 Shephard, *War of Nerves*, 355–57.

96 Carol MacDonald, Kerry Chamberlain, and Nigel Long, "Posttraumatic Stress Disorder (PTSD) and Its Effects in Vietnam Veterans: The New Zealand Experience," *NZ Journal of Psychology* 24, 2 (December 1995): 63.

97 Jones and Wessely, *Shell Shock to PTSD*, 129–32, 234–38; and Shorter, *A History of Psychiatry*, 304–5.

98 Simon Wessely, "War and Psychiatry: A Story in Three Acts," lecture, Global History Seminar, London Centre of the University of Notre Dame, March 27, 2013; Garton, *The Cost of War*, 109–10; Dancey, "The Interaction of the Welfare State and the Disabled," 274–77; and Dancey, "Treatment in the Absence of Pensioning," 347.

99 Australian War Memorial, "Vietnam War 1962–75," 2013, http://www.awm.gov.au/atwar/vietnam.asp.

100 Department of Veterans' Affairs, "Australia and the Vietnam War: Public Opinion," http://vietnam-war.commemoration.gov.au/public-opinion/index.php.

101 Downs, "Australia," 15–17, 22–24.

102 Ibid.

103 Department of Veterans' Affairs, *Factsheet HSV133: Psychology and Other Mental Health Services for Veterans – Information for the Veteran Community* (Canberra: Government of Australia, January 2001).

104 Australian Centre for Posttraumatic Mental Health, "Our History," November 4, 2010, http://phoenixaustralia.org/.

105 Canada, Parliament, House of Commons Standing Committee on Veterans Affairs, *Minutes of Proceedings*, 2nd session, 39th Parliament, Meeting No. 93, June 3, 2008 (Mr. Adam Luckhurst).

106 Khalida Ismail and Glyn Lewis, "Multi-Symptom Illnesses, Unexplained Illness and Gulf War Syndrome," *Philosophical Transactions: Biological Sciences* 361, 1468, *Health of Gulf War Veterans* (April 29, 2006): 543–44, 548–49.

107 Brig. Gen. (Rtd.) G.E. Sharpe, "The Sand beneath Our Feet: The Changing Mandate in the Croatia Inquiry," Veteran Voice.info, 2011, http://veteranvoice.info/ARCHIVE/info_11may_Paper_ShiftingSands_byBGen_Sharpe.pdf; Veterans Health Administration, *VHA/DoD Clinical Practice Guideline for the Management of Medical Unexplained Symptoms: Chronic Pain and Fatigue* (Washington, DC: US Department of Defense, 2001), 1.

108 Lt.-Gen. Roméo Dallaire was commander of the UN Assistance Mission to Rwanda from 1993 to 1994. After witnessing atrocities in Rwanda, Dallaire suffered from depression. Parliament of Canada, "Roméo Dallaire – Senate Biography," 2013, http://www.parl.gc.ca/SenatorsMembers/Senate/SenatorsBiography/isenator_det.asp?senator_id=2772&M=M&Language=E.

109 Department of National Defence, "Caring for Our Own: A Comprehensive Approach for the Care of CF Ill and Injured Members and Their Families," (Ottawa: Department of National Defence, 2014), 9, 19; and Office of the Auditor General of Canada, *Report of the Auditor General of Canada* (Ottawa: Office of the Auditor General of Canada, 2014), 5–6.

110 Kathy Darte, Lt.-Col. Stéphane Grenier, Alexandra Heber, and Donald Richardson, "Combining Clinical Treatment and Peer Support: A Unique Approach to Overcoming Stigma and Delivering Care," in *Human Dimensions in Military Operations – Military Leaders' Strategies for Addressing Stress and Psychological Support* (Brussels: NATO, 2006), 2.

111 Ibid.

112 Department of National Defence, "Caring for Our Own," 23; and Canada, House of Commons Standing Committee on National Defence, *Minutes of Proceedings*, 2nd session, 39th Parliament, Meeting No. 18, March 13, 2008 (Mr. Raymond Lalonde).

113 Veterans Affairs Canada, "Veterans Bill of Rights," http://www.veterans.gc.ca/eng/about-us/veterans-bill-of-rights/vbor.

114 Office of the Veterans Ombudsman, "Improving the New Veterans Charter: The Parliamentary Review" (Ottawa: Office of the Veterans Ombudsman, January 2013), 3.

115 Ibid.

116 Ibid., Message from the Veterans Ombudsman.

117 Ibid., 5.

118 Office of Veterans Ombudsman, "Improving the New Veterans Charter: The Actuarial Analysis," (Ottawa: Office of the Veterans Ombudsman, June 2013), 4.

119 John Paul Tasker, "Ottawa Revives Harper-Era Legal Arguments to Block Pensions for Injured Vets," CBC News, June 15, 2016, http://www.cbc.ca/news/politics/ottawa-pensions-injured-vets-equitas-lawsuit-1.3637155.

120 Kieron Lang, "Feds Spend $694K in Legal Fight against Veterans," CTV News, January 28, 2015, http://www.ctvnews.ca/canada/feds-spent-694k-in-legal-fight-against-veterans-1.2209816.

121 Joseph Boaz, "Former Soldiers Blast Their Treatment by Veterans Affairs," *Chilliwack Progress*, January 2015, https://issuu.com/blackpress/docs/i20150121090100450/3.

122 Office of the Veterans Ombudsman, "Supporting Severely Impaired Veterans: Report on the New Veterans Charter Permanent Impairment Allowance and Permanent Impairment Allowance Supplement," (Ottawa: Office of the Veterans Ombudsman, June 2014).

123 Director Casualty Support Management, "Guide to Benefits, Programs, and Services for Serving and Former CAF Members and Their Families," (Ottawa: Department of National Defence, May 13, 2014), 14–15.

124 Ibid.

125 Mandy Kovacs, "Canadian Veterans Remain Critical of Government," Global News, January 28, 2015, http://globalnews.ca/news/1798943/canadian-veterans-remain-critical-of-government/.

126 Office of the Auditor General of Canada, *Report of the Auditor General of Canada*, 3.

127 Ibid., 5.

128 Ibid., 8.

129 Ibid., 10–11.

130 Laura Stone, "Julian Fantino Out as Veterans Affairs Minister," Global News, January 5, 2015, http://globalnews.ca/news/1755468/julian-fantino-out-as-veterans-affairs-minister-report/.

131 David Pugliese, "The Battle for Veterans' Votes: Conservatives a Target for Some Former Military," *Ottawa Citizen*, February 2, 2015, http://ottawacitizen.com/news/politics/the-battle-for-veterans-votes-conservatives-the-target-for-some-former-military.

132 Office of Auditor General of Canada, *Report of the Auditor General of Canada*, 1.

133 Helen McCartney, "The Military Covenant and the Civil-Military Contract in Britain," *International Affairs* 86, 2 (2010): 412–13.

134 Tristan McGeorge, Jamie Hacker Hughes, and Simon Wessely, "The MoD PTSD Decision: A Psychiatric Perspective," *Occupational Health Review* 122 (July/August 2006): 21.

135 Ibid.

136 Sima Kotecha, "Care for UK Military Veterans Is 'Flawed,' Medical Experts Say," BBC News, October 29, 2014. http://www.bbc.com/news/uk-29807947.

137 Deirdre MacManus, N. Jones, S. Wessely, N.T. Fear, E. Jones, and N. Greenberg, "The Mental Health of the UK Armed Forces in the 21st Century: Resilience in the Face of Adversity," *JRAMC* 160, 2 (2014): 125.

138 MacManus et al., "The Mental Health of the UK Armed Forces," 2; Ministry of Defence, "Suicide and Open Verdict Deaths in the UK Regular Armed Forces 1985–2013," March 27, 2014, https://www.gov.uk/government/uploads/system/uploads/attachment_data/file/416463/20150326_UK_AF_Suicide_National_Statistic_2015_Data_O.pdf; and "Myth Busters," Combat Stress, 2015, http://www.combatstress.org.uk/veterans/myth-busters/#VeteransAndSuicide.

139 British Army, "Veterans and Reserves Mental Health Program (Formerly Medical Assessment Program)," Ministry of Defence, 2013.

140 Ibid.

141 David Rutter, "Veterans Mental Health Policy: What Is the Future?" Paper presented at the Veterans' Mental Health – Facts, Fiction and Future Conference, February 11, 2015, King's College London; "Innovations in Mental Health Care by the NHS & Charitable Sector: Panel Discussion," Veterans' Mental Health – Facts, Fiction and Future Conference, February 11, 2015, King's College London.

142 Christopher Dandeker, Simon Wessely, Amy Iversen, and John Ross, "What's in a Name? Defining and Caring for 'Veterans': The UK in International Perspective," *Armed Forces and Society* 32 (January 2006): 161–77.

143 Howard Burdett, Charlotte Woodhead, Amy Iversen, Simon Wessely, Christopher Dandeker, and Nicola T. Fear, "Are You a Veteran? Understanding of the Term 'Veteran' among UK Ex-Service Personnel: A Research Note," *Armed Forces and Society* 39, 4 (2013): 1.

144 Simon Wessely, "Time Bombs or Tidal Waves: What Do We Know about the Health and Well Being of Serving and Ex-Serving Members of the UK Armed Forces?" Veterans'

Mental Health – Facts, Fiction and Future Conference, February 11, 2015, King's College London.

145 Canada, Parliament, House of Commons Standing Committee on Veterans Affairs, *Minutes of Proceedings*, 2nd session, 39th Parliament, Meeting No. 93, June 3, 2008 (Mr. Adam Luckhurst); and Downs, "Australia," 16.

146 GAC programs include "caregiver initiatives, alternative housing, long-term and continuing care, health promotion and rehabilitation, departmental research," and "dementia research." Veterans Affairs Canada, "The Gerontological Advisory Council" August 20, 2012, http://www.veterans.gc.ca/eng/about-us/advisory-groups/gerontological.

147 Veterans Affairs NZ, "Case Management Information Sheet," October 6, 2012, http://www.veteransaffairs.mil.nz/info-sheets-forms/case-management.html; (accessed on 6 October 2012); Department of Veterans' Affairs, *Factsheet HCS01: Veterans Home Care* (Canberra: Government of Australia, 2013).

148 Department of Veterans' Affairs, ibid.

149 Ivan P. Ryan, Korea Veterans Association of Australia, email to author, May 24, 2012; and Les Peate, Korea Veterans Association of Canada, email to author, June 16, 2012.

150 Canada, House of Commons Standing Committee on National Defence, *Minutes of Proceedings*, 2nd session, 39th Parliament, Meeting No. 18, March 13, 2008 (Ms. Rachel Corneille Gravel).

151 Ivan P. Ryan, Korea Veterans Association of Australia, email to author, May 24, 2012.

152 Canada, Parliament, House of Commons Standing Committee on Veterans Affairs, *Minutes of Proceedings*, 2nd session, 39th Parliament, Meeting No. 46, June 5, 2007 (Mr. Pierre Allard).

153 Office of the Auditor General of Canada, *Report of the Auditor General of Canada*, 18–19.

154 Canada, House of Commons Standing Committee on Veterans Affairs, *Minutes of Proceedings*, 2nd session, 39th Parliament, Meeting No. 16, March 6, 2008.

155 Smyttan Common, as quoted in Tom Hickman, *The Call-Up: A History of National Service* (London, UK: Headline, 2004), 271.

156 Canada, House of Commons Standing Committee on National Defence, *Minutes of Proceedings*, 2nd session, 39th Parliament, Meeting No. 18, March 13, 2008 (Mr. Doug Clorey).

157 The Department of Veterans' Affairs funded the Monash University study. Researchers were able to track remaining veterans through service/government records. Malcolm Sims, Jillian Ikin, and Dean McKenzie, *Health Study 2005: Australian Veterans of the Korean War* (Melbourne: Department of Epidemiology and Preventative Medicine, Faculty of Medicine, Nursing and Health Sciences, Monash University, 2005), 11–12.

158 Ibid.

159 No comparable studies have been carried out on Commonwealth veterans or prisoners of war, but there is a small body of literature on American veterans. Like the Monash report, these articles suggest heightened levels of PTSD and other mental health problems. However, the majority of studies involve only a small number of men, and participants usually responded to advertisements in order to take part. Consequently, they were not randomly chosen but self-selected individuals. Examples include: Patricia B. Sutker and Albert N. Allain Jr., "Assessment of PTSD and Other Mental Disorders in World War II and Korean Conflict POW Survivors and Combat Veterans," *Psychological Assessment* 8, 1 (1996): 18–25; Brian Engdahl, Thomas N. Dikel, Raina Eberly, and Arthur Blank Jr., "Comorbidity and Course of Psychiatric Disorders in a Community Sample of Former Prisoners of War," *American Journal of Psychiatry* 155, 12 (December 1998): 1740–45; Edward M. McCranie and Leon A. Hyer, "Posttraumatic Stress Disorder Symptoms in Korean Conflict and World War II Combat Veterans Seeking Outpatient Treatment," *Journal of*

Traumatic Stress 13, 3 (2000): 427–39; and Cynthia Lindman Port, Brian Engdahl, and Patricia Frazier, "A Longitudinal and Retrospective Study of PTSD among Older Prisoners of War," *American Journal of Psychiatry* 158, 9 (September 2001): 1474–75.

160 In the aftermath of the war, a UN Memorial Cemetery was established in Busan. A number of other Commonwealth memorials were erected throughout Korea. While the war has long been recognized on national monuments across the Commonwealth, the first dedicated Korean War memorial was not built until 1996. Commemorative sites and their dedication dates include: Korean War Memorial Wall, Brampton, ON, Canada (1996); Korean War Memorial, Canberra, Australia (1999); Veterans Memorial Garden Alrewas, Staffordshire, England (2000); Korean War Memorial, Belfast, Northern Ireland (2010).

161 Jennifer Morse, "Year of the Korean War Veteran Announced," *Legion Magazine*, March 12, 2013, http://legionmagazine.com/en/index.php/2013/03/year-of-the-korean-war-veteran-announced/; Joe Shute, "Britain's Korean War Veterans Win Their Final Fight," *Telegraph*, November 29, 2014, http://www.telegraph.co.uk/history/britain-at-war/11260575/Britains-Korean-War-veterans-win-their-final-fight.html.

162 James Meikle, "Korean War Veterans Say Sacrifice Finally Honoured as Memorial Is Unveiled," *Guardian*, December 3, 2014, http://www.theguardian.com/world/2014/dec/03/korean-war-memorial-unveiled-london.

163 Ibid.

164 Foreign and Commonwealth Office, "Press Release: Memorial to the Korean War Unveiled in London," December 3, 2014, https://www.gov.uk/government/news/memorial-to-the-korean-war-unveiled-in-london.

165 Her Majesty Queen Elizabeth II, quoted in Sarah Kim, "Queen Praises Korean War Memorial in London," *Korea Joongang Daily*, December 5, 2014, http://koreajoongangdaily.joins.com/news/article/article.aspx?aid=2998125.

Conclusion

Epigraph: John Bushy Burke, as quoted in Richard Trembeth, *A Different Sort of War: Australians in Korea 1950-53* (Melbourne: Australian Scholarly Publishing, 2005), 150.

1 Capt. J.J. Flood, "Psychiatric Casualties in UK Elements of Korean Force: Dec. 1950 – Nov. 1951," *Journal of the Royal Army Medical Corps* 100, 1 (January 1954): 46; and 25 Canadian Field Dressing Station (25 FDS) War Diaries, 1951–53, Library and Archives Canada (LAC): RG 24-C-3, vols. 18395–97.

2 David French, *Army, Empire and the Cold War: The British Army and Military Policy, 1945-1971* (Oxford: Oxford University Press, 2012), 141; Max Hastings, *The Korean War* (London: Macmillan, 2000), 286–87; and Gen. Bruce C. Clarke, interview by Jerry N. Hess, January 14, 1970, Harry S. Truman Library and Museum, http://www.trumanlibrary.org/oralhist/clarkeb.htm.

3 25 FDS War Diaries, 1951–53, LAC: RG 24-C-3, vols. 18395–97; War Office, Report on Health of Army 1951–52, The National Archives at Kew (TNA): WO 279/610.

4 Liam Clarke, "The Opening of Doors in British Mental Hospitals in the 1950s," *History of Psychiatry* 4 (1993): 527–51; Ivan Patrick Ryan, Korea Veterans Association of Australia, email message to author, May 24, 2012; Les Peate, Korea Veterans Association of Canada, email message to author, June 16, 2012; and Canadian Mental Health Association, "History of CMHA," http://ontario.cmha.ca/about-us/history-of-cmha/#.WC99MubQeUk.

5 Alice Aiken and Amy Buitenhuis, *Supporting Canadian Veterans with Disabilities* (Kingston, ON: Defence Management Studies Program, Queen's University, 2011), 6; Travis E. Dancey, "The Interaction of the Welfare State and the Disabled," *Canadian Medical Association Journal* 103 (August 1, 1970): 274–77; and Travis E. Dancey, "Treatment in the

Absence of Pensioning for Psychoneurotic Veterans," *American Psychiatric Journal* 107 (1950): 347.

6 Ivan Patrick Ryan, Korea Veterans Association of Australia, email message to author, May 24, 2012.

7 Les Peate, Korea Veterans Association of Canada, email message to author, June 16, 2012; and Dept. of Health and Social Security – Central Advisory Committee on War Pensions, Minutes of 97th Meeting, November 18, 1981, TNA: PIN 88/90.

8 Richard Trembeth, *A Different Sort of War: Australians in Korea 1950-1953* (Melbourne: Australian Scholarly Publishing, 2005), 48.

9 Ibid.

10 Lt.-Col. Herbert Fairlie Wood, *Strange Battleground: The Operations in Korea and Their Effects on the Defence Policy of Canada* (Ottawa: Queen's Printer and Controller of Stationery, 1966), 257; Gen. Sir Anthony Farrar-Hockley, *The British Part in the Korean War,* vol. 2, *An Honourable Discharge* (London: HMSO, 1995), ix; Ian McGibbon, *New Zealand and the Korean War,* vol. 2, *Combat Operations* (Auckland: Oxford University Press, 1996), vii; Trembeth, *A Different Sort of War,* 1; and BBC, "WW2 People's War: Fact File: Commonwealth and Allied Forces," March 2012, http://www.bbc.co.uk/history/ww2peopleswar/timeline/factfiles/nonflash/a6651218.shtml.

11 Lt. Col. D.K. Palit, "Military Lessons of the Korean War," *United Services Institute of India Journal* 82, 348, 349 (July-October 1952): 157-74; Wood, *Strange Battleground,* 13.

12 Ibid.

13 As quoted in Joy Damousi, *Living with the Aftermath: Trauma, Nostalgia and Grief in Post-War Australia* (Cambridge: Cambridge University Press, 2001), 44.

14 As quoted in ibid., 46.

15 Don Leier, as quoted in Ted Barris, *Deadlock in Korea: Canadians at War 1950-1953* (Toronto: Macmillan of Canada, 1999), 304-5.

16 French, *Army, Empire and the Cold War,* 141; Hastings, *The Korean War,* 286-87; Gen. Bruce C. Clarke, interview by Jerry N. Hess, January 14, 1970, Harry S. Truman Library and Museum, http://www.trumanlibrary.org/oralhist/clarkeb.htm.

17 Associated Press, "New Zealand Pulls Troops Out of Afghanistan," Fox News, April 4, 2013, http://www.foxnews.com/world/2013/04/04/new-zealand-pulls-troops-out-afghanistan/; Postmedia News, "End of Afghan Mission Leaves Vets Grappling with Their Return to Canada," *National Post,* February 27, 2012, http://news.nationalpost.com/2012/02/27/end-of-afghan-mission-leaves-vets-grappling-with-their-return-to-canada/; Pakistan Kakhuda Hafiz: Leading Alternative Policy Institute, "A Review of the 12 Years of British Troops in Afghanistan," July 24, 2013, http://www.pakistankakhudahafiz.com/opinion/a-review-of-the-12-years-of-british-troops-in-afghanistan/; Luis Martinez, "US Veterans: By the Numbers," ABC News, November 11, 2011, http://abcnews.go.com/Politics/us-veterans-numbers/story?id=14928136#1.

18 James Wright, "Have Americans Forgotten Afghanistan?" *Atlantic,* March 25, 2013, http://www.theatlantic.com/international/archive/2013/03/have-americans-forgotten-afghanistan/274331/.

19 Oliver Miles, "Why Are We Still in Afghanistan?" London Review of Books, July 10, 2013, http://www.lrb.co.uk/blog/2013/07/10/oliver-miles/why-are-we-still-in-afghanistan/.

20 As quoted in Eric Taylor, *Wartime Nurse: One Hundred Years from the Crimea to Korea, 1854-1954* (London: Robert Hale, 2001), 207.

Appendices

1 83 (1950). Resolution of June 27, 1950 [S/1511], as quoted in Evan Luard, *A History of the United Nations,* vol. 2, *The Years of Western Domination 1945-55* (London: Macmillan, 1982), 241-42.

2 Commonwealth prisoners of war numbered as follows: United Kingdom, 977; Canada, 32, Australia, 26; New Zealand, 1. Walter G. Hermes, *Truce Tent and Fighting Front, United States Army in the Korean War* (Washington, DC: Office of the Chief of Military History, 1966).

3 Neither North Korean nor Chinese forces recognized the 1949 Geneva Conventions on the treatment of prisoners of war. Commonwealth troops were subjected to ill treatment including but not limited to solitary confinement, denial of toilets, and denial of clothing and bedding. Throughout the war, attempts were also made to indoctrinate POWs with communist ideology. Ministry of Defence, *Treatment of British Prisoners of War in Korea*, 1955, The National Archives at Kew (TNA): ADM 1/25760; and Jonathan F.W. Vance, *Objects of Concern: Canadian Prisoners of War through the Twentieth Century* (Vancouver: UBC Press, 1994), 217–34.

4 Captain N.G. Fraser, Monthly Psychiatric Report August 1953, September 1953, Library and Archives Canada (LAC): RG 24-C-3, vol. 18397.

5 Ibid.

6 Ibid.

7 Ibid.

8 Ibid.

Bibliography

Archival Records

Australian National Archives

Digital Collections
A462   Department of Prime Minister and Cabinet/Department of Foreign Affairs and Trade, Central Office – Australian High Commission Correspondence Files
A5954   Sir Frederick Shedden Collection

Australian War Memorial

Digital Collections
AWM 85, Class 1   Headquarters, 28th British Commonwealth Brigade Group
          Class 2   1 Battalion, The Royal Australian Regiment
          Class 3   2 Battalion, The Royal Australian Regiment
          Class 4   3 Battalion, The Royal Australian Regiment
          Class 5   Headquarters British Commonwealth Forces in Korea

Canadian War Museum

Textual Records
Papers of Major David Spencer Whittingham (1923–94)

Directorate of History and Heritage, Department of National Defence
File Nos.   000.8 (D96)
          112.3H1.009 (D113)
          1326–2676
          361.003 (D1)
          681.013 (D48)

Harry S. Truman Library and Museum
Audiovisual Materials Collection

Imperial War Museum
The Sound Archive

Legasee: The Veteran Video Archive
Korean War Collection

Library and Archives Canada
MG 31   Sneath Papers
RG 24   National Defence files from commands, schools, units, ships, bases, and formations

Liddell Hart Centre for Military Archives
Reference Material: Postwar, 1945–70, Papers, 1927–72

National Library of Australia
Trove Collections

Private Papers of Dr. N.G. Fraser

The National Archives at Kew (United Kingdom)

ADM 1	Admiralty and Ministry of Defence, Navy Department: Correspondence and Papers
DEFE 3	Admiralty: Operational Intelligence Centre
DEFE 7	Ministry of Defence prior to 1964: Registered Files (General Series)
DEFE 10	Ministry of Defence: Major Committees and Working Parties: Minutes and Papers
DEFE 11	Ministry of Defence: Chiefs of Staff Committee: Registered Files
DEFE 24	Ministry of Defence: Defence Secretariat Branches and their Predecessors: Registered Files
FO 371	Foreign Office: Political Departments: General Correspondence from 1906 to 1966
MH 79	Ministry of Health: Confidential Registered Files
MH 95	Board of Control: Entries Files
PIN 14	Ministry of Pensions and successors: Codes and Instructions
PIN 15	Ministry of Pensions and successors: War Pensions, Registered Files (GEN Series) and other records
PIN 18	Ministry of National Insurance and successors: Registered Files (F Series)
PIN 19	Ministry of National Insurance and successors: Registered Files (NI Series)
PIN 47	Ministry of National Insurance and successors: Registered Files (STA Series)
PIN 59	Ministry of Pensions and successors: War Pensions Policy, Registered Files (WPP Series)
WO 32	War Office and successors: Registered Files
WO 163	War Office and Ministry of Defence and predecessors: War Office Council, later War Office Consultative Council, Army Board and their various committees: Minutes and Papers
WO 216	Office of the Chief of the Imperial General Staff: Papers
WO 231	War Office: Directorate of Military Training, later Directorate of Army Training: Papers
WO 279	War Office and Ministry of Defence: Confidential Print
WO 281	War Office: British Commonwealth Division of United Nations Force: War Diaries, Korean War
WO 308	British and Commonwealth Forces: Historical Records and Reports, Korean War
WO 342	War Office: Army Operational Research Group, later Army Operational Research Establishment: Registered Files
WO 348	Military Personnel Research Committee and Sub-committees, later Army Personnel Research Committee: Minutes and Papers
WO 279	War Office and Ministry of Defence: Confidential Print
WO 281	British Commonwealth Division of United Nations Force: War Diaries, Korean War

WO 291   Ministry of Supply and War Office: Military Operational Research Unit, successors and related bodies: Reports and Papers

United States Army Academy of Health Sciences, Stimson Library
Digital Collections

United States National Archives and Records Administration
RG 112   Records of the United States Army Surgeon General

Wellcome Library and Archives
Royal Army Medical Corps Muniments Collection

Other Sources

Agnew, G.H. "The Shortage of Hospital Beds." *Canadian Medical Association Journal* 46, 4 (April 1942): 373–74.

Aiken, Alice, and Amy Buitenhuis. *Supporting Canadian Veterans with Disabilities.* Kingston, ON: Defence Management Studies Program, School of Public Policy, Queen's University, 2011.

Alamo, C., P. Clervoy, E. Cuenca, F. López Muñoz, and G. Rubio. "History of the Discovery and Clinical Introduction of Chlorpromazine." *Annals of Clinical Psychiatry* 17, 3 (2005): 113–35.

Allison, William. "Review of *War of Patrols: Canada's Army Operations in Korea* by William Cameron Johnston." *Canadian Historical Review* 85, 4 (2004): 805.

Allport, Alan. *Demobbed: Coming Home after the Second World War.* New Haven, CT: Yale University Press, 2009.

Anderson, Donald. "Navy, Army, and Air Force Institutes in War and Peace." *Royal United Services Institute Journal* 85, 537 (1940): 64–72.

Anderton, Geoffrey. "The Birth of the British Commonwealth Division Korea." *Journal of the Royal Army Medical Corps* 99, 2 (January 1953): 43–54.

Andrade, Ernest Jr. "Review of *Morale: A Study of Men and Courage: The Second Scottish Rifles at the Battle of Neuve Chapelle, 1915* by John Baynes." *Military Affairs* 32, 2 (October 1968): 91.

Andrew, J.E., and K.A. Hunter. "The Royal Canadian Army Medical Corps in the Korean War." *Canadian Medical Association Journal* 72 (February 1, 1955): 178–84.

–. "The Royal Canadian Army Medical Corps in the Korean War." *Canadian Services Medical Journal* (July/August 1954): 5–15.

Arbuckle, James V. *Military Forces in 21st Century Peace Operations: No Job for a Soldier?* New York: Routledge, 2006.

Associated Press. "New Zealand Pulls Troops Out of Afghanistan." Fox News, April 4, 2013. http://www.foxnews.com/world/2013/04/04/new-zealand-pulls-troops-out -afghanistan/.

Australian Centre for Posttraumatic Mental Health. "Our History." http://phoenixaustralia. org/.

"Australian Force to go to Korea." *West Australian,* July 27, 1950.

Australian War Memorial. "Captain Reg Saunders." http://www.awm.gov.au/exhibitions/ korea/faces/saunders/.

–. "Korean War, 1950–1953." http://www.awm.gov.au/atwar/korea.asp.

–. "People Profiles: General Francis George (Frank) Hassett, AC, KBE, CB, DSO." http:// www.awm.gov.au/people/8445.asp.

–. "Vietnam War 1962–75." http://www.awm.gov.au/atwar/vietnam.asp.
–. "War at Sea: The Royal Australian Navy in Korea." http://www.awm.gov.au/exhibitions/korea/ausinkorea/navy/.
Babington, Anthony. *Shell-Shock: A History of the Changing Attitudes to War Neurosis.* London: Leo Cooper, 1997.
Ban, Thomas A. "Fifty Years Chlorpromazine: A Historical Perspective." *Neuropsychiatric Diseases and Treatment* 3, 4 (August 2007): 495-500.
Barclay, Cyril Nelson. *The First Commonwealth Division: The Story of British Commonwealth Land Forces in Korea, 1950–1953.* Aldershot: Gale and Polden, 1954.
Barham, Peter. *Forgotten Lunatics of the Great War.* New Haven, CT: Yale University Press, 2004.
Bartlet, Leslie. "A National Service Psychiatrist's Story." *Journal of the Royal Army Medical Corps* 156, 4 (December 2010): 273-75.
Barris, Ted. *Deadlock in Korea: Canadians at War 1950–1953.* Toronto: Macmillan of Canada, 1999.
BBC. "WW2 People's War: Fact File: Commonwealth and Allied Forces," March 2012. http://www.bbc.co.uk/history/ww2peopleswar/timeline/factfiles/nonflash/a6651218.sthml.
Belenky, Gregory, ed. *Contemporary Studies in Combat Psychiatry.* Contributions in Military Studies 62. Westport, CT: Greenwood, 1987.
Bercuson, David J. *Blood on the Hills: The Canadian Army in the Korean War.* Toronto: University of Toronto Press, 1999.
Binneveld, Hans. *From Shell Shock to Combat Stress: A Comparative History of Military Psychology.* Amsterdam: Amsterdam University Press, 1998.
Blaxland, John C. "The Armies of Canada and Australia: Closer Collaboration?" *Canadian Military Journal* 3, 3 (Autumn 2002): 45-54.
Blood, Christopher G., and Eleanor D. Gauker. "The Relationship between Battle Intensity and Disease Rates among Marine Corps Infantry Units." *Military Medicine* 158, 4 (1993): 340-44.
Bogousslavsky, Julian, and Laurent Tatu. "French Neuropsychiatry in the Great War: Between Moral Support and Electricity." *Journal of the History of the Neurosciences: Basic and Clinical Perspectives* 22, 2 (2013): 144-54.
Brady, Anne-Marie, and Douglas Brown, eds. *Foreigners and Foreign Institutions in Republican China.* New York: Routledge, 2013.
Bretland, P.M. "The Principles of Prevention of Cold Injuries: Notes on the Problem as Encountered, and the Methods Used, in Korea." *Journal of the Royal Army Medical Corps* 100, 2 (April 1954): 88-98.
Brill, Norman Q., and Gilbert W. Beebe. "Psychoneuroses: Military Applications of a Follow-up Study." *United States Armed Forces Medical Journal* 3 (1952):15-33.
Brosseau, Bernard L.P. "Notes From Korea: Medical Services." *Canadian Army Journal* 8, 1 (April 1953): 107-20.
Burdett, Howard, Charlotte Woodhead, Amy Iverson, Simon Wessely, Christopher Dandeker, Nicola T. Fear. "Are You a Veteran? Understanding of the Term 'Veteran' among UK Ex-Service Personnel: A Research Note." *Armed Forces and Society* 39, 4 (2013): 751-59.
Byron-Watson, Brent. *Far Eastern Tour: Canadian Infantry in Korea, 1950–1953.* Montreal and Kingston: McGill-Queen's University Press, 2002.
Canada. House of Commons Standing Committee on National Defence. 39th Parliament, 2006-08.
–. House of Commons Standing Committee on Veterans Affairs. 39th Parliament, 2006-08.

"Canadian Armed Forces: News of the Medical Services." *Canadian Medical Association Journal* 62, 3 (March 1950): 297.

"Canadian Armed Forces: News of the Medical Services." *Canadian Medical Association Journal* 62, 6 (June 1950): 712.

"Canadian Armed Forces: News of the Medical Services." *Canadian Medical Association Journal* 63, 3 (September 1950): 304.

"Canadian Armed Forces: News of the Medical Services." *Canadian Medical Association Journal* 63, 6 (December 1950): 612–13.

"Canadian for Australian Army Course." *Cairns Post*, December 19, 1950.

Canadian Forces Advisory Council. *The Origins and Evolution of Veterans Benefits in Canada*. Ottawa: Veterans Affairs Canada, 2004.

Canadian Mental Health Association. "History of CMHA." http://ontario.cmha.ca/about-us/history-of-cmha/#.WC99MubQeUk.

Canadian Mental Health Association, Ontario Branch. "Remembering & Celebrating a Good Life: The Jack Griffin Education and Research Endowment Fund." Canadian Mental Health Association, n.d. http://ontario.cmha.ca/files/2013/04/jack_griffin_brochure.pdf.

Canadian Psychiatric Association. "In Memoriam." *Canadian Psychiatric Journal* (January 2010). http://ww1.cpa-apc.org/Publications/Archives/CJP/2001/September/memoriam.asp.

Carew, Tim. *The Commonwealth at War*. London: Cassell, 1967.

Catchpole, Brian. "The Commonwealth in Korea." *History Today* 48, 11 (November 1998). http://www.historytoday.com/brian-catchpole/commonwealth-korea.

Catignani, Sergio. "Motivating Soldiers: The Example of the Israeli Defence Forces." *Parameters* 34, 3 (Autumn 2004): 108–21.

Clark-Coulthard, Christopher. *Duntroon: The Royal Military College of Australia, 1911–1986*. Sydney: Allen and Unwin, 1986.

Clarke, Liam. "The Opening of Doors in British Mental Hospitals in the 1950s." *History of Psychiatry* 4 (1993): 527–51.

Clever, W.G. "A Brief History: British Canadian Military Medical Services." *Canadian Army Journal* 8, 4 (October 1954): 134–53.

Coates, H.J. "Morale on the Battlefield." *Australian Defence Force Journal* 45 (March/April 1984): 5–16.

"Cold in Korea." *Lancet* 260, 6727 (August 2, 1952): 233.

"Cold Weather Clothing for Korea." *British Medical Journal* 2, 4745 (December 15, 1951): 1457–58.

Cole, Howard N. *NAAFI in Uniform*. Lewes, East Sussex, UK: Navy, Army and Air Force Institute, 1982.

Combat Stress. "About Us: The History of Combat Stress." http://www.combatstress.org.uk/about-us/history-of-combat-stress/.

"Commonwealth Forces' Record in Korea: 'A Successful Experiment.'" *Times of London*, July 21, 1953.

Cooling, Franklin B. "Allied Interoperability in the Korean War." *Military Revie* 63, 6 (June 1983): 26–52.

Cooter, Roger. "Medicine and the Goodness of War." *Canadian Bulletin of History* 7 (September 1990): 147–59.

Copp, Terry, and Bill McAndrew. *Battle Exhaustion: Soldiers and Psychiatrists in the Canadian Army 1939–1945*. Montreal and Kingston: McGill-Queen's University Press, 1990.

Copp, Terry, and Mark Osborne Humphries. *Combat Stress in the 20th Century: The Commonwealth Perspective*. Kingston, ON: Canadian Defence Academy Press, 2010.

Cowdrey, Albert E. *The Medics' War: The United States Army in Korea.* Washington, DC: US Army Center of Military History, 1987.

Crammer, J.L. "Comment: Britain in the Fifties: Leucotomy and Open Doors." *History of Psychiatry* 5, 19 (1994): 393–95.

Cunningham-Boothe, Ashley, and Peter Farrar, eds. *British Forces in the Korean War.* West Yorkshire: British Korean Veterans Association, 1989.

Damousi, Joy. *Living with the Aftermath: Trauma, Nostalgia and Grief in Post-War Australia.* Cambridge: Cambridge University Press, 2001.

Dancey, Travis E. "The Interaction of the Welfare State and the Disabled." *Canadian Medical Association Journal* 103, 3 (August 1, 1970): 274–77.

–. "Treatment in the Absence of Pensioning for Psychoneurotic Veterans." *American Psychiatric Journal* 107 (1950): 347.

Dandeker, Christopher, Simon Wessely, Amy Iverson, and John Ross. "What's in a Name? Defining and Caring for 'Veterans': The UK in International Perspective." *Armed Forces and Society* 32 (January 2006): 161–77.

Davies, John D. "Malaise of General Practice." *British Medical Journal* 2, 5414 (10 October 1964): 948.

Day, Francis Martin, Phyllis Spence, and Barbara Ladouceur, eds. *Memoirs of the Canadian Red Cross Corps.* Vancouver: Ronsdale Press, 1998.

Dean, Eric T. Jr. *Shook over Hell: Post-Traumatic Stress, Vietnam and the Civil War.* Cambridge, MA: Harvard University Press, 1997.

Deane, Hugh. *The Korean War, 1945–1953.* San Francisco: China Books and Periodicals, 1999.

Department of Veterans' Affairs. "Australia and the Vietnam War: Public Opinion." http://vietnam-war.commemoration.gov.au/public-opinion/index.php.

–. *Factsheet HCS01: Veterans Home Care.* Canberra: Government of Australia, 2013.

–. *Factsheet HSV133: Psychology and Other Mental Health Services for Veterans – Information for the Veteran Community* (Canberra: Government of Australia, January 2001).

–. *Pensioner Summary.* Canberra: Government of Australia, December 2011.

Developing Leaders: A Sandhurst Guide. Camberley: Ministry of Defence, 2012.

Devine, P. "La Belle Alliance – Lessons for Coalition Warfare from the Korean War, 1950–1953." *Australian Defence Force Journal* 118 (May/June 1996): 47–48.

Directorate of History and Heritage, Department of National Defence. *Canada and the Korean War.* Ottawa: Art Global, 2002.

–. *Historical Report No. 72: Canadian Participation in the Korean War Part II.* Ottawa: Government of Canada, 1955.

"Discussion on Military Medical Problems in Korea." *Proceedings of the Royal Society of Medicine* 46 (June 10, 1953): 1037–46.

Downs, G.J. "Australia." *Journal of International and Comparative Social Welfare* 10, 1 (1994): 6–27.

"Editorial Comments: A Health Survey of Canada." *Canadian Medical Association Journal* 50, 4 (April 1944): 364.

Edwards, Paul M. *The Korean War.* American Soldiers' Lives: Daily Life through History. Westport, CT: Greenwood, 2006.

Ekins, Ashley, and Elizabeth Stewart, eds. *War Wounds: Medicine and the Trauma of Conflict.* Wollombi, NSW: Exisle Publishing, 2011.

Engdahl, Brain, Thomas N. Dikel, Raina Eberly, and Arthur Blank Jr. "Comorbidity and Course of Psychiatric Disorders in a Community Sample of Former Prisoners of War." *American Journal of Psychiatry* 155, 12 (December 1998): 1740–50.

Fairlie-Wood, Herbert. *Strange Battleground: The Operations in Korea and Their Effects on the Defence Policy of Canada.* Ottawa: Queen's Printer and Controller of Stationery, 1966.

Farley, John. *Brock Chisholm, the World Health Organization, and the Cold War.* Vancouver: UBC Press, 2008.

Farquhar, William R. Jr., and Henry A. Jeffers Jr. *Building the Imjin: Construction of Libby and Teal Bridges during the Korean War (October 1952 – July 1953).* Studies in Military Engineering No. 5. Fort Belvoir, VA: United States Army Corps of Engineers, 1989.

Farrar-Hockley, Sir Anthony. *The British Part in the Korean War.* Vol. 1, *A Distant Obligation.* London: HMSO, 1990.

–. *The British Part in the Korean War.* Vol. 2, *An Honourable Discharge.* London: HMSO, 1995.

Feasby, W.R. *Official History of the Canadian Medical Services, 1939–1945.* Vol. 2, *Clinical Subjects.* Ottawa: Queen's Printer and Controller of Stationery, 1953.

Feigin, Simon L. "Neuropsychiatric Casualties as a Result of Combat Involving Hill 266 ('Old Baldy')." *Medical Bulletin of the United States Army Far East* 1, 8 (July 1953): 134–36.

Fensome, Jason Timothy. "The Administrative History of National Service in Britain, 1950–1963." PhD dissertation, Cambridge University, 2001.

Flood, J.J. "Psychiatric Casualties in UK Elements of Korean Force: December 1950 – November 1951." *Journal of the Royal Army Medical Corps* 100, 1 (January 1954): 40–47.

Foreign and Commonwealth Office. "Press Release: Memorial to the Korean War in London," December 3, 2014. https://www.gov.uk/government/news/memorial -to-the-korean-war-unveiled-in-london.

"Forty Million Pounds." *British Medical Journal* 1, 4760 (March 29, 1952): 697–98.

French, David. *Army, Empire and the Cold War: The British Army and Military Policy, 1945–1971.* Oxford: Oxford University Press, 2012.

Frohman, I. Philips. "The Barbiturates." *American Journal of Nursing* 54, 4 (April 1954): 432–34.

Gabriel, Richard A. *No More Heroes: Madness and Psychiatry in War.* New York: Hill and Wang, 1967.

Gal, Reuven. "Unit Morale: From Theoretical Puzzle to an Empirical Illustration – An Israeli Example." *Journal of Applied Social Psychology* 16, 6 (1986): 549–64.

Garton, Stephen. *The Cost of War: Australians Return.* Melbourne: Oxford University Press, 1996.

Ginzberg, E., J.K. Anderson, S.W. Ginsburg, and J.L. Herma. *The Lost Divisions.* New York: Columbia University Press, 1959.

Glass, Albert Julius. "History and Organization of a Theater Psychiatric Service before and after 30 June 1951." In *Recent Advances in Medicine and Surgery: Based on Professional Medical Experiences in Japan and Korea 1950–1953.* Vol. 2. Medical Science Publication No. 4. Washington, DC: Walter Reed Army Medical Service Graduate School, 1954.

–. "Psychiatry in the Korean Campaign: A Historical Review." *US Armed Forces Medical Journal* 4 (1953): 1387–1401.

–. "Psychotherapy in the Combat Zone." *American Journal of Psychiatry* 110, 10 (1954): 725–31.

Golden, Robert, Jeffrey L. Lieberman, Joseph McEvoy, and Scott Stroup. "Drugs of the Psychopharmacological Revolution in Clinical Psychiatry." *Psychiatric Services* 51, 10 (October 1, 2000): 1254–58.

Gorman, J.H., J.S. Logan, and D.A.D. Montgomery. "Historical Review: The Evacuation of Burma: Fifty Years Ago." *Ulster Medical Journal* 61, 2 (October 1992): 166–74.

Granatstein, J.L. *Canada's War: The Politics of the Mackenzie King Government, 1939–1945.* Toronto: University of Toronto Press, 1990.

Granatstein, J.L., and Peter Neary, eds. *The Veteran's Charter and Post World War II Canada.* Montreal: McGill-Queen's University Press, 1998.

Gray, Hub. *Beyond the Danger Close: The Korean Experience Revealed: 2nd Battalion Princess Patricia's Canadian Light Infantry.* Calgary: Bunker to Bunker Books, 2003.

Grey, Jeffrey. *Australian Brass: The Career of Lieutenant General Sir Horace Robertson.* Cambridge: Cambridge University Press, 1992.

–. *The Commonwealth Armies and the Korean War: An Alliance Study.* Manchester: Manchester University Press, 1988.

Griffin, J.D.M. "Review Essay/Note Critique: Cameron's Search for a Cure." *Canadian Bulletin of Medical History* 8 (1991): 121–26.

Griffith, James. "Measurement of Group Cohesion in US Army Units." *Basic and Applied Social Psychology* 9, 2 (1988): 149–71.

Grint, Keith. *The Arts of Leadership.* Oxford: Oxford University Press, 2001.

Hanson, H.E., and R.F. Goldman. "Cold Injury in Man: A Review of Its Etiology and Discussion of Its Prediction." *Military Medicine* 134, 11 (October 1969): 1307–16.

Hastings, Max. *The Korean War.* Pan Grand Strategy Series. London: Pan Macmillan Books, 2000.

H.E.M. "Editorial Comments: Nursing Service Problems in Hospitals." *Canadian Medical Association Journal* 47, 2 (August 1942): 157.

Henderson, David, and R.D. Gillespie. *A Textbook of Psychiatry for Students and Practitioners.* 7th ed. London: Oxford University Press, 1950.

Henderson, William D. *Cohesion: The Human Element in Combat.* Washington, DC: National Defense University Press, 1985.

Hermes, Walter G. *Truce Tent and Fighting Front, United States Army in the Korean War.* Washington, DC: Office of the Chief of Military History, 1966.

Hickey, Michael. "The Korean War: An Overview." BBC History, March 21, 2011. http://www.bbc.co.uk/history/worldwars/coldwar/korea_hickey_01.shtml.

–. *The Korean War: The West Confronts Communism 1950–1953.* London: John Murray, 2000.

Hickman, Tom. *The Call-Up: A History of National Service.* London, UK: Headline, 2005.

"High US Honor for Australian." *Barrier Miner,* March 28, 1951.

Horn, Bernd, and Robert W. Walker, eds. *The Military Leadership Handbook.* Toronto: Dundurn Press and Canadian Defence Academy Press, 2008.

Howson, Susan. "The Origins of Cheaper Money, 1945-7." *Economic History Review,* New Series 40, 3 (August 1987): 433–52.

Human Dimensions in Military Operations – Military Leaders' Strategies for Addressing Stress and Psychological Support. Brussels: NATO, 2006.

Ingraham, Larry H., and Frederick J. Manning. "Psychiatric Battle Casualties: The Missing Column in a War without Replacements." *Military Review* 60, 8 (1980): 18–29.

Ismail, Khalida, and Glyn Lewis. "Multi-Symptom Illnesses, Unexplained Illness and Gulf War Syndrome." *Philosophical Transactions: Biological Sciences* 361, 1468, *Health of Gulf War Veterans* (April 29, 2006): 543–51.

Janowitz, Morris. *The Professional Soldier: A Social and Political Portrait.* Glencoe, IL: Free Press, 1960.

Johnson, Mark. *At the Front Line: Experiences of Australian Soldiers in World War II.* Cambridge: Cambridge University Press, 1996.

Johnston, William Cameron. *A War of Patrols: Canadian Army Operations in Korea.* Vancouver: UBC Press, 2003.

Jones, Edgar. *Morale, Psychological Wellbeing of UK Armed Forces and Entertainment: A Report for the British Forces Foundation.* London: King's College London Institute of Psychiatry at the Maudsley, January 2012.

–. "Shell Shock." Lecture, King's College London, 2010.

Jones, Edgar, and Ian Palmer. "Army Psychiatry in the Korean War: The Experience of 1 Commonwealth Division." *Military Medicine* 165, 4 (2000): 257–59.

Jones, Edgar, and Simon Wessely. "Hearts, Guts and Minds: Somatisation in the Military from 1900." *Journal of Psychosomatic Research* 56 (2004): 425–29.

–. "Psychiatric Battle Casualties: An Intra- and Interwar Comparison." *British Journal of Psychiatry* 178 (March 2001): 242–47.

–. *Shell Shock to PTSD: Military Psychiatry from 1900 to the Gulf War.* London: Taylor and Francis, 2005.

Jones, Franklin D., Linette R. Sparacino, and Joseph M. Rothberg, eds. *Psychiatry in the US Army: Lessons for Community Psychiatry.* Bethesda, MD: Uniformed Services University of Health Sciences, 2005.

Jones, Franklin D., Linette R. Sparacino, Victoria L. Wilcox, and Joseph M. Rothberg, eds. *Military Psychiatry: Preparing in Peace for War.* Washington, DC: US Government Printing Office, 1994.

Keshen, Jeffrey A. *Saints, Sinners, and Soldiers: Canada's Second World War.* Vancouver: UBC Press, 2004.

Kim, Sarah. "Queen Praises Korean War Memorial in London." *Korea Joongang Daily,* December 5, 2014. http://koreajoongangdaily.joins.com/news/article/article. aspx?aid=2998125.

Kolata, Gina Bari. "New Drugs and the Brain." *Science,* New Series 205, 4408 (August 24, 1979): 774.

"Korea Scandal: Report That Will Shock You." *Sunday Dispatch,* January 6, 1952.

Koren, Lindsey. "Smithsonian Traveling Exhibition Offers Fascinating Look at Military Mail and Communications." Mail Call, Smithsonian Institution Traveling Exhibition Service, 2011. http://www.sites.si.edu/exhibitions/exhibits/mailCall/#press.

L'Etang, H.J.C.J. "A Criticism of Military Psychiatry in the Second World War: Part III Historical Survey." *Journal of the Royal Army Medical Corps* 97, 5 (November 1951): 316–27.

Law Commission. *A New Support Scheme for Veterans: A Report on the Review of the Revised Pensions Act 1954.* Wellington, NZ: Law Commission, May 2010.

Leese, Peter. *Shell Shock: Traumatic Neurosis and the British Soldiers of the First World War.* London: Palgrave Macmillan, 2002.

Lehmann, Heinz E. "Introduction of Chlorpromazine Treatment of Mental Illness in North America." Canadians for Health Research. http://www.chrcrm.org/en/salute -excellence/introduction-chlorpromazine-treatment-mental-illness-north-america.

Lewis, Martin M. "The Promotion and Maintenance of Mental Health in the Military Community: Part II." *Journal of the Royal Army Medical Corps* 96, 2 (February 1951): 102–14.

Linklater, Eric. *Our Men in Korea.* London: Her Majesty's Stationery Office, 1952.

Local Army Welfare Officer. "Six Years of Army Welfare." *Royal United Services Institute Journal* 91, 561 (1946): 52–53.

Lowe, Peter. "An Ally and a Recalcitrant General: Great Britain, Douglas MacArthur and the Korean War, 1950–1951." *English Historical Review* 105, 416 (July 1990): 624–53.

Luard, Evan. *A History of the United Nations.* Vol. 2, *The Years of Western Domination 1945–55.* London: Macmillan, 1982.

Luke, Claude F. "The Work of the Navy, Army and Air Force Institutes Entertainment Branch." *Royal United Services Institute Journal* 86, 541 (1941): 88–95.

MacDonald, Callum. *Britain and the Korean War*. Oxford: Basil Blackwell, 1990.

MacDonald, Carol, Kerry Chamberlain, and Nigel Long. "Posttraumatic Stress Disorder (PTSD) and Its Effects in Vietnam Veterans: The New Zealand Experience." *New Zealand Journal of Psychology* 24, 2 (December 1995): 63–68.

Macmillan, Duncan. "Recent Developments in Community Mental Health." *Lancet* 281, 7281 (March 16, 1963): 567–68.

Martinez, Luis. "US Veterans: By the Numbers." ABC News, November 11, 2011. http://abcnews.go.com/Politics/us-veterans-numbers/story?id=14928136#1.

McCranie, Edward M., and Leon A. Hyer. "Posttraumatic Stress Disorder Symptoms in Korean Conflict and World War II Combat Veterans Seeking Outpatient *Treatment*." *Journal of Traumatic Stress* 13, 3 (2000): 427–39.

McGeorge, Tristan, Jamie Hacker Hughes, and Simon Wessely. "The MoD PTSD Decision: A Psychiatric Perspective." *Occupational Health Review* 122 (July/August 2006): 21–28.

McGibbon, Ian. *New Zealand and the Korean War*. Vol. 1, *Politics and Diplomacy*. Auckland: Oxford University Press, 1992.

–. *New Zealand and the Korean War*. Vol. 2, *Combat Operations*. Auckland: Oxford University Press, 1996.

McIntyre, Darryl. "Australian Army Medical Services in Korea." In *Australia in the Korean War 1950–1953*. Vol. 2, *Combat Operations*, by Robert J. O'Neill, 570–83. Canberra: Australian War Memorial and the Australian Government Publication Service, 1985.

McManners, Hugh. *The Scars of War*. London, UK: HarperCollins, 1994.

Melady, John. *Korea, Canada's Forgotten War*. Toronto: Macmillan of Canada, 1983.

Menninger, Roy W., and John C. Nemiah, eds. *American Psychiatry after World War II (1944–1994)*. Washington, DC: American Psychiatric Press, 2000.

Mileham, Patrick, Richard Lane, David Rowland, and Philip Wilkinson. "Panel – Morale in the Armed Forces." *Royal United Service Institute Journal* 146, 2 (2001): 46–53.

Miles, Oliver. "Why Are We Still in Afghanistan?" London Review of Books, July 10, 2013. http://www.lrb.co.uk/blog/2013/07/10/oliver-miles/why-are-we-still-in-afghanistan/.

Moncrieff, Joanna. "An Investigation into the Precedents of Modern Drug Treatment in Psychiatry." *History of Psychiatry* 10 (1999): 475–90.

Morse, Jennifer. "Year of the Korean War Veteran Announced." *Legion Magazine*, March 12, 2013. http://legionmagazine.com/en/index.php/2013/03/year-of-the-korean-war-veteran-announced/.

Newman, Richard A. "Combat Fatigue: A Review of the Korean Conflict." *Military Medicine* (October 1964): 921–28.

Nicholson, G.W.L. *Canada's Nursing Sisters*. Toronto: Samuel Stevens, 1975.

Noble, Douglas, Marion E. Roudebush, and Douglas Price. "Studies of Korean War Casualties, Part I: Psychiatric Manifestations in Wounded Men." *American Journal of Psychiatry* 108, 7 (January 1, 1952): 495–99.

Nolan, Victoria. *Military Leadership and Counterinsurgency: The British Army and Small War Strategy since World War II*. London: Tauris, 2012.

Norbury, Frank B. "Psychiatric Admissions in a Combat Division in 1952." *Medical Bulletin of the United States Army Far East* 1, 8 (July 1953): 130–33.

Norton-Taylor, Richard. "Executed WWI Soldiers to Be Given Pardons." *Guardian*, August 16, 2006. http://www.theguardian.com/uk/2006/aug/16/military.immigrationpolicy.

Oates, David. "Memories of Kure Japan: A Personal Experience." Memories of Kure: A Medic in the Korean War, http://www.kurememories.com/page4.htm.

O'Neill, Robert J. *Australia in the Korean War 1950–1953*. Vol. 1, *Strategy and Diplomacy*. Canberra: Australian War Memorial and the Australian Government Publication Service, 1981.

–. *Australia in the Korean War 1950–1953*. Vol. 2, *Combat Operations*. Canberra: Australian War Memorial and the Australian Government Publication Service, 1985.

Pakistan Kakhuda Hafiz: Leading Alternative Policy Institute. "A Review of the 12 Years of British Troops in Afghanistan," July 24, 2013. http://www.pakistankakhudahafiz.com/opinion/a-review-of-the-12-years-of-british-troops-in-afghanistan/.

Palmer, Robert R. *The Procurement of Enlisted Personnel: The Problem of Quality*. Washington, DC: United States Government Printing Office, 1948.

Palit, D.K. "Military Lessons of the Korean War." *United Services Institute of India Journal* 82: (July-October 1952), 348–49.

Parliament of Canada. "Roméo Dallaire – Senate Biography." http://www.parl.gc.ca/SenatorsBio/senator_biography.aspx?senator_id=2772&Language=E&sortord=.

Parr, Alison. *Silent Casualties: New Zealand's Unspoken Legacy of the Second World War*. North Shore, NZ: Tandem Press, 1995.

Peate, Les. "Korean War: Food for thought." *Esprit de Corps*, March 1997. https://www.thefreelibrary.com/Korean+War%3A+food+for+thought.-a030448491.

Peterson, Donald B., and Rawley E. Chambers. "Restatement of Combat Psychiatry." *American Journal of Psychiatry* 109, 4 (October 1952): 249–54.

Pols, Hans, and Stephanie Oak. "War & Military Mental Health: The United States Psychiatric Response in the 20th Century." *American Journal of Public Health* 97, 12 (December 2007): 2133–42.

Pope, Rex. "British Demobilisation after the Second World War." *Journal of Contemporary History* 30, 1 (January 1995): 69–71.

Port, Cynthia Lindman, Brian Engdahl, and Patricia Frazier. "A Longitudinal and Retrospective Study of PTSD among Older Prisoners of War." *American Journal of Psychiatry* 158, 9 (September 2001): 1474–79.

Postmedia News. "End of Afghan Mission Leaves Vets Grappling with Their Return to Canada." *National Post*, February 27, 2012. http://news.nationalpost.com/2012/02/27/end-of-afghan-mission-leaves-vets-grappling-with-their-return-to-canada/.

Pozner, Harry. "Some Aspects of Post-War Army Psychiatry." *Journal of the Royal Army Medical Corps* 94, 1 (January 1950): 44–45.

"Psychiatry: Condensed from an Article Written by Brigadier Alfred Torrie, MB and Major RH Ahrenfeldt." *Journal of the Royal Army Medical Corps* 95, 6 (June 1948): 327–33.

Queen Alexandra's Royal Army Nursing Corps. "Information and History about Netley Royal Victoria Military Hospital." QARANC, http://www.qaranc.co.uk/netleyhospital.php.

Rawling, Bill. *Death Their Enemy: Canadian Medical Practitioners and War*. Quebec: AGMV Marquis, 2001.

–. *The Myriad Challenges of Peace: Canadian Forces Medical Practitioners since the Second World War*. Ottawa: Canadian Government Publishing, 2004.

Reid, Fiona. "Distinguishing between Shell-Shocked Veterans and Pauper Lunatics: The Ex-Services' Welfare Society and Mentally Wounded Veterans after the Great War." *War in History* 14, 3 (July 2007): 347–71.

Reister, Frank A. *Battle Casualties and Medical Statistics: United States Army Experience in the Korean War*. Washington, DC: Surgeon General, Department of the Army, 1973. US Army Medical Department, Office of Medical History, http://history.amedd.army.mil/booksdocs/korea/reister/reister.html.

Remembering: Scotland at War. "It Was Easier to Put Me in the Black Watch 'National Service.'" http://www.rememberingscotlandatwar.org.uk/Accessible/Exhibition/87/It-was-easier-to-put-me-in-the-Black-Watch-National-Service.

Remploy. "Who We Are." http://www.remploy.co.uk/about-us/whoweare.ashx (accessed 17 March 2013).

Reynolds, David. "From World War to Cold War: The Wartime Alliance and the Post-War Transitions, 1941–1947." *Historical Journal* 45, 1 (March 2002): 211–27.

Ritchie, Elspeth Cameron. "Psychiatry in the Korean War: Perils, PIES and Prisoners of War." *Military Medicine* 167, 11 (2002): 898–903.

Rivard, Jeffrey R. "Bringing the Boys Home: A Study of the Canadian Demobilization after the First and Second World Wars." MA thesis, University of New Brunswick, 1999.

Roberts, Adrian. *Synopsis of Causation: Cold Injury.* London: Ministry of Defence, 2008.

Robinson, R.H. "Future Medical Officers for the Army." *Journal of the Royal Army Medical Corps* 96, 2 (February 1951): 130–36.

–. "Future Medical Officers for the Army Part III: Some Suggestions." *Journal of the Royal Army Medical Corps* 96, 3 (March 1951): 182–91.

Russell, Harold. "24th Canadian Field Ambulance, Royal Canadian Army Medical Corps." *Canadian Military History* 8, 1 (Winter 1999): 65–74.

Sampson, James B. "Anxiety as a Factor in the Incidence of Combat Cold Injury: A Review." *Military Medicine* 149 (February 1984): 89–91.

Sandler, Stanley. *The Korean War: No Victors, No Vanquished.* Lexington, KY: University of Kentucky Press, 1999.

Sargant, William. "Physical Treatment of Acute War Neuroses." *British Medical Journal* 2 (1942): 574–76.

–. *The Unquiet Mind: The Autobiography of a Physician in Psychological Medicine.* London: Heinemann, 1967.

Savage, Paul L., and Richard A. Gabriel. "Cohesion and Disintegration in the American Army: An Alternative Perspective." *Armed Forces and Society* 2 (1976): 340–76.

Scolnick, Meyer, and Joseph L. Packer. "Evolution of the Army and Air Force Exchange Service." *United States Air Force Judge Advocate General Law Review* 8, 5 (1966): 19–36.

Scott, L.V. *Conscription and the Attlee Governments: The Politics and Policy of National Service 1945–1951.* Oxford: Oxford University Press, 1993.

Scull, Andrew. *Hysteria: The Disturbing History.* Oxford: Oxford University Press, 2005.

–. "Psychiatrists and Historical 'Facts' Part One: The Historiography of Somatic Treatments." *History of Psychiatry* 6 (1995): 225–41.

Scurfield, Raymond M. *A Vietnam Trilogy, Veterans and Post Traumatic Stress: 1968, 1989, 2000.* New York: Algora Publishing, 2004.

Segal, David R., and H. Wallace Sinaiko, eds. *Life in the Rank and File: Enlisted Men and Women in the Armed Forces of the United States, Australia, Canada, and the United Kingdom.* Washington, DC: Pergamon-Brassey's International, 1986.

Sharpe, G.E. "The Sand beneath Our Feet: The Changing Mandate in the Croatia Inquiry." Veteran's Voice.info, 2011. http://veteranvoice.info/ARCHIVE/info_11may_Paper_ShiftingSands_byBGen_Sharpe.pdf.

Shephard, Ben. *A War of Nerves: Soldiers and Psychiatrists in the Twentieth Century.* Cambridge, MA: Harvard University Press, 2001.

Sims, Malcolm, Jillian Ikin, and Dean McKenzie. *Health Study 2005: Australian Veterans of the Korean War.* Melbourne: Department of Epidemiology and Preventative Medicine, Faculty of Medicine, Nursing and Health Sciences, Monash University, 2005.

Shorter, Edward. *A History of Psychiatry: From the Era of the Asylum to the Age of Prozac.* New York : John Wiley and Sons, 1997.

Smurthwaite, David, and Linda Washington. *Project Korea: The British Soldier in Korea, 1950–1953.* London: National Army Museum, 1988.

Snape, Michael Francis. *God and the British Soldier: Religion and the British Army in the First and Second World Wars.* London: Routledge, 2005.

Sobel, Raymond. "Anxiety-Depressive Reactions after Prolonged Combat Experience – the 'Old Sergeant Syndrome.'" *Bulletin of the United States Army Medical Department* (1949): 137–46.

Stacey, Charles Perry. "The Development of the Canadian Army." *Canadian Army Journal* 6, 4 (July 1952): 1–10.

Steger, Byron L. "Medical Societies in Korea." *Medical Bulletin of the United States Army Far East* 1, 6 (May 1953): 92.

Strachan, Hew, ed. *The British Army, Manpower and Society into the Twenty-First Century.* London: Frank Cass, 2000.

Stueck, William Whitney. *The Korean War: An International History.* Princeton, NJ: Princeton University Press, 1995.

Sutker, Patricia B., and Albert N. Allain Jr. "Assessment of PTSD and Other Mental Disorders in World War II and Korean Conflict POW Survivors and Combat Veterans." *Psychological Assessment* 8, 1 (1996): 18–25.

Tasker, John Paul. "Ottawa Revives Harper-Era Legal Arguments to Block Pensions for Injured Vets." CBC News, June 15, 2016. http://www.cbc.ca/news/politics/ottawa-pensions-injured-vets-equitas-lawsuit-1.3637155.

Taylor, Eric. *Wartime Nurse: One Hundred Years from the Crimea to Korea, 1854–1954.* London: Robert Hale, 2001.

"Teaching Mental Health: Discussion by the Royal Medico-Psychological Association." *Lancet* 265, 6861 (February 26, 1955): 449.

Tosh, John. *The Pursuit of History: Aims, Methods and New Directions in the Study of Modern History.* Rev. 3rd ed. London, UK: Longman, 2002.

Trembeth, Richard. *A Different Sort of War: Australians in Korea 1950–1953.* Melbourne: Australian Scholarly Publishing, 2005.

United Kingdom. *Hansard Parliamentary Debates,* 5th ser., vols. 536–615.

United States Army Medical Department. *Recent Advances in Medicine and Surgery: Based on Professional Medical Experiences in Japan and Korea 1950–1953.* Vol. 2. Medical Science Publication No. 4. Washington, DC: Walter Reed Army Medical Service Graduate School, 1954.

United States Army Medical Research Laboratory. *Cold Injury – Korea 1951–1952.* Fort Knox, KY: United States Army Medical Research Laboratory, 1953.

Uttley, Stephen. "New Zealand." *Journal of International and Comparative Social Welfare* 10, 1 (1994): 40–57.

Vance, Jonathan F.W. *Objects of Concern: Canadian Prisoners of War through the Twentieth Century.* Vancouver: UBC Press, 1994.

Veterans Affairs Canada. "The Gerontological Advisory Council?" http://www.veterans.gc.ca/eng/about-us/advisory-groups/gerontological.

–. "Ste Anne's Hospital – Our History." http://www.veterans.gc.ca/eng/steannes/stannehis5 (accessed 6 June 2013).

Veterans Health Administration. *VHA/DoD Clinical Practice Guideline for the Management of Medically Unexplained Symptoms: Chronic Pain and Fatigue.* Washington, DC: US Department of Defense, 2001.

Watt, J.C. *Surgeon at War*. London: George Allen and Unwin, 1955.

Wessely, Simon. "The Life and Death of Private Harry Farr." *Journal of the Royal Society of Medicine* 99 (September 2006): 440–43.

–. "War and Psychiatry: A Story in Three Acts." Lecture, Global History Seminar, London Centre of the University of Notre Dame, March 27, 2013.

Whelan, Richard. *Drawing the Line: The Korean War, 1950–1953*. London: Faber and Faber, 1990.

Wilson, Roland. *Official Year Book of the Commonwealth of Australia No. 37: 1946 and 1947*. Canberra: Commonwealth Bureau of Census and Statistics, 1948.

Wollen, Peter. *Signs and Meaning in the Cinema*. 5th ed. London: Macmillan, 2013.

World Veterans Federation. *Social Affairs Rehabilitation, Comparative Report: Legislation Affecting Disabled Veterans and Other War Victims*. WVF- DOC/830. Paris: World Veterans Federation, September 1955.

Wright, Harold M. *Salute to the Air Force Medical Branch on the 75th Anniversary, Royal Canadian Air Force*. Ottawa: H.M. Wright, 1999.

Wright, James. "Have Americans Forgotten Afghanistan?" *Atlantic*, March 25, 2013. http://www.theatlantic.com/international/archive/2013/03/have-americans-forgotten-afghanistan/274331/.

Wrobel, Sylvia. "Science, Serotonin, and Sadness: The Biology of Antidepressants." *Journal of the Federation of American Societies for Experimental Biology* 21, 13 (November 2007): 3404–17.

Index

Note: "(i)" after a page number indicates an illustration or map

accidental wounds, 72–74, 138n101
Adam, Major J.M., 71
Addison, Christopher, 14
Adjutant General (AG) A Branch, 51, 56, 58–59
Afghanistan, 105
aircraft (soldier evacuations), 79, 82
Allan Memorial Institute, 14
American Expeditionary Force, 11
American Psychiatric Association (APA), 17
American Psychological Association (APA), 93–94
Anderton, Colonel Geoffrey, 30, 32, 37
Andrade Jr., Ernest, 40
Andrew, Colonel J.E., 3, 34–35
antidepressants, 92
Anzac Club, 54
ANZUS treaty, 24
Argyll and Sutherland Highlanders (1st Battalion), 24, 47
Army Council Secretariat (ACS), 21
Army Kinema Corps, 56
Assistant Director of Army Psychiatry (ADA Psych) UK, 14, 20, 21
Assistant Director of Medical Services (ADMS), 29–30, 72
associations (veterans), 89, 90–91, 93–94, 98, 99, 103
Attlee, Prime Minister Clement, 13–14
Auditor General (Canada), 96–97
Australian armed forces: bond with Canada, 35–36; evacuation and repatriation, 79, 84, 141n163; pension application process, 89; psychiatric-care research, 100, 149n157; PTSD research, 94; recruitment, 24, 25; rotation policy, 65–66; veteran's poem, 86–87; veterans' associations, 89, 90–91, 94. *See also* 1st Commonwealth Division; Royal Australian Regiment (RAR)
Australian Army Canteen Service (AACS), 53–54(i)
Australian Centre for Posttraumatic Mental Health (ACPMH - Phoenix Australia), 94
Australian General Hospital (130th). *See* British Commonwealth General Hospital (BCGH)/No.29 British General Hospital

Balkans (Canadian deployment), 95
Ban, Dr. Thomas A., 92
Barris, Ted, 90
Bartlet, Dr./Lieutenant Leslie, 64, 68, 81
battle exhaustion: limits to endurance studies, 46; names for, 68–69, 136n64; soldier, 70(i); statistics, 69; symptoms, 3
Belenky, Gregory, 64
Benny, Jack, 58
Bercuson, David J., 55, 65
Berenberg, Albert N., 71
Beswick, Dr. John, 84
Black Watch (1st Battalion), 43–44
Bolocan, Dr. Hyam, 68, 75
Bouchier, Air Vice Marshal Cecil, 33
brigade and battalion commanders, 37
British Armed Forces: court-martial and execution, 9; demobilization, 12–15; doctors, 15–17, 119n55; evacuation and repatriation, 83, 85; food rations, 49; funding, 12–13; leadership, 41; officer training selection, 20–21; psychiatric care, 22, 89, 92–94, 97–98; psychiatric casualty statistics, 67, 98; psychiatry schools, 19–20; rank discrimination,

89, 92–93; recruitment, 15–16, 21–22, 24, 121n88; relations with Canada, 36; rotation policy, 66–67; veterans' lawsuit, 97–98; welfare services administration, 51; winter clothing, 48, 130n64. *See also* 1st Commonwealth Division; 27th British Commonwealth Infantry Brigade

British Commonwealth Communications Zone Medical Unit (BCCZMU), 32, 37, 125n78

British Commonwealth General Hospital (BCGH)/No.29 British General Hospital: medical support, 26(i), 27, 123n31; post-combat syndromes, 70; psychiatric casualties, 63, 79, 80, 81, 140n144; renamed, 30. *See also* hospitals

British Commonwealth Occupation Force (BCOF), 26

British Ex-Services Mental Welfare Society, 90

British Expeditionary Force (BEF), 9–10

British Medical Association (BMA), 15–16

British Medical Journal (BMJ), 6, 16, 71

British Mental Health Act (1959), 92

British Second Army, 69

Brodie, Brigadier Thomas, 37

Bullock, Samuel C., 71

Byron-Watson, Brent, 55, 65

Camp, Dr. Norman, 75

Canadian Army Active Force, 15

Canadian Army Special Force (CASF), 24, 25, 48–49, 64–65

Canadian Broadcasting Corporation, 56

Canadian Defence Medical and Dental Advisory Board, 69

Canadian Forces (CF): clubs, 55, 132n92; demobilization, 12–15, 17; inter-allied relations, 28, 29, 35–36; manpower shortages, 13; mobility policy, 34–35; older vs younger veterans, 99–100; pension system, 95–97; personnel selection officers, 18–19; psychiatric care, 83(i)–84, 94, 95, 99; recruitment, 15–16, 21–22, 24, 25, 121n88; repatriation and convalescence, 83(i)–84; role in divisional medicine, 4; veterans, 95, 96,

99–100, 147n108; winter clothing, 48. *See also* 1st Commonwealth Division; 25th Canadian Infantry Brigade

Canadian Medical Association (CMA), 13, 34

Canadian Mental Health Association, 14

Canadian Red Cross, 55, 132n92

canteens and clubs, 51, 52(i)–55, 75, 131n79, 132n92

Cantlie, Sir Neil, 17, 72

Carr, Carole, 58

Carriage, R.J., 44

Cassels, Major General Jim, 29, 36–37, 40–41(i), 42–43, 72–74

Catignani, Dr. Sergio, 40

Chalke, Major Franklin Cyril Rhodes, 19, 64, 65, 120n66

chaplains, 58–59

character disorder, 3, 68

Chief of the Imperial General Staff (CIGS), 31

Chiefs of Staff (COS), 26, 28, 34, 41

China, 2, 28

chlorpromazine (medical drug), 92

cigarettes, 49

Clark, General Mark, 41(i), 43

Clarke, General Bruce, 39, 43

Clever, Captain W.G., 36

clothing (winter), 48

Coad, Brigadier Basil, 24, 25, 42, 47

Coates, Major General H.J., 39

cohesion (definition), 46

cold injury, 3, 4, 8, 71–72

Cole, Lieutenant Colonel Howard, 53

Colonel Davey (Lieutenant Colonel David Rose), 44, 128n29

combat fatigue, 69, 136n64. *See also* battle exhaustion

Combat Stress (association), 98

commanding officer (CO), 35, 36–37, 40–42, 43–45, 72, 73. *See also individual commanders*

Common, Smyttan, 100

Commonwealth Division. *See* 1st Commonwealth Division

Commonwealth Rehabilitation Scheme, 86

concerts, 58, 75

Cooter, Roger, 5

Copeland, Lieutenant Colonel N., 20, 21
Croatia Board of Inquiry (Sharpe
Inquiry), 95
Crookshank, Harry, 16
Crown News, 130*n*72
Crown Radio, 56, 58

Dailley, Lieutenant-Colonel G.D., 18
Dallaire, Lieutenant-General/Senator
Roméo, 95, 96, 147*n*108
Dalziel, Major W.R., 30
Damousi, Joy, 104
Danckwerts, Harold, 16
Davies, Major R.G., 81
Davis, Captain A.J.M., 18(i)
Deane, Hugh, 45
Delay, Jean, 92
Deniker, Pierre, 92
Department of Veterans' Affairs
(Australia DVA), 94
Deputy Chief of Staff to the Commander-
in-Chief of UN Forces, 33–34
Deputy Director of Medical Services
(DDMS), 29–30, 37
*Diagnostic and Statistical Manual of
Mental Disorders (DSM-III)*, 93–94
Director of Army Psychiatry (DA Psych)
UK, 14, 19
Director General of Army Medical
Services (DGAMS), 17, 19
Director General of Medical Services
(DGMS) Canada, 17, 68
Director General of Military Training, 47
Disability Benefits Program (Canada), 97
disability pensions, 85–89, 142*n*12
doctors (armed forces), 13–14, 15, 17, 31,
119*n*55
drugs. *See* medical drugs

Easton, Alex, 44
Ebisu Leave Centre, 54–55
education (vocational training), 59,
86–87, 89–90
8054th Evacuation Hospital, 62. *See also*
hospitals
Eisenhower, President Dwight D., 103
Eli Lilly and Company, 77
Elizabeth II, Queen, 101
Empire Club, 54

entertainment, 56, 57(i), 58, 75
Equitas case, 96
Executive Committee of the Army
Council (ECAC), 20

Fallon, Michael, 101
Fantino, Julian, 97
Far Eastern Land Force (FARELF), 31, 73
Farr, Private Harry, 9, 22
Farrar Hockley, General Sir Anthony, 24
female staff (canteens and clubs), 55
field ambulances and dressing stations:
about, 30; early days of war, 26;
mobility, 31–32, 35; nationalistic feeling,
34–35; psychiatric assessments, 76–77;
psychiatric casualties, 61. *See also
individual names of field ambulances
and dressing stations*
Fields, Gracie, 58
films, 45, 56, 57(i), 58, 75
1st Commonwealth Division: about, 2–3;
beginnings, 27–30; benefits, 30–31;
brigade and battalion commanders,
37; challenges and obstacles, 2–3, 8,
31–35; compromise and cooperation,
35–37, 102, 105; deployment reasons,
44–45; entertainment, 56, 57(i), 58;
food rations, 48–49; group cohesion,
46–48; headquarters, 30; leadership,
40–44; living conditions, 55; manpower
shortages, 17, 31–32, 119*n*55; medical
units, 17, 29–30, 119*n*55; mental health
and morale, 7, 39–60, 104; national
differences, 32–35; officer selection,
20–21, 36–37; opposition to, 27–28;
prisoners of war (POWs), 113, 152*nn*2–
3; psychiatric care and convalescence,
75–84, 139*n*131, 140*n*144, 141*n*163;
psychiatric casualties, 3, 4, 67–75,
135*n*47, 136*n*64, 137*n*80, 138*n*101; racism,
45; raids, 42–43; recreation services,
51, 52(i)–55, 131*n*79, 132*n*92; recruit
screening, 64–65; return to unit (RTU)
rates, 78–79, 85, 102, 139*n*131; rotation
policy, 65–67; social services, 58–59; as
success, 23, 37–38; supply chains, 25, 31;
tours of duty, 44–46; welfare services,
48–51; winter clothing, 48
First World War, 9–11, 22

Flieger, Don, 91
Flood, Captain J.J., 3, 63, 67, 78, 80–81
food rations, 48–49
forward psychiatry, 11, 75, 93, 105
Foulkes, Lieutenant General Charles, 27
Fraser, Captain N.G., 64, 68, 74, 77, 81, 113
French, David, 35, 43–44
Fuller, Major R., 81–82
Fuller, Samuel, 45

Gabriel, Richard A., 129*n*54
Gal, Reuven, 46
Garton, Stephen, 88
gastrointestinal conditions, 4, 69
General Office Commanding (GOC), 29, 31
Gerontological Advisory Council (GAC), 99, 149*n*146
Gillespie, Dr. Robert D., 67
Glass, Colonel Albert J., 63, 66, 77, 78
Godfrey, Captain R.G., 79
Goldman, R.F., 71
"great bug out," 62
Grey, Jeffrey, 6, 27–28, 36, 66
group cohesion, 46–48
group rotation policy, 47
Gulf War Syndrome, 95
gunshot wounds (GSWs), 72

Hanking, Sergeant Major, 9
Hanson, H.E., 71
Harsant, Major General A.G., 31
Hassett, Lieutenant Colonel Francis, 37
Hastings, Max, 2
healthcare system (civilian), 13
Heidelberg Hospital, 99
Help for Heroes (association), 98
Henderson, Sir David K., 19, 67
Hering, Captain (US Marine surgeon), 46
Hickman, Tom, 49, 100
hockey, 56, 57(i)
Hood, Sir Alexander, 19, 20–21
hospitals: first integrated unit, 26(i), 27, 123*n*31; psychiatric casualties, 62, 63, 79, 80, 81(i)–82, 140*n*144; renamed, 27, 30; ships, 79–80(i); veterans, 83(i)–84, 89, 99
Howerd, Frankie, 58
Hunter, Brigadier Ken A., 3, 14, 34–35

Hutton, Dr. G.H., 17
hypothermia, 3, 4, 8, 71–72
hysteria, 74

India, 26–27, 123*n*30
Indian Army Medical Service (IAMS), 26–27
Indian Field Ambulance (60th), 26, 30
inter-allied command. *See* 1st Commonwealth Division
Inter-Service Medical Committee (ISMC Canada), 15
International Security Assistance Force (ISAF), 105
Iraq, 105
"Iron Mike" (Lieutenant General John W. O'Daniel), 29, 42

James, Captain W.J., 26
James, Deputy Assistant Chaplain General W.S., 58–59
Japan, 26(i), 27, 123*n*31
Japan News, 130*n*72
Johnston, Major J.L., 64, 66, 69, 81
Jones, Edgar, 3, 4, 7–8, 14, 39, 56, 72
Journal of the Royal Army Medical Corps (JRAMC), 3, 15, 40, 67, 78
Jowitt, Sir William, 13

Kaye, Danny, 58
Kayforce (16 New Zealand Field Artillery Regiment), 25, 37
Keightley, General Sir Charles, 73
Kendall, Lieutenant General Paul, 43
King's Centre for Military Health Research, 3
King's Own Scottish Borderers (KOSB), 25
King's Scottish Light Infantry (KSLI), 25
KO teams (mobile psychiatric detachments), 64, 134*n*20
Kookaburra Club, 54(i)
Korea Veterans Association of Australia, 89, 91, 99, 103
Korea Veterans Association of Canada, 103
Korean peninsula (1950-53), xiii(i)
Korean War: armistice, 74–75; army living conditions (rats), 55; army racism, 45;

beginnings, 23–25, 62; casualty statistics, 23, 67, 136n47; chronology of events, 107–12; deployment, 24–25, 103; films, 45; as "forgotten war," 1–2; "great bug out," 62; historical importance, 104–5; infrastructure and roads, 53, 79; inter-allied cooperation, 35, 105; memorials, 101, 103, 150n160; military operations, 69, 113; as police action, 103, 104; psychological scars of, 61–84; public perception, 39, 104; reasons for, 44–45; veterans' treatment, 103–4; winter tours of duty, 45–46
Koren, Lindsey, 50–51

Laborit, Henri, 92
Ladell, Officer W.S.S., 71
Lavin, Captain Robert J., 69
laws and legislation, 16–17, 88, 89, 92, 95–96
lawsuits (veterans), 96, 97–98
leadership, 40–44
Leier, Don, 104
Lewis, Dr. Aubrey, 19
Lewis, Major Martin, 40
libraries, 59
Lifton, Dr. Robert J., 93
Lynn, Vera, 58

MacArthur, General Douglas, 2, 23, 29
Mackenzie King, Prime Minister, 28
magazines, 50, 130n72
Maine (hospital ship), 79–80(i)
Maple Leaf Club, 55, 132n92
Maple Leaf Park, 132n92
Marion, Private Arthur, 90
Martin, James A., 64
Matthews, Private Heath, 70(i)
Mays, Luther L., 71
McCannel, Colonel J.S. (ADMS), 34, 37
McGrath, Major J.J., 81
McKechney, Robin, 53
McLeod, Keith, 90
McNally, Lieutenant-Colonel N.H., 70
medical drugs, 12, 77, 91, 92
medical officers (MOs), 31–32, 37, 77, 84
medical symptoms. *See* psychiatric symptoms

medical units. *See* field ambulances and dressing stations
memory, 6
Meneces, Colonel N.T., 37
mental health and morale, 39–60
mental illness stigma, 8, 10, 89, 90, 100–1
Middlesex Regiment (1st Battalion), 24, 47
Miles, Oliver, 105
Military Covenant (UK), 97
military hospitals. *See* hospitals
military operations, 69, 113
military vs psychiatry relationship, 5, 15, 21
Ministry of Defence (MoD) post-traumatic stress disorder case (UK), 97–98
Ministry of Pensions and National Insurance (MPNI), 88, 93
Monash University, 100, 149n157
monoamine oxidase inhibitors (MAOIs), 92
Moodie, Lieutenant Colonel J.W., 37
morale: cigarettes, 49; entertainment, 56, 57(i), 58, 75; female staffers, 55; food rations, 48–49; group cohesion, 46–48; increase, 75; leadership, 40–44; magazines, 50, 130n72; mental health, 39–60; newspapers, 130n72; postal system, 49, 50(i), 51; recreation services (canteens and clubs), 51, 52(i)–55, 131n79, 132n92; reflections on, 59–60; social services, 58–59; tour-of-duty limits, 44–46; welfare services role, 48–51
Morland, Jessie, 104
Morrison, Mr., 15

Nathan Committee (1945 UK), 15
National Health Service (NHS), 16, 98
National Service Act, 16–17
National Veterans Resource Project (NVRP), 93
Navy, Army, and Air Force Institute (NAAFI UK), 51, 52(i), 53
New Veterans Charter (NVC), 96
New Zealand (NZ), 24, 25, 39, 94
New Zealand Defence Force, 94

New Zealand Field Artillery Regiment
(16 NZ Fd Regt), 25, 37
newspapers, 130*n*72
Nicholson, G.W.L., 36
No. 6 Convalescent Depot, 81(i)–82
No. 29 British General Hospital. *See*
British Commonwealth General
Hospital (BCGH)/No.29 British
General Hospital
non-commissioned officers (NCOs),
43–44
Norbury, Lieutenant Frank B., 40
North Atlantic Treaty Organization
(NATO), 24, 95, 105
North Korean People's Army (NKPA),
23–24
Nye, Colonel C.W., 29–30, 37

O'Brien, Private Vin, 50(i)
O'Connor, Sir Richard, 20–21
O'Daniel, Lieutenant General John
W. (Iron Mike), 29, 42
O'Neill, Robert J., 40, 65
O'Toole, Erin, 96
Oates, Dr. David, 82, 106
Office of the Veterans Ombudsman
(OVO), 96
officer selection, 20–21, 36–37
"old sergeant syndrome," 46
ombudsman (veterans), 96
130th Australian General Hospital,
26(i), 27, 123*n*31. *See also* British
Commonwealth General Hospital
(BCGH)/No.29 British General
Hospital
Operation Big Switch, 113
Operation Commando, 69
Operation Homeward Bound, 113
Operation Little Switch, 113
Operation Showdown, 69
operational stress injury (OSI)
clinics, 95
Operational Trauma and Stress Support
Centre (OTSSC), 95
other ranks (OR), 10, 11, 36, 89

Parker, Private Bob, 50(i)
Pearson, Prime Minister Lester B., 27–28
Peate, Les, 49, 103

pension systems: adaptation and change,
91–100; application process, 87–89;
compensation, 8, 9, 11, 86–87; laws and
legislation, 88, 89, 92, 95–96; rights,
85–89; types, 85–86, 142*n*12. *See also*
veterans
personnel officers (POs), 59
physical exercise, 81(i)–82
poems, 86–87
Pope, Rex, 12
post-combat syndrome, 69–71, 137*n*80
Post-Traumatic Stress Disorder (PTSD):
associations, 98; first mention, 93–94;
lawsuits, 97–98; research, 1, 93–94,
100, 149*n*157, 149*n*159; socio-cultural
context, 5; statistics, 98. *See also*
psychiatric symptoms
post-traumatic syndrome (first mention),
136*n*64
postal system, 49, 50(i), 51
Pozner, Lieutenant Colonel Harry, 67
Princess Patricia's Canadian Light
Infantry (1PPCLI), 57(i)
Princess Patricia's Canadian Light
Infantry (2PPCLI), 25, 41–42, 90. *See
also* 25th Canadian Infantry Brigade
prisoner-of-war camps, 45
prisoners of war (POWs), 113, 152*nn*2–3
proximity, immediacy, expectancy (PIE),
11. *See also* forward psychiatry
Psychiatric Advisory Committee
(PAC), 19
psychiatric care: assessments, 76–77;
change and adaptation, 91–100;
convalescence and physical exercise,
81(i)–82; effectiveness, 7–8; forward
psychiatry, 11, 75, 93, 105; goals, 11;
medical drugs, 92; psychotherapy,
77–78; reflections on, 84; religion as
alternative, 59; research study, 100,
149*n*157, 149*n*159; return to unit
(RTU), 78–79, 85, 102, 139*n*131;
screening programs, 11–12; sedation,
77, 80
psychiatric casualties: discharge statistics,
90; evacuation and repatriation, 63–64,
79, 82–83; prisoners of war (POWs),
113; statistics, 22, 23, 62, 67, 90, 136*n*47;
stigma, 8, 10, 89, 90, 100–1; types, 3, 4

psychiatric symptoms: battle exhaustion
and names for, 3, 68–69, 136n64;
character disorder, 3, 68; cold
injuries, 3, 4, 8, 71–72; gastrointestinal
conditions, 4, 69; hysteria, 74;
post-combat syndrome, 69–71,
137n80; psychoneurosis, 3, 67–68;
psychosomatic disorders, 3, 4, 6, 8, 71,
80; respiratory problems, 4, 69; self-
inflicted wounds (SIWs), 3, 8, 72–74,
138n101; shell shock, 9, 10, 69, 136n64;
skin reactions, 4, 69; truce exhaustion,
74–75. *See also* Post-Traumatic Stress
Disorder (PTSD)
psychiatry: forward psychiatry (PIE), 11,
75, 93, 105; vs military relationship, 5,
15, 21; mistrust of, 21; officer training,
20–21; psychiatrists, 11, 17, 63–64, 75–77,
80–81, 119n55; schools, 19–20
psychoneurosis, 3, 67–68
psychosomatic disorders, 3, 4, 6, 8, 71, 80
psychotherapy, 77–78
PTSD Resolution (association), 98
PULHEMS/PULHEEMS recruitment
screening tool (physique, upper limbs,
locomotion, hearing, eyesight, mental
functioning, and stability), 21–22,
121n88

radio broadcasting, 56
Rangaraja, Lieutenant Colonel A.G., 26
rats and wildlife (living conditions), 55
Rawling, Bill, 3, 6
Rayner, Louis, 104
recreation services, 51, 52(i)–55, 131n79,
132n92
reflections on: inter-allied command
success, 37–38; military psychiatric-
care history, 22; morale, 59–60;
psychiatric care, 84; veterans, 100–1
Regimental Aid Post (RAP), 76(i)
Regimental Medical Officers (RMOs), 26,
75–76
regimental system (value), 47–48
religion, 58–59
research methodology, 4, 5–6
respiratory problems, 4, 69
return to unit (RTU) rates, 78–79, 85, 102,
139n131

Returned and Services League (RSL),
90–91
Reynolds, Lieutenant M.F., 43
Rhône-Poulenc, 92
Ridgway, General Matthew, 44–45
roadhouses, 53, 75
Robertson, Lieutenant General Sir
Horace, 25–26, 28–29, 32–33(i), 34, 41,
47
Robinson, Colonel R.H., 15
Robitaille, Major R.J.A., 64
Rockingham, Brigadier John, 34, 37,
57(i)
Rose, Lieutenant Colonel David (Colonel
Davey), 44, 128n29
Rosie, Brigadier Robert James, 14, 118n39
rotation policy, 47
Royal 22é Régiment (R22er), 57(i), 65. *See
also* 25th Canadian Infantry Brigade
Royal Army Chaplain's Department
(RAChD), 58–59
Royal Army Educational Corps (RAEC),
56, 57(i), 58, 59
Royal Army Medical College
(Millbank), 20
Royal Army Medical Corps (RAMC):
demobilization, 14–15; psychiatric
care and casualties, 61–62, 63,
67, 79; relations with Canada, 36;
reorganization, 19; staff shortages,
16–17, 30, 31, 119n55
Royal Australian Air Force (RAAF),
79, 90
Royal Australian Army Medical Corps
(RAAMC), 29–30, 47
Royal Australian Regiment (1 RAR), 65
Royal Australian Regiment (3 RAR),
25, 37, 44, 47, 65–66, 76(i). *See also*
28th British Commonwealth Brigade
Group; Australian armed forces
Royal Australian Regimental Aid Post
(RAP) 3rd Battalion, 76(i)
Royal Canadian Army Medical Corps
(RCAMC): demobilization, 14–15,
17; mental health training, 18(i);
nationalistic mobility policy, 34–35;
psychiatric care, 4, 62, 67; psychiatrists,
64; relations with UK, 36; staff
shortages, 16, 31

Royal Canadian Army Service Corps
    (RCASC), 91
Royal Canadian Regiment, 65, 70(i). *See
    also* 25th Canadian Infantry Brigade
Royal Legion, 90–91
Royal Leicestershire Regiment, 25
Royal Military College (Australia), 35–36
Royal Military College (Canada), 35–36
Royal Victoria Hospital Netley, 83
Rutherford, Captain, 47, 66
Rwanda, 95, 147*n*108
Ryan, Ivan Patrick, 89, 103

Salmon, Thomas, 11
Sandiford, Brigadier H.A., 14, 19
Sargant, William, 77
Saunders, Captain Reg, 44
Savage, Paul L., 129*n*54
Seaforth Highlanders, 36
Second World War, 12–15, 18, 22, 23,
    103, 104
sedation (psychiatric care), 77, 80
self-inflicted wounds (SIWs), 3, 8, 72–74,
    138*n*101
service patient programs, 89
service pensions, 85
Sharpe, Colonel Joe, 95
shell shock, 9, 10, 69, 136*n*64. *See also*
    battle exhaustion
Shephard, Ben, 78
Sheppard, Rex, 55
Shier, Colonel Stanley, 68
ships, 79–80(i)
Shoosmith, Major General Steven, 34
"shorter time syndrome," 47
skin reactions, 4, 69
Slater, Eliot, 77
Slim, Field Marshal Sir William, 31, 37, 47,
    72–74
Smillie, Major R.A., 32
Smith, Colonel G.L. Morgan, 32, 37,
    70–71, 84
Snow, Colonel J.E., 30
Sobel, Major Raymond, 46
social services, 58–59
sodium amytal, 77
somatic disorders, 3, 4, 6, 8, 71, 80
Sparacino, Linette R., 64
sporting competitions, 56, 57(i)

St. Laurent, Prime Minister Louis, 24,
    27–28
Staffordshire Regiment, 25
Stars and Stripes, 130*n*72
Ste-Anne-de-Bellevue Hospital,
    83(i)–84, 99
Stone, Lieutenant Colonel, 41–42
Stone, Ruth, 79–80
Strachan, Hew, 46
Strachey, John, 17
supply chains, 25, 31

Task Force Smith, 23–24
"The Wounded Man Speaks" (veteran's
    poem), 86–87
Thermega Limited, 90
38th Parallel Medical Society, 77
Thomas, Al, 58
Thompson, Brigadier Clifford S., 17
361 Station Hospital, 63. *See also* hospitals
Torrie, Colonel Alfred, 14
Tosh, John, 6
tours of duty, 44–46
trauma, 5, 10
Trembeth, Richard, 103
Trevett, Bill, 55
tricyclic antidepressants (TCAs), 92
truce exhaustion, 74–75
Truman, President Harry S., 45, 103
24th Canadian Field Ambulance, 37
25th Canadian Field Ambulance, 30, 35
25th Canadian Field Dressing Station
    (25 FDS): about, 30; administrative
    policy and behavioural problems,
    68; chaplains, 59; evacuation and
    repatriation, 113; manpower
    shortages, 31–32; mobility, 31–32, 35;
    psychiatric care, 4, 65, 69, 76, 77;
    psychiatrists, 64
25th Canadian Infantry Brigade, 29, 34,
    37, 132*n*92. *See also* 1st Commonwealth
    Division; Canadian Forces (CF)
26th British Field Ambulance, 26, 30
27th British Commonwealth Infantry
    Brigade, 24–25, 26, 29, 41–42, 63. *See
    also* 1st Commonwealth Division;
    British Armed Forces
28th British Commonwealth Brigade
    Group, 29

29th Independent Infantry Brigade Group (29 Brigade), 25, 26, 37, 63

UN forces/UN Command (UNC), 2, 23–24, 27, 28, 33–34, 41(i)
UN peacekeeping forces, 105
US Army: in Afghanistan, 105; battle exhaustion, 69; beginnings of war, 2, 23–24; convalescent camps, 82; food rations, 48–49; inter-allied leadership relationship, 27, 42–43; psychiatric casualties, 62(i), 67, 79, 136n47; reasons for war, 44–45; return to unit (RTU) rates, 78–79; rotation policy, 47, 66, 129n54; veterans' associations, 93. *See also* 1st Commonwealth Division
US Army Medical Corps, 7, 27, 63, 64, 77
US Army Medical Research Laboratory, 71
US Eighth Army, 44–45
US I Corps, 42–43
US 7th Infantry Division, 69

Van Fleet, General James, 45
veterans: associations, 89, 90–91, 93–94, 98, 99, 103; compensation schemes, 86–87; definition, 98–99; education and vocational training, 86–87, 89–90; hospitals, 83(i)–84, 89, 99; laws and legislation, 88, 89, 92, 95–96; lawsuits, 96, 97–98; medical care, 89–91; mental illness stigma, 8, 10, 89, 90, 100–1; older vs younger, 99–100; ombudsman, 96; poems, 86–87; psychiatric-care research study, 100, 149n157, 149n159;

rank and care quality, 89; service patient programs, 89; support denial, 103. *See also* pension systems
Veterans Affairs Canada (VAC), 95, 96–97
Veterans Bill of Rights (Canada 2007), 95–96
Veterans Independence Program (VIP), 99
Veterans and Reserves Mental Health Programme (VRMHP), 98
Vietnam Veterans Against the War (VVAW), 93
Vietnam Veterans Counselling Service (VVCS), 94, 95
Vietnam War (1961-1975), 93–94, 104
vocational training, 59, 86–87, 89–90

Walker, General, 28–29
War Office (WO), 12, 15–16, 21, 33, 48
War Office Selection Boards (WOSBs), 20
war pensions committee (WPC), 87–88
Wayne and Shuster, 58
welfare services, 48–51, 75
Wessely, Simon, 4, 14
West, General Michael, 31, 37, 43
West Yorkshire Regiment (1st Battalion), 9
Wetenhall, J.P., 13
Windsor, R. (British civil servant), 93
winter clothing, 48
World Health Organization (WHO), 14
Wright, Harold M., 82
Wright, James, 105

Zhou Enlai, Premier, 28

STUDIES IN CANADIAN MILITARY HISTORY

John Griffith Armstrong, *The Halifax Explosion and the Royal Canadian Navy: Inquiry and Intrigue*

Andrew Richter, *Avoiding Armageddon: Canadian Military Strategy and Nuclear Weapons, 1950–63*

William Johnston, *A War of Patrols: Canadian Army Operations in Korea*

Julian Gwyn, *Frigates and Foremasts: The North American Squadron in Nova Scotia Waters, 1745–1815*

Jeffrey A. Keshen, *Saints, Sinners, and Soldiers: Canada's Second World War*

Desmond Morton, *Fight or Pay: Soldiers' Families in the Great War*

Douglas E. Delaney, *The Soldiers' General: Bert Hoffmeister at War*

Michael Whitby, ed., *Commanding Canadians: The Second World War Diaries of A.F.C. Layard*

Martin Auger, *Prisoners of the Home Front: German POWs and "Enemy Aliens" in Southern Quebec, 1940–46*

Tim Cook, *Clio's Warriors: Canadian Historians and the Writing of the World Wars*

Serge Marc Durflinger, *Fighting from Home: The Second World War in Verdun, Quebec*

Richard O. Mayne, *Betrayed: Scandal, Politics, and Canadian Naval Leadership*

P. Whitney Lackenbauer, *Battle Grounds: The Canadian Military and Aboriginal Lands*

Cynthia Toman, *An Officer and a Lady: Canadian Military Nursing and the Second World War*

Michael Petrou, *Renegades: Canadians in the Spanish Civil War*

Amy J. Shaw, *Crisis of Conscience: Conscientious Objection in Canada during the First World War*

Serge Marc Durflinger, *Veterans with a Vision: Canada's War Blinded in Peace and War*

James G. Fergusson, *Canada and Ballistic Missile Defence, 1954–2009: Déjà Vu All Over Again*

Benjamin Isitt, *From Victoria to Vladivostok: Canada's Siberian Expedition, 1917–19*

James Wood, *Militia Myths: Ideas of the Canadian Citizen Soldier, 1896–1921*

Timothy Balzer, *The Information Front: The Canadian Army and News Management during the Second World War*

Andrew B. Godefroy, *Defence and Discovery: Canada's Military Space Program, 1945–74*

Douglas E. Delaney, *Corps Commanders: Five British and Canadian Generals at War, 1939–45*

Timothy Wilford, *Canada's Road to the Pacific War: Intelligence, Strategy, and the Far East Crisis*

Randall Wakelam, *Cold War Fighters: Canadian Aircraft Procurement, 1945–54*

Andrew Burtch, *Give Me Shelter: The Failure of Canada's Cold War Civil Defence*

Wendy Cuthbertson, *Labour Goes to War: The CIO and the Construction of a New Social Order, 1939–45*

P. Whitney Lackenbauer, *The Canadian Rangers: A Living History*

Teresa Iacobelli, *Death or Deliverance: Canadian Courts Martial in the Great War*

Graham Broad, *A Small Price to Pay: Consumer Culture on the Canadian Home Front, 1939–45*

Peter Kasurak, *A National Force: The Evolution of Canada's Army, 1950–2000*

Isabel Campbell, *Unlikely Diplomats: The Canadian Brigade in Germany, 1951–64*

Richard M. Reid, *African Canadians in Union Blue: Volunteering for the Cause in the Civil War*

Andrew B. Godefroy, *In Peace Prepared: Innovation and Adaptation in Canada's Cold War Army*

Nic Clarke, *Unwanted Warriors: The Rejected Volunteers of the Canadian Expeditionary Force*

David Zimmerman, *Maritime Command Pacific: The Royal Canadian Navy's West Coast Fleet in the Early Cold War*

Cynthia Toman, *Sister Soldiers of the Great War: The Nurses of the Canadian Army Medical Corps*

Daniel Byers, *Zombie Army: The Canadian Army and Conscription in the Second World War*

J.L. Granatstein, *The Weight of Command: Voices of Canada's Second World War Generals and Those Who Knew Them*

Colin McCullough, *Creating Canada's Peacekeeping Past*

Douglas E. Delaney and Serge Marc Durflinger, eds., *Capturing Hill 70: Canada's Forgotten Battle of the First World War*

Brandon R. Dimmel, *Engaging the Line: How the Great War Shaped the Canada–US Border*

Geoffrey Hayes, *Crerar's Lieutenants: Inventing the Canadian Junior Army Officer, 1939–45*